AFTER DANTE: POETS IN PURGATORY

After Dante:
Poets in Purgatory
Translations by Contemporary Poets

Edited by Nick Havely
with Bernard O'Donoghue

2021

Published by Arc Publications
Nanholme Mill, Shaw Wood Road
Todmorden, OL14 6DA, UK
www.arcpublications.co.uk

Design by Tony Ward
Printed in Great Britain by
TJ Books, Padstow, Cornwall

978 1908376 76 3 (pbk)

The publishers are grateful to the authors and translators
and, in the case of previously published material,
to their publishers, for allowing their work
to be included in this anthology.

Cover image
William Blake, 'Dante and Statius sleeping, Virgil watching'
(illustration to the 'Divine Comedy', *Purgatorio* XXVII)
Image © Ashmolean Museum, University of Oxford.

**'Arc Classics: New Translations
of Great Poets of the Past'
Series Editor: Jean Boase-Beier**

In memory of

Michael O'Neill
(1953-2018)
poet and scholar

'the soul's free to change its chamber'
Purgatorio 21. 62
(translated by Michael O'Neill)

CONTENTS

Postscript
Around *Purgatorio* – lyrics by Dante,
his predecessors and contemporaries

Resurrecting Dead Poetry

qui la morta poesì resurga
Purgatorio 1. 7

After the struggle of the descent through the labyrinths of Hell, Dante and Virgil have climbed back to the surface of the earth, and now at dawn on Easter Sunday they look up to the sky brightening over the sea. As a prelude to this renewal, at the opening of *Purgatorio's* first canto, a rebirth of the poem itself is announced:

> Let this be the place where we resurrect dead poetry
> *Purg.* 1. 7

Dante's journey will now be a reconstructive pilgrimage. It will explore the forms of penance rather than those of punishment, and the nature of community rather than that of conflict, enacting the purposeful 'movement of the spirit' (*moto spiritale, Purg.* 18. 32), with migrant souls winding up the terraces of a mountain, not trapped down in the vicious circles of Hell's hollowness. Escaping the travesties of creation, represented by the monsters and grotesque transformations of the *Inferno*, the *Purgatorio* will also frequently portray forms of creativity – human and divine – and amongst its communities whose members often address each other as 'brother' there will be a fraternity of poets. This is how Dante's guide Virgil speaks to a fellow Latin poet at a moment of recognition (*Purg.* 21. 131), and it is the form used too by several of the Italian poets whom the pilgrim 'Dante' encounters on this journey. So, when this Dante-persona recognizes his predecessor Guido Guinizelli in the 'refining fire' of the mountain's final terrace, he describes him as a 'father' (*padre*), but Guinizelli's response implicitly rejects the tribute and points the pilgrim towards the wider poetic community:

> 'My brother', he said, 'this one I'd rather refer
> to', and he indicated a spirit ahead of us,
> 'as a better crafter of the vernacular'.[1]

---

[1] *Purg.* 26. 115-17, as translated here by Alvin Pang.

Dante's Purgatory draws upon the medieval Christian belief – evolved over a long period and formally defined during Dante's time – in a 'middle state' between Heaven and Hell, where those whose sins had been forgiven during life would have to make satisfaction for them. In the *Purgatorio*, therefore, souls are portrayed making atonement over the course of time, and in a place that, as the poem reminds its readers, will not last for ever. Yet, as imagined here – a rugged mountain rising from the sea in the southern hemisphere and lit by a circling sun – the *Purgatorio* places the Dante-persona, Virgil his guide and the readers of the poem on more firmly familiar ground than either of the other afterworlds of the *Comedy*. In the words of a modern American poet who translated the *Purgatorio*:

> Here the times of the day recur with all the sensations and associations that the hours bring with them, the hours of the world we are living in as we read the poem.[2]

The *Purgatorio* thus represents a transient world, but unlike the permanent realms of the *Inferno* and the *Paradiso*, it is a world marked by the passing of time and by the motion and development of humanity in transition. On their way through the mountain's lower levels and up the higher terraces towards the Earthly Paradise at its summit, Dante and Virgil encounter groups of souls who embody the strengths and shortcomings of developing human communities: political, religious, artistic, poetic. Indeed, a recent guide to Dante has suggested that this is the part of the *Comedy* 'in which Dante's concern for the state of humanity on earth is most fully developed and articulated [...] the most human of the three *cantiche*'.[3]

The progress of souls and of the poem itself is frequently imagined in the *Comedy* as a kind of voyage – prosperous, difficult, or even disastrous. At the opening of *Purgatorio*'s first canto (translated here by Mary Jo Bang), the poet speaks

---

[2] From W. S. Merwin's Introduction to his verse translation of the *Purgatorio* (Random House, 2000).
[3] Peter Hainsworth & David Robey, *Dante: A Very Short Introduction* (Oxford University Press, 2015), p. 83.

of how 'My mind's little skiff' (*la navicella del mio ingegno*) now hoists sail. The act of raising and rising continues to apply to a poem which, having come through the 'bitter sea' of the *Inferno*, now sets a new course as it looks 'to travel over better waters'. So forceful is the metaphor of voyaging in this prologue to the *Comedy*'s 'second realm' that it led many of the poem's early illustrators to imagine Dante and Virgil themselves arriving on the shores of Mount Purgatory by boat, rather than (as they actually do in the poem) from the dead centre of the earth.[4]

A few decades later in Dante's own century, another vernacular poet would recognize and adapt the significance of this new departure. Embarking on the second book of his *Troilus*, Chaucer's poet-persona aligned the hopes of the storm-driven Trojan lover with the improving prospects of his own narrative voyage:

> Owt of thise blake wawes for to saylle,
> O wynd, o wynd, the weder ginneth clere;
> For in this see the boot hath swych travaylle,
> Of my connyng, that unneth I it stere.
> This see clepe I the tempestous matere
> Of disespeir that Troilus was inne;
> But now of hope the kalendes bygynne.

> ['Sailing out of these dark waves, I pray to the wind as the weather begins to clear, for in such a sea the vessel of my skill is so buffeted that I can scarcely steer it. The sea I speak of is the stormy state of despair that Troilus was in, but now is the time of dawning hope'.][5]

Hope is, as Chaucer recognized, the virtue that literally keeps the groups of migrant souls in the *Purgatorio* going, and its symbolic green colour recurs frequently in this part of Dante's poem. Hope of a more earthly kind also has significance for the English vernacular writer following in Dante's wake. In drawing upon the prologue to the *Comedy*'s second kingdom, the opening of the second book of the *Troilus* marks a new departure for the English poem: a moment

---

[4] Dante's fascination with the imaginary sea-voyage had been reflected earlier in his sonnet addressed to his friend and fellow-poet, Guido Cavalcanti, translated as the first lyric in the Postscript to this volume.
[5] Chaucer, *Troilus & Criseyde*, 2. 1-7.

when Chaucer turns from a domestic scene in his story's main source (a romance by Boccaccio) and looks ambitiously to place his narrative and art within the tradition of Dante's journey. Emulating the visionary poet of the *Purgatorio* may have taken a further form in Chaucer's time. Towards the end of the *Purgatorio* – the Earthly Paradise at the summit of the mountain – the problematic reunion of Dante and Beatrice may have influenced another great English medieval vernacular writer: the anonymous poet of *Pearl*, who makes a similarly idyllic setting the scene for an encounter between a visionary dreamer and his dead daughter, developing a dialogue which also leads in unexpected directions.[6]

Returning to the beginning of Dante's poem: following their arrival at the foot of Mount Purgatory, the pilgrim and his guide Virgil linger uncertainly on the shore of the island, looking out to sea. Here they see in the distance a 'light and swift vessel' propelled by the wings of an angelic helmsman and bringing a group of souls who, as the boat approaches, can be heard singing with one voice a psalm of deliverance from captivity: 'When Israel went out of Egypt'.[7] As these souls disembark and ask for directions, Virgil has to reply *noi siam peregin, come voi siete*: 'we are outsiders, just the same as you'.[8] The word *peregrino* also means 'pilgrim'; it is used here for the first time in the *Commedia*, and its significance will gather force through the rest of the poem. Dante, the traveller, and those he encounters throughout the ascent of the mountain, are part of a Christian community on the move.

Another common metaphor describing such a community at this time – and one that Dante will allude to elsewhere – is that of St Peter's ship; hence the group of souls coming ashore on his purgatorial island can be imagined as a kind of itinerant church. This kind of arrival finds a parallel – and some comparable complexities – in seventeenth-century English writing. Andrew Marvell's boatload of saintly exiles crossing the 'Oceans bosome' in his poem 'The Bermudas' approach their Edenic island in a similar spirit, singing their

---

[6] See the translation of canto 30 here by Jane Draycott, who has also translated the Middle English *Pearl* (Carcanet / Oxford Poets, 2011).
[7] Psalm 114 (113 in the Vulgate).
[8] *Purg.* 2. 63, as translated here by Bernard O'Donoghue.

own psalm of deliverance:

> Thus sung they in the English boat,
> An holy and a chearful Note
> And all the way, to guide their Chime,
> With falling Oars they kept the time.[9]

Despite the differences of political and religious context –
and the possible ironies of the Puritan pilgrims' vision – they
still bear a striking resemblance to Dante's redeemed souls in
their angelic vessel, maintaining a similar harmony and singing
in unison the psalm that reflects both their transitional state
and their unity of purpose as they approach the new world:

> *'When Israel emerged out of Egypt'*,
> They all sang together with one voice,
> and all that is written after in that Psalm.
> *Purg.* 2. 46-8

That liberated voice can be heard again in a twenty-first-
century account of actual migrants crossing the sea and
celebrating deliverance. A recent account of the 2015 refugee
crisis by Patrick Kingsley describes the moment when three
hundred Eritreans were rescued at sea north of Libya:

> For the majority, this is a time to rejoice. Seemingly without
> discussion they organise themselves in neat rows on the
> packed deck. One man rises from their midst, stands before
> them, and begins to sing. Then the hundreds sitting below
> him join in unison – they all know the words. A series of
> Christian hymns wafts over the waters of the Mediterranean.
> Minutes after being rescued, this huge crowd of Eritreans are
> thanking God for letting them live.[10]

For Dante's migrants arriving on the shore of Purgatory,
song continues to serve a celebratory purpose. From this
group of 'new people' a single figure emerges to greet Dante
as a much-loved friend (*Purg.* 2. 76-7). Of the many souls to

---

[9] Marvell, 'Bermudas', ll. 37-40. A recent view of the poem's complexities and
contexts is by Timothy Raylor, 'The Instability of Marvell's "Bermudas"',
in the *Marvell Newsletter*, Winter 2014, online at: https://marvell.wp.st-
andrews.ac.uk/newsletter/the-instability-of-marvells-bermudas/.
[10] Patrick Kingsley, *The New Odyssey: The Story of Europe's Refugee Crisis*
(*Guardian* / Faber, 2016).

be recognized and identified during Dante's ascent of the mountain, this first acquaintance is a fellow-artist: a musician about whom little else is known. Known to have set the work of at least one other Tuscan poet to music, the soul identified simply as 'Casella' is then made to mark the harmonious reunion of the living and the dead by setting to music one of Dante's own *canzoni*:

> 'Love which speaks to me within my mind'
> he started then to sing so very sweetly
> that the memory of it still echoes deep within me.[11]

The song holds its audience of poets and pilgrims briefly enchanted before being broken off by the guardian of the mountain brusquely reminding all of them that they have a 'more pressing concern' that should move them on towards the ascent of the mountain. But the singer's tribute draws together for a moment elements of the poet's social, intellectual and artistic past, strengthening the bond of community between travellers in Purgatory.

Recollection of friends and fellow artists amid the pressure of other needs and circumstances would lead another English poet to evoke this scene in the *Purgatorio* when he says of a contemporary musician:

> Dante shall give fame leave to set thee higher
> Than his Casella, whom he wooed to sing,
> Met in the milder shades of Purgatory.[12]

Written in 1646, towards the end of the first Civil War, John Milton's tribute 'To Mr H[enry]. Lawes on his Airs' addresses the composer who had set to music the songs of the poet's early masque *Comus*. Milton's Dantean conclusion to this sonnet not only celebrates a fellow-artist's achievement, but also subtly acknowledges the painful fact that in what one of the combatants called 'this war without an enemy', the

---

[11] *Purg.* 2. 112-14, translated here by Bernard O'Donoghue. The poem that Casella sets to music (the *canzone*, 'Amor che ne la mente mi ragiona') is also translated in the Postscript to this volume (lyric no. 2).
[12] For the text of Milton's sonnet 'To Mr H. Lawes' (no. XIII), see *John Milton: Complete Shorter Poems*, ed. J. Carey (Longman, 1968) and many other editions.

Parliamentarian poet and the Royalist musician had taken different sides. Locating and imagining a meeting 'in the milder shades of Purgatory' probably implies comparison with the coming challenges of ascending Dante's rugged mountain, thus suggesting that Lawes and Milton each now have a harder journey ahead of them.

For Milton, closer engagement with the doctrines of Dante's *Purgatory* would have been problematic, and the fact that a third of Dante's poem is devoted to what British Protestant readers regarded as a 'Popish superstition' could partly explain why it took so long to appear in English translation. A seventeenth-century English poet with a Catholic background would, however, respond vividly to the central ethos and imagery of the *Purgatorio*. John Donne mentions Dante on several occasions, owned a copy of the *Convivio* (which he inscribed in Italian), and in his Fourth Satire may well be referring to the *Inferno* when he speaks of one 'who dreamt he saw hell'. But it is in a well-known passage towards the end of his Third Satire that Donne seems to come closest to the experience and significance of Dante's ascent of the 'holy mountain':

> ... On a huge hill,
> Cragged and steep, Truth stands, and hee that will
> Reach her, about must, and about must goe;
> And what th' hills suddennes resists, winne so;
> Yet strive so, that before age, deaths twilight,
> Thy Soule rest, for none can worke in that night.[13]

Several features of Donne's 'hill' in Satire 3 parallel those of Dante's *santo monte*: for instance, the idealized feminine figure on its summit and night as the time when the climbing cannot progress. But it is the sense of energetic yet circuitous progression ('about must, and about must goe') that registers Donne's strongest response to Dante's ascent, which the pilgrim describes in powerfully paradoxical terms here (in Andrew Fitzsimons's translation) as:

---

[13] For the texts of Donne's satires, see *The Satires, Epigrams and Verse Letters of John Donne*, ed. W. Milgate (Clarendon Press, 1967) and many other editions. On Donne and Dante, see N. Havely, *Dante's British Public: Readers & Texts* (Oxford UP, 2014), pp. 78-9 with notes 66 and 68.

the climbing and circling of this mountain,
which straightens you whom the world has twisted.[14]

With the revival of interest in Dante during the early
nineteenth century, an English Romantic poet would have no
hesitation in engaging more explicitly and sustainedly with
this part of the *Commedia*. For Percy Shelley, as for Milton, the
second canto of the *Purgatorio* seems to have carried especial
appeal. In a letter to Leigh Hunt long after the poet's death,
Mary Shelley wrote:

> Can any thing be so wondrously poetical as the approach of
> the boat with souls from earth to Purgatory – Shelley's most
> favourite passage [in Dante][15]

and Shelley himself (also in a letter to Leigh Hunt) had earlier
spoken of 'the spirit coming over the sea in a boat like Mars
rising from the vapours of the horizon' as displaying 'all the
exquisite tenderness & sensibility, in which Dante excelled all
poets except Shakespeare'.[16]

In the same letter, Shelley identified another such scene from
the *Purgatorio*: the portrayal at the beginning of canto 28 of the
Dante-pilgrim's entry into the Edenic 'Earthly Paradise' at the
summit of the mountain. Around 1820-1, Shelley translated
the first half of the canto; and along with another unfinished
project, *The Triumph of Life*, the verse of his translation from
Purgatorio 28 represents an experiment in *terza rima* that
remains one of the most extensive and significant translations
of Dante by a major English poet.[17] In Shelley's version of the
scene, the tracing of Dante's gradual but expectant progress
through 'the divine wood' towards Matelda responds vividly
to the canto's vision of recovering Paradise, as does the English
poet's portrayal of the 'bright lady' herself , when at the end of
the fragment she appears

---

[14] *Purg.* 23. 125-6, where Dante combines the verbs *salendo* and *rigirando*.
[15] *Letters of Mary Wollstonecraft Shelley*, ed. B. T. Bennett (Johns Hopkins UP, 1980-8), 2: 283.
[16] *Letters of Percy Bysshe Shelley*, ed. F. L. Jones (Oxford UP, 1964), 2: 112.
[17] Shelley's translation is re-edited here by Timothy Webb, and the canto is completed by Michael O'Neill.

like Proserpine ...
                        ... singing here
And gathering flowers, at that time when
She lost the spring and Ceres her ... more dear.

Shelley's preference for the 'tenderness & sensibility' of the *Purgatorio*'s poet, as opposed to the 'severe' and 'hell-darkening' Dante of Hazlitt and others, would soon be echoed by a number of influential Victorian writers. In his *Lectures on the History of Literature* (1838), Thomas Carlyle noted, and to some extent shared, the popular fascination with the 'dark' Dante of the *Inferno*, but – perhaps following in the tracks of Donne's Third Satire – he also asked whether the *Purgatorio* might not be thought

> a better and greater thing on the whole. It is very beautiful to see them get up into that black great mountain in the western ocean, where Columbus had not yet been. To trace *giro* after *giro*, the purification of souls is beautiful exceedingly; the sinner's repentance, the humble hope...[18]

In a later lecture on *The Hero as Poet* (1840), Carlyle continued to develop the idea, attributing the contemporary preference for the *Inferno* to 'our general Byronism of taste' and portraying Dante's 'Mountain of Purification' as 'an emblem of the noblest conception of that age'. In this lecture, the *Purgatorio*'s dramatisation of urgent penitence and 'never-dying Hope' seem for Carlyle to embody an ideal of combining social solidarity and self-help:

> The joy too of all, when one has prevailed; the whole Mountain shakes with joy, and a psalm of praise rises, when one soul has perfected repentance and got its sin and misery left behind![19]

The *Purgatorio* would also carry particular significance – exemplifying 'special points of contact between Dante and the genius of our own century' – for a later Victorian critic, Walter Pater. In his 1892 introduction to the first volume of a verse-translation of Dante's poem by his Oxford friend Charles Lancelot Shadwell, Pater identified these 'special points' as

---

[18] In *Dante in English Literature,* ed. Paget Toynbee (Methuen, 1909), 2: 491.
[19] *Ibid.,* 2: 505.

> a minute sense of the external world [...] a minute sense
> of the phenomena of the mind [...] a demand for wide and
> cheering outlooks in religion [and] for a largeness of spirit in
> its application to life ... [20]

Like Carlyle, Pater stressed the primacy of hope among
the souls in Dante's 'second realm', and he identified amid the
religious scepticism of his own age

> a development of religious hope or hopefulness, similar in
> tendency to the development of the doctrine of Purgatory in
> the church of the Middle Age...[21]

'Hopefulness' and 'cheering outlooks' were features of
Victorian culture that annoyed T. S. Eliot. For him, they stood
alongside 'optimism' as representing 'a great deal of what one
hated in the nineteenth century'.[22] In his 1929 essay *Dante*, in
Faber's 'Poets on the Poets' series (from which that last phrase
is quoted), Eliot's reading of the *Purgatorio* reacts sharply
against the ethos of critics like Carlyle and Pater. In the same
passage, he also claims that 'Pre-Raphaelite imagery', too, got
in the way of his due 'appreciation of Beatrice'.[23] Eliot may have
had in mind here such mid-Victorian visualizations as Dante
Gabriel Rossetti's watercolour of *Purgatorio* 30 'The Meeting
of Dante and Beatrice in [the Earthly] Paradise' (1853-4), and
its sentimentalizing of an encounter which, in Eliot's view,
dramatises 'the passionate conflict of the old feelings with the
new', and which embodies 'the greatest *personal* intensity in
the whole poem'.[24]

Eliot does of course acknowledge the obvious importance
of hope as giving purpose to the sufferings of souls on the
terraces of the mountain, and thus distinguishing them from
the hopeless inhabitants of Dante's 'blind prison'. But – unlike
Carlyle, Rossetti and Pater – he is concerned from the start
to stress the difficulty of the *Purgatorio* and the importance
of the reader's learning from it 'that a straightforward

---

[20] *The Purgatory of Dante Alighieri: an Experiment in Literal Translation* (Macmillan, 1892), p. xxiii.
[21] Pater, Introduction to *The Purgatory of Dante Alighieri*, p. xx.
[22] T. S Eliot, *Dante* (Faber, 1929), p. 42.
[23] *Ibid.*, p. 42.
[24] *Ibid.*, p. 44.

philosophical statement can be great poetry'.[25] As Eliot's essay later makes clear, he has in mind particularly the 'suspension of belief' required for that modern reader to grapple with the discourses of the *Purgatorio*'s (and the *Commedia*'s) central cantos. Discourses such as Virgil's on the nature of love in canto 17 (91-139) are thus for Eliot examples of 'the philosophy of that world of poetry which we have entered'.[26]

Encounters with Dante's ancestors from that 'world of poetry' are for Eliot among the 'easier' episodes in the *Purgatorio*, and his discussion of them in the 1929 essay has a bearing upon his own poetic practice. His account of 'the meeting with Dante's predecessors', Guido Guinizelli and Arnaut Daniel – along with his revision of the prose translation of the 'superb verses' that comprise Arnaut Daniel's prayer of hope and plea for Dante's remembrance (*Purg.* 26. 140-7) – reflects the significances that the episode of the souls 'purged in flame' had carried and would continue to carry for him.[27] Dante's portrayal of the twelfth-century Occitan poet Arnaut had been invoked at least three times in Eliot's poetry before that: the opening of his plea for remembrance *Ara vus prec* ('And so I pray you') was the title of a 1920 collection of poems, and Arnaut's return into 'that fire which refines them' (*Purg.* 26. 148) had been quoted in the original in the final section of *The Waste Land*, where the title that Guido Guinizelli gives him in *Purgatorio* 26 (*il miglior fabbro* 'the better craftsman') had been applied to Eliot's fellow-poet (and devotee of Arnaut) Ezra Pound, by way of dedication.

Eliot's developing ascetic style and his quest for what he would later call 'Purgatorial [...] effect' would continue to be informed by Dante's poets on the last terrace of the penitents (canto 26). Arnaut's plea for intercession – *Sovegna vos* ('be mindful') – is quoted in the fourth section of *Ash Wednesday* (1930), amid what one critic sees as the 'churchyard melancholy' of that penitential poem.[28] In the last of the *Four Quartets*

---

[25] *Ibid.*, p. 29.

[26] T. S. Eliot, *op. cit.*, p. 40.

[27] Eliot's rendering of Arnaut's lines (*Dante*, p. 34) represents one of his furthest departures from the Temple Classics version which he normally uses for translating the original in the 1929 essay.

[28] Alison Milbank, *Dante and the Victorians* (Manchester UP, 1998), p. 227.

(composed in 1942), the speech of Eliot's 'dead master' enacts a form of linguistic and spiritual purification and imagines a 'refining fire' like that of *Purgatorio* 26, where 'the exasperated spirit […] must move in measure, like a dancer' ('Little Gidding' II). Here the poets and lovers in the flames of the last terrace of Dante's *Purgatorio* seem to join forces with the 'sages standing in God's holy fire' who had become the poet's initial 'singing-masters' in Yeats's 'Sailing to Byzantium' – a poem which itself had begun in a Dantean way with a voyage and in two earlier drafts had perhaps even alluded to the pilgrim's arrival and his ascent to the Gate of Purgatory.[29]

The *Purgatorio* was, in even more extensive ways, a 'singing school' for a major poet of the later twentieth century: Seamus Heaney. Heaney's 1991 collection *Seeing Things*, with its 'Markings', 'Drawings' and 'Squarings' is a kind of builders' yard in which Dante is the poetic foreman; and the *Commedia*'s presence is evident: from the beginning – where the ghost of Larkin quotes the opening lines of *Inferno* 2 in Heaney's own translation – to the end, where the poet re-enacts the 'crossing' of the Acheron in *Inferno* 3. *Seeing Things* also invokes Dante's metaphor for his own craft in the *Purgatorio*. One of the earlier poems in the collection, 'The Biretta', (pp. 26-7) transforms a priest's hat – being held by the young Heaney as altar boy – first into a child's 'paper boat' and then (from the adult poet's point of view) into the vessel that 'wafts into / The first lines of the *Purgatorio*'.

Heaney here harks back to Dante's rhetorical throat-clearing as he emerges from the mouth of hell and enters the 'second realm' of his poem (*Purg.* 1. 1-12), albeit with a hint of scepticism. In a later interview he describes how, as an altar boy being handed the priest's biretta, 'there was a momentary temptation to launch it into the sanctuary like a paper dart' and how in the poem he decided to turn it into Dante's 'boat of the imagination' (the *navicella del mio ingegno* of *Purg.* 1. 2).[30] The irreverent context for this allusion to the key poem of Catholic culture – like the turning 'upside down' of the biretta

---

[29] Earlier versions of the poem included the mariners 'singing at the oars' during the journey and a 'marble stair' at the narrator's entrance to the city (drafts b1r and b2r).

[30] Dennis O'Driscoll, *Stepping Stones: Interviews with Seamus Heaney* (Faber, 2008), p. 327.

that precedes it – looks to be of a piece with Heaney's gently subversive portrayal of priestly authority in 'The Biretta', but it also reflects the continuing Dantean 'impulse' behind *Seeing Things* as a whole.

A few years before *Seeing Things*, Heaney had interrogated the language of *Purgatorio* more harshly and in a more explicitly political context. In *Station Island* (1984) he had staged a Dantean encounter with a relative and victim of sectarian assassination who appears to rebuke the poet for 'evasion' of that event and the brutal 'fact' of violence. Drawing upon the purgatorial context of the ancient pilgrimage site where the encounter is imagined to take place (St Patrick's Purgatory on Lough Derg), Heaney's 'second cousin' now questions whether his kinsman is making any kind of atonement for using the 'lovely blinds' of Dante's *Purgatorio* in an earlier elegy – 'The Strand at Lough Beg: In Memory of Colum McCartney' in *Field Work* (1979) – and having, in that poem's final scene, 'saccharined' the brute facts of Colum's death 'with morning dew.'[31]

Part of the allusion here is once again to the opening canto of the *Purgatorio* and the dew with which Virgil ritually washes away 'the muck and mire of Hell' from the pilgrim Dante's 'tear-stained cheeks' (1. 121-9). The cousin's parting words in *Station Island* VIII also seem to 'accuse directly' the earlier poem in *Field Work* (1979) where Heaney had commemorated his death. 'The Strand at Lough Beg' uses as its epigraph Dorothy Sayers's translation of Dante's evocative water-music, describing the waves breaking on the shores of Mount Purgatory and the 'tall rushes' that grow there out of 'the oozy sand' (*Purg.* 1. 100-2).[32]

The last scene of Heaney's poem re-imagines the Purgatorial ritual in the 'early mist' and 'squeaking sedge' of the Northern Irish lough.[33] Like the later encounter in *Station Island* VIII, the scene in 'The Strand at Lough Beg' does not shy away from the marks of the murder itself – the 'blood and roadside muck' – and its concluding image of the 'rushes that shoot green again' could well hint at renewed violence as well as

---

[31] Heaney, *Station Island* (Faber, 1984), p. 83.
[32] *Dante: "The Divine Comedy"* II translated by Dorothy L. Sayers (Penguin Classics, 1955), p. 76.
[33] Heaney, *Field Work* (Faber, 1979), p. 18.

rebirth. Yet – as the resort to elaborate similes suggests ('Like a dull blade [...] Fine as the drizzle...') – uneasy questions about poetic 'evasion' may still remain.

In *Station Island* meanwhile, a kind of 'atonement' for that earlier use of 'the lovely blinds of the *Purgatorio*' does already seem to be under way, by means of an encounter with another victim of sectarian violence (the shopkeeper, Willie Strathearn), in the section preceding the meeting with McCartney. In *Station Island* VII, the atrocity is confronted tersely through low-key dialogue and direct description of the 'shock' with which the pilgrim dwells on the 'ravaged forehead' of his dead friend. There may be a parallel here with a Dantean soul whose death was due to political violence and whose appearance comes a shock to the pilgrim in the *Purgatorio*: the Ghibelline leader Manfred, whose face is likewise suddenly seen to have 'one eyebrow split with a blow' and who directs the Dante-persona to look at the fatal wound to his chest.[34] A possible parallel between *Station Island* and Dante's political vision remains unspoken, but Heaney is likely to have responded to the *Purgatorio*'s portrayal of factional conflict (in *Purg.* 3 and elsewhere), as he had earlier done to internecine strife in the *Inferno*.[35]

In a different cultural context, Dante's 'shaping influence' would also be evident at the end of *Station Island*, through an episode which shows the *Purgatorio* helping to articulate a sense of the poet's role within a literary and linguistic community. The final encounter in Heaney's whole sequence is with the detached, self-exiled 'old father', James Joyce, whose voice is heard here 'eddying with the vowels of all rivers' and who, as Heaney later argued, 'qualifies as a poet more than most writers of verse'.[36] Heaney's Joyce draws the pilgrim back on to the mainland, urging him now to 'Take off from here' beyond the 'circle' of conventional politics or religion – '... it's time to swim'.[37]

As Heaney later understood it: 'in the fiction of the poem, the advice is given to somebody who has been "in the swim"

---

[34] *Purgatorio* 3. 108, as translated in this volume by A. E. Stallings.
[35] As in Heaney's 'Ugolino' (*Field Work*, pp. 61-4).
[36] Dennis O'Driscoll, *op. cit.*, p. 249.
[37] Heaney, *Station Island*, pp. 93-4.

of Lough Derg [the pilgrimage site] [...] rather than out on his own'.[38] And although Heaney does not spell out the parallel, 'Joyce's' role and speech here – his emphasis on the opportunity and need 'to write for the joy of it' – powerfully echo Virgil's final words to Dante as the pilgrim nears the end of his journey in the *Purgatorio*:

> 'lo tuo piacere omai prendi per duce;
> fuor sei de l'erte vie, fuor sei de l'arte'.

> ['now let pleasure be your guide,
> for you are past the steep and narrow rut'.][39]

The 'Joyce' of *Station Island* also rejoices with his fellow Irish writer that 'The English language / belongs to us' – a claim that might have been advanced by several non-English anglophone poets who translated or imagined the *Purgatorio*.

The actual Joyce of *A Portrait of the Artist* himself appropriated several scenes from this cantica – notably Stephen Dedalus's epiphanic encounter with the 'bird-girl':

> She was alone and still, gazing out to sea; and when she felt his presence and the worship of his eyes her eyes turned to him in quiet sufferance of his gaze, without shame or wantonness. Long, long she suffered his gaze and then quietly withdrew her eyes from his and bent them towards the stream, gently stirring the water with her foot hither and thither.[40]

The exchange of glances at a liminal moment in Joyce's narrative is paralleled by the pilgrim's gazing at Matelda by the stream in canto 28 of the *Purgatorio*.[41] And Joyce's colleague and compatriot, Samuel Beckett – another writer who likewise (to quote Heaney's words again) 'qualifies as a poet more than most writers of verse' – would draw upon the *Purgatorio* from his early fiction through to his late dramas, where the resonances of Dante's second afterworld would converge with those from the *Inferno*.[42] In Beckett's most famous Dantean

---

[38] O'Driscoll, *op. cit.*, p. 250.
[39] *Purg.* 27. 131-2, translated here by Alvin Pang.
[40] Joyce, *A Portrait of the Artist* IV,. pp. 867-71.
[41] James Robinson, 'Purgatorio in the Portrait', in *Dante in the Nineteenth Century* (Peter Lang, 2011), pp. 267-70.
[42] Hugh Haughton, 'Purgatory Regained? Beckett and Dante', in *Dante's Modern Afterlife* (Macmillan, 1998), p. 146.

reinvention, the 'listless' and sceptical Belacqua – found lingering on the lower slopes of Purgatory – becomes 'the dirty low-down Low Church Protestant high-brow' protagonist of *More Pricks than Kicks* (1934). The original Belacqua's 'lazy manner and curt remark provoked a slight smile' of recognition from the poet (*Purg.* 4. 121-2). As Hugh Haughton has pointed out, by the end of the Irish writer's career, 'Dante's friend has become Beckett's', and in the late autobiographical fiction, *Company* (1980), Belacqua takes a curtain call as 'the old lutist cause of Dante's first quarter-smile'.[43]

English-language poets have thus, from medieval to modern times, reinvented, alluded to and quoted from the *Purgatorio* and recognized its importance as a 'singing school'; but not many of them so far have produced complete translations. Two of those who have done so are American: H. W. Longfellow in the nineteenth century and W. S. Merwin in the twentieth. Longfellow's lengthy progress towards a verse rendering of the whole *Commedia* (not completed till 1867) began with the *Purgatorio*. He lectured on it at Harvard in 1838 and in a collection of poems the following year published versions of passages from cantos 2 (13-51), 28 (1-33) and parts of cantos 30-31, thus reflecting and sustaining the Romantic interest in Dante's 'Celestial Pilot' and his 'Terrestrial Paradise', whilst perhaps prefiguring the mid-nineteenth-century cult of Beatrice. Shortly afterwards he would embark upon the whole cantica over the course of ten years, from 1843 to 1847.

Like Longfellow, Merwin is expert in Romance literature, and his complete *Purgatorio* (2000) is a relatively recent addition to a long list of translations from many languages that includes several major medieval European texts, such as *The Poem of the Cid* (1959) and *The Song of Roland* (1963). Recognizing 'the impossibility of ever really translating the *Divine Comedy*', Merwin's *Purgatorio* aims to deploy what he calls 'convocations' of English words that will have a 'thrust and sense' comparable to those of Dante.

Merwin's interest in the *Purgatorio* as a prime example of 'poetry that was written from perspectives revealingly different from our own' is shared by the sixteen contributors to this collection. The

---

[43] Haughton *op. cit.*, pp. 160-1, quoting *Company* p. 85 and alluding to the encounter in *Purg.* 4: 97-135.

poets translating this *Purgatorio* draw upon a variety of different cultures: Australian, Caribbean, English, Irish, Italian, North American, Scottish, Singaporean. All of them also draw upon their experience of translating verse from different languages (including Italian). Two of them have already published versions of the *Inferno* and have now completed voyages through the 'better waters' of this second cantica.[44]

The translations here thus render the *Purgatorio* in a number of different voices, reflecting a range of contemporary cultures, concerns and techniques. For example, Lorna Goodison's account of canto 12 is informed by the language, landscape and politics of Jamaica, whilst Colin Donati's version of cantos 19 and 20 draws upon Scottish vocabulary, and John Kinsella in canto 32 engages with environmental issues. Verse here also reflects the potential of a variety of metrical forms for the re-voicing of the poem. Steve Ellis, for example, uses the seven- or eight-syllable verse that featured in his telegraphically compact version of *Hell*; and another translator of the *Inferno*, Mary Jo Bang, intersperses terse six-syllable lines among the longer ones; whilst versions by two eminent translators of medieval English poetry – Bernard O'Donoghue and Jane Draycott – reflect the capacities of five-stress meter. A number of the renderings – such as those by Michael O'Neill, Andrew Fitzsimons and Alvin Pang – frequently approximate Dante's original rhyme scheme; Angela Leighton follows a four-beat rhythm, reflecting the predominant stress pattern in the *Commedia*'s line; and two of the translators – A. E. Stallings and Patrick Worsnip – use different forms of full *terza rima*.

The debate about appropriate voices and verse forms for rendering Dante's *Commedia* into English goes back at least to the earliest British translations of the whole poem, and it seems set to continue.[45] Meanwhile, that poem's versatility is illustrated by the various versions that follow here in this 'Poets' *Purgatorio*'.

Nick Havely

---

[44] Steve Ellis's translation of the complete *Divine Comedy* was published by Vintage in 2019, and Mary Jo Bang's version of the *Purgatorio* is published by Graywolf.
[45] The debate has recently been enlivened by the 70 versions of *Inferno* cantos in *To Hell and Back: an Anthology of Dante's Inferno in English Translation* (1782-2017), ed. Tim Smith and Marco Sonzogni (John Benjamins, 2017).

Prelude: About *Purgatorio*
Four poems by contemporary poets

1. Jan Kemp

Crux Australis – Te Paki o Autahi – The Southern Cross[1]

'I turned to the right and considered the other pole,
and I saw four stars never seen except by the first people.'
Purg. 1. 22-4

He never saw this kite of four stars,
yet knew they existed – heart map of home, our palm, hemisphere,
where we know where we are upside down near the pole.

Somehow, he knew Eden is here,
& we hand on the sunrise
from Mt Hikurangi, a flaming canna.

And Dante, pilgrim, could have climbed up out of the shaft,
plumb opposite Jerusalem, to stand ankle deep in the Pacific,
on a shoal near the Kermadecs

awestruck at seeing his cardinal virtues,
incarnate, white, on the milk near Centaurus –
Justice, Prudence, Temperance & Fortitude,
rocks the gods had flung out of the back yard,
making space to plant the herbs
of faith, hope and *aroha*.

---

[1] From Jan Kemp, *Dante's Heaven* (Puriri Press, 2006).

2. Jamie McKendrick

il tremoto[2]

Inside the mountain earth begins to move
its joints and spring the links that pegged it down
– the fans of schist, the chocks and wedges of

feldspar and chert. A daylight owl screws back
from rock that spilling derelicts her nest
then quiet plugs the ear, a twist of wax.

Behind the quiet a core of silence hums
until earth moves again – this time in earnest:
dumb matter's rigid-tongued delirium

wrung at the verge of the crack that gapes at
the heart of things, that widens the Norman watchtower
from its sunken gateway to the parapet

as the tide uncoils. This means in Purgatory
a soul pinned to the rock has broken free.

---

[2] From 'The Mountain' in Jamie McKendrick, *Selected Poems* (Faber, 2016).

3. Angela Leighton

Dante on Reflection: Canto X, Purgatorio[3]

So this is the way to go, however
you summarise the sin, calibrate the soul:
to follow a road to the ends of the world.

That door clanged shut – was I out or in?
(Over my shoulder Eurydice lapsed.
Lot's wife was salted to an upright stack.)

But he and I pressed on through a chink –
stonewalled, yet finding some permissive path
that pitched and rolled under our feet.

My dear poet warned me: 'Now use your art.
Just dance, balance – dare to dream
how a passage might carry you through and out.'

It was madness, I knew – sheer lunacy to think
we could find our way in the waning moonlight,
squeeze our shapes through the eye of a needle

to clear this world and discover another.
But we did, somehow, emerging elsewhere
on a plain, a blank, a flatness so sheer

we stepped out blindly, trying to find our feet,
dizzied by a ground that stretched to nowhere –
lonely as hell, barren as a waste.

And though it seemed endless, measureless to man,
yet a mountain rose, and near where we sat
an edge gave suddenly onto nothingness.

---

[3] From Angela Leighton, *One, Two* (Carcanet, 2021)

I searched the fathomless scene all round,
trying to map that country of the mind,
its wild carousel of heights and depths;

and that was when I saw, suddenly quite close,
a cliff of white rising beside me.
Impassable it seemed, a marble sheet,

but beautifully, finely carved in relief,
finer than porcelain, sharper than light,
than icicles shaped by nature overnight.

And I traced an angel with the grace of a man
announcing *All Hail*, wings riffled with flight.
The words in my ears from the hollow of his mouth

matched my deepest heart's desire –
as if the scappled marble sliced
sounds out of air – was it memory's knife? –

and a palombino whiteness met
like breathlessness my outstretched hand.
I could dream-caress each dumb-found sense.

In death's harsh land of pain and penitence,
where sweating, wounded souls staggered up
their helix track – sorry flesh-bound shades

bound for the summit to be freed from themselves –
I paused to follow the stone's allure,
its speaking lines figuring a cry

ancient as story, rehearsed every day
in wishing litanies, faithful prayers.
And then I remembered my own art's hoard

of echoes gathered from ages before:
the river from which no soul returns;
three times that shade fled, fugitive as dream.

My sweet poet nudged me. It was time to go,
but I ducked, delayed, slunk round to stay
gazing at that angel's momentous invitation:

to sing death's *ninna-nanna* to a child;
while, pierced with foresight any mother denies,
she knelt to answer with heart-broken eyes.

So something truer than right or wrong,
than measured dues and heavenly rewards,
gave me pause – and held me dreaming, where

that marble effigy gentled the cliff face.
How know art's knowhow, its slow skill to feel?
Where else but elsewhere the dream's own place?

I searched sin's calculus, to discover art's grace.

4. Michael O'Neill

Detained[4]

Day after day, the sky a tempered blue
that hardly changed in hue, you sat,
trying to grasp the *Purgatorio*.

The envious with eyelids sewn, their late
errors forgiven but not quite forgotten,
the slothful racing ahead, soon out of sight,

the discourse, and the glimmerings of Heaven –
all these detained you from the summer's slow,
accelerating slide towards oblivion,

the swimmers and the waters' undertow,
the paunches and the tough resolves in tatters,
the minor torments dealt by midge and mosquito,

and too much sun, inertia over great matters,
the rubbing sandal and the brand-new blister,
the hint of violence after silence shatters,

the litany intoned each night of other,
if also flawed, accounts of being. You
erased them all, content to be there, where

no rain nor hail nor snow nor dew
could fall[5], and where *thought grew
into a dream*[6] whose substance had not vanished,

as if belief survived, as if, in fact, it flourished.

---

[4] From Michael O'Neill, *Gangs of Shadow* (Arc, 2014)
[5] As in Michael O'Neill's version of *Purgatorio* 21, here, ll. 46-7.
[6] A version of the last line of *Purgatorio* 18.

Dante
Purgatorio

ABBREVIATIONS AND PRINTED SOURCES

Aen.   Virgil, *Aeneid*

AV   Bible, 1611 Authorized Version

BGLD *Blackwell's Guides to Literature: Dante*, Nick Havely (Oxford, 2007)

Boyde *Dante Philomythes and Philosopher: Man in the Cosmos*, Patrick Boyde (Cambridge, 1981)

CL   *Dante Alighieri: Commedia*, ed. Anna Maria Chiavacci Leonardi (Milan, 1991-7), 3 vols

Conv. Dante, *Convivio*

DBC   Lucan, *De bello civico*, also known as *Pharsalia*

DE   *The Dante Encyclopedia*, ed. R. Lansing (New York & London, 2000)

DM   *The Divine Comedy of Dante Alighieri*, ed. & tr. Robert Durling, introduction & notes by Robert Durling & Ronald Martinez (Oxford, 1996-2013), 3 vols

DVE   Dante, *De vulgari eloquentia*

Inf.   Dante, *Inferno*

JB   *The New Jerusalem Bible: Standard Edition,* ed. H. Wansborough (London, 1985)

Met.   Ovid, *Metamorphoses*

Mon.   Dante, *Monarchia*

Par.   Dante, *Paradiso*

Purg. Dante, *Purgatorio*

Theb. Statius, *Thebaid*

VN   Dante, *Vita Nova*

ONLINE RESOURCES:
'Dante Worlds' at danteworlds.laits.utexas.edu includes images, textual commentary and audio-recordings.

The Princeton Dante Project at etcweb.princeton.edu includes original texts, translations, recitation of the *Commedia* in Italian, and historical and interpretive notes.

Dante Then and Now

It was a life that had – and still has – political, popular and poetic dimensions.

Most of Dante's works – including the *Commedia* – were the product of his banishment from his native city. He was, as he mentions in the *Commedia*, born and baptised in Florence; this was some time between late May and early June 1265. It was there in the early 1290s that he composed his collection of poems and commentaries, portraying the development of his relationship with Beatrice: the *Vita nova*. Later in that decade he embarked upon a political career, being elected to high office in the city at the turn of the century. This was why in the *Commedia* he dates his 'middle of life' crisis to 1300. Around then he fell foul of the Papacy and Florentine political rivals and was subsequently sentenced to exile early in 1302. The rest of his life would be spent under the protection and patronage of various rulers of other cities and regions in Northern Italy; and while this would involve constantly 'going up and down other men's stairs', it would also enable him to compose works such as a treatise on vernacular poetry, an unfinished philosophical encyclopedia (the *Convivio*), and the hundred cantos of the *Commedia*, which he began around 1307-10. In one of those Northern Italian cities, Ravenna, he died, 700 years ago, in September 1321.

Dante's writing during those years of exile constantly reflected his political commitments. Not only did he write forceful invective in the *Inferno* against political opponents in Florence and corrupt Popes at Rome and Avignon, to make them, as his ancestor in Paradise would say, 'scratch where they itch'; he also developed a positive vision of renewal in the governance of Church and State. Early in the second decade of the fourteenth century, when he was writing the *Purgatorio*, it seemed that there was a faint chance of uniting much of Europe under a new Holy Roman Emperor, and Dante responded to that moment in public letters and in the political utterances of the *Purgatorio* itself. That project ended in failure, but his concern for political and religious reform continued to be voiced in his later work. Around 1317, a few years before his death, he wrote a treatise on world monarchy in which he also argued for the restriction of the Church's temporal power; and even in the *Paradiso* – the journey of celestial enlightenment that concludes the *Commedia* – there is a constant regard for the earthly order; for time as well as eternity; for the human as well the heavenly 'populace'.

The wider earthly populace has always been part of Dante's readership and audience. Although he speaks of his challenging voyage through Paradise being followed only by 'few', nearly all of his verse is in the Florentine vernacular, not Latin, and an epitaph written very shortly after his death describes him as 'the author most loved by the people'. From Dante's time to the present the *Commedia* has been appreciated by a wide range of readers, and it has been publicized by performers, from Boccaccio lecturing in a church in fourteenth-century Florence, to Benigni reciting in twenty-first-century town-squares and theatres.

Writers and artists of all sorts have responded strongly and frequently to Dante's work over the past seven centuries, and the *Commedia* has produced a vigorous afterlife in the popular genres of the novel, drama and cinema. The *Inferno* especially continues to generate compelling visual imagery in the form of illustration, film, video and graphic fiction. Continuing translation of the *Comedy* into languages from Arabic to Yiddish testifies to what has been called the 'generosity' of Dante's text; and some of the translators have themselves been poets. The versatility of Dante's vision and language – and his power as a precedent for ambitious projects – has been appreciated by poets from Chaucer to Heaney and beyond. Dante himself entered into dialogue with other poets in his early *Vita nova* and here in the *Purgatorio* (especially cantos 21-2, 24 and 26). And, as the voices in this translation make clear, that dialogue still goes on.

CANTO 1
Mary Jo Bang

Heading over waters getting better all the time
my mind's little skiff now lifts its sails,
letting go of the oh-so-bitter sea behind it.

The next realm, the second I'll sing,
is here where the human spirit gets purified   5
and made fit for the stairway to heaven.

Here's where the kiss of life restores the reign
of poetry – O true-blue Muses, I'm yours –
and where Calliope jumps up just long enough

to sing backup with the same bold notes   10
that knocked the poor magpie girls into knowing
their audacity would never be pardoned.

The fluid blue of the eastern sapphire
pooling in the cloudless mid-sky,
clear down to the first curved horizon-line,   15

was an even more delightful sight,
having left behind the sad-making dead air
that had so messed with my chest and eyes.

The gorgeous planet that says yes to love
was turning the east into a total glitter fest,   20
veiling the fish that formed her entourage.

I looked right; focusing on the South Pole,
I saw four stars that had gone unseen
since the first human beings.

It was like the sky was having a wild night   25
with these tiny blinking lights; O sad-eyed lady North,
widowed of a sight you would so love to see!

After this mini stargazing party,
I turned a bit toward the other pole,
where the shuddering Bear had already lumbered off.   30

Nearby, I saw a man all alone;
he looked like an elder statesman, one worthy
of no less respect than a child owes a parent.

His beard was long and salted white,
ditto his hair, which fell forward   35
onto his chest in two thick bands.

The rays of the four sacred stars
gave his face the glint of a minted coin;
I pictured a searchlight sun in front of him.

'Who are you, who've turned the dead-end river   40
on its head by getting out of jail without a card?'
he said, his venerable feathers ruffled.

'Who guided you, or acted like a flashlight,
when you fled the fathomless night-gloom
that keeps the Infernal Valley forever in the dark?   45

Have the laws of the Abyss been broken?
Or has Heaven weakened the law, so you damned ones
can come right up to my rockface anytime you like?'

My teacher gave me a look, then using head-nods
and hand gestures made me kneel   50
and bend my head in deference.

'I didn't come here on my own,' he said.
'A woman came down from Heaven
and begged me to help this one by coming with him.

But since you want to hear the whole story,   55
the unabridged version of how and why
we came to be here, I can't say no to that.

This man hasn't seen his final evening hour;
playing a fool's game, however, he was so close
there was very little time for a turnaround.   60

As I told you, I was sent to help him stay alive;
there was no other way to do that
except the one I set for myself.

I've shown him the guilty ones,
and now I need to show him the spirits   65
who purify themselves under your sovereign say-so.

It's a long story, how I brought him this far;
power descended from on high and helped me
bring him to this place, where he can see and hear you.

I hope you'll agree to his coming here.   70
He's seeking freedom, the price of which is known
by those who give their lives for it.

You know this. Death for the sake of it wasn't bitter
in Utica, where you shuffled off your mortal coil,
which will be so bright on that one fine day.   75

We haven't violated any eternal edicts:
he's alive and I'm not tied to Minos;
I'm in the circle where the innocent eyes of your Marcia

show how much she longs to still belong
to your pure and most-most loving breast.   80
For her love then, I hope you'll give us the go-ahead.

Let us travel through your seven kingdoms;
I'll take word of your kindness back to her,
that is, if you don't mind your name being dropped below.'

'I so loved setting eyes on Marcia   85
when I was far from here,' he said,
'that I never said no to whatever she asked for.

But now that she's on the far side of the river of pain,
she no longer moves me – that law was decreed
when I was airlifted out of there.   90

But if, as you say, a Heavenly woman moves you
to act and acts as your handler, there's no need
to flatter; it's enough to ask in her name.

So, go, tie a simple reed around his waist,
and wash his filthy face –   95
make sure you scrub off all the grime.

There's no way he can go in front
of the first of the ministers of Paradise
looking as if he got caught in a smoke cloud.

All around this small island, at its lowest-most point   100
where the sea-waves' sway tugs at the rough stones,
rushes grow in the soft silt.

Plants with leaves or woody stalks don't last there;
they get badly broken
by the surf's steady rasp and after-rasp.   105

Don't travel back this way;
the sun, now coming up, will show you how
to take an easier route up the mountain.'

With that, he vanished into thin air.
I got up without speaking and turned to my teacher,   110
looking straight into his eyes.

He said, 'Son, you can follow me.
Let's go back. The plain slopes that way
down to its lowest point.'

Dawn was outracing the after-midnight hours   115
running in front of it. I could see,
even from this distance, the fluttering edge of the shore.

We made our way over the desolate plain
like someone looking for a lost path,
who, until it's found, feels like it's all in vain.   120

When we came to an area where,
because of a cool breeze, the dew held its own
against the sun's evaporative reach,

my teacher opened both hands
and placed his palms lightly on the wet grass;   125
now seeing what he had in mind,

I offered him my tear-stained cheeks,
and, right there, he revealed all my true colours,
which Hell had kept hidden.

We then went down to the deserted coastline,   130
which had never seen anyone navigate its waters
and come back after the fact.

There, he tied the reed around my waist
as the other had directed: Oh, one for the books!
When he pulled up the lowly plant by its roots,   135

another at once sprang up in its place.

NOTES TO CANTO 1
Mary Jo Bang & Nick Havely

11-12. Ovid in *Met.* 5. 294-678 tells how the Pierides, the nine daughters of King Pieros, challenged the Muses to a singing contest. Calliope (identified with epic poetry), representing the Muses, won and afterwards changed the Pierides into magpies as punishment for their hubris.

19-21. Venus ('the gorgeous planet') was thought to have two manifestations, chaste love and lustful desire. Her 'entourage' is composed of the stars in the constellation Pisces (the fish).

23-27. Dante would have known of actual stars in the Southern Hemisphere, but his 'four stars' here are traditionally interpreted as representing the cardinal virtues (fortitude, justice, prudence and temperance) with which humanity had originally been endowed). After the Fall, Adam and Eve would have relocated from the Terrestrial Paradise to the Northern Hemisphere, where they and their descendants would have been deprived, or 'widowed,' of these stars. The song 'Sad-Eyed Lady of the Lowlands' was written by Bob Dylan (*Blonde on Blonde*, 1966).

30. The northern constellation Ursa Major is also known as the Great Bear. T. S. Eliot, 'Gerontion': 'De Bailhache, Fresca, Mrs. Cammel, whirled / Beyond the circuit of the shuddering Bear / In fractured atoms.'

31. The guardian of Purgatory is much later in this canto (ll. 73-5) identified as Cato the Younger (95-46 BCE), a late Roman Republic statesman and follower of Stoicism who opposed Caesar and sided with Pompey. In 46 BCE, after Caesar prevailed in the Battle of Thapsus, Cato took his own life in Utica, rather than serve Caesar; see Lucan's foretelling of this in *DBC* 2. 306-13. As a suicide and opponent of the Roman Empire, he seems a surprising choice for this role in *Purg.*; see *DE* 146-9. The idea of Cato as the warden of Purgatory may have come from Virgil's description of Aeneas's shield which shows 'righteous souls set apart, with Cato administering justice to them' (*Aen.* 8. 670).

47. The divine 'law' separating Hell from Purgatory and Paradise was, as Cato later says (ll. 89-90), established at the death of Christ and the release of virtuous pre-Christian souls such as his from Limbo (see *Inf.* 4. 52-63).

53-54. The 'woman' is Beatrice. Alerted to Dante's plight by St. Lucy, she came down from Heaven to Limbo to entreat Virgil to help Dante (*Inf.* 2. 52-114).

78-80. Marcia, Cato's wife and the mother of three of his children, resides in Limbo with Virgil and other pre-Christian figures (*Inf.* 4. 128).

93. The reed signifies humility. Dante was also girded in the *Inferno*, there with a knotted cord like those worn by Franciscan friars.

130-4. In the original, the rhyme scheme recalls the account of Ulysses's disastrous voyage towards Mount Purgatory in *Inf.* 26, and the phrase describing Virgil's obedience to Cato's instructions (*com'altrui piacque*, lit. 'as it pleased another') echoes that which has in the *Inferno* conveyed the divine judgment on Ulysses. Here as elsewhere in the *Commedia*, the Dante-persona's journey is deliberately compared or contrasted with those of his pagan predecessors.

136. The canto ends with a reminder of another epic journey. The golden bough plucked by Aeneas at the start of his visit to the underworld is also said to have miraculously regenerated (*Aen.* 6. 143-4).

CANTO 2
Bernard O'Donoghue

Already the Sun had reached the west horizon
of the meridian cycle bisected at Jerusalem
which is where it attains its highest point,

and Night, spinning the opposite way
was emerging over the Ganges out of the Scales   5
that fall from her hand when day's duration's ended

so that the white-red complexion of radiant Dawn
was turning yellow-hued where I was standing,
gone russet with the passage of the hours.

We were still there along the seashore   10
like people who are pondering the way,
resolved to go but rooted to the spot,

when, just as at the break of dawn
through thick mists Mars still burns red
low in the West above the ocean floor,   15

there appeared to me – and may I live to see again! –
a light coming so fast across the sea
that no aerial flight could equal it.

After I'd turned my eyes slightly aside
to put another question to my leader,   20
I looked back to find it bigger, brighter.

Then on each side of it there appeared to me
something white I could not make out, and underneath
bit by bit another whiteness coming from it.

My Master didn't speak a word as yet   25
until the first whitenesses emerged as wings,
and then he knew well who the pilot was

and cried out 'Bend your knees! Bend them down;
behold the Angel of God. Join your hands together.
From now on you'll deal with such authorities.   30

See how he is above all human implements
and needs neither oars nor sails but just his wings
that carry him between such far-flung shores.

See how he points them upward to the heavens,
beating the air with his everlasting wings   35
which do not change like earthly plumage does.'

Then, as the godlike creature of the air
came nearer and nearer to us, he became so clear
that my eyes could hardly bear his closeness

and I lowered them. He came onwards to the shore   40
with a vessel so light and speedy
that the water took no impression from it.

On the stern stood the heavenly steersman
in such a form that he seemed inscribed as blessed
and more than a hundred spirits sat inside it.   45

'When Israel emerged out of Egypt',
they all sang together with one voice,
and all that is written after in that Psalm.

Then he made the Sign of the Cross to them,
at which they all threw themselves on to the strand,   50
and he left again as quickly as he had come.

The throng that stayed behind seemed foreign
to the place, looking around
like someone who is weighing up new things.

From all sides the Sun was shooting forth   55
the day, and with his well-aimed arrows
had chased Capricorn from the heights of heaven

when these new people lifted up their faces
to us, saying: 'If you know it,
please point out to us the way up the mountain.'   60

Virgil said 'I think you must believe
that we know all about arrangements here;
but we are outsiders, just the same as you are.

We'd only just arrived here before you,
but by so rough and arduous a route   65
that the climb will seem as nothing from here on.'

The spirits who had spotted by my breathing
that I was still alive, were so astonished
that they all turned pale; and just the way

a crowd will gather to hear the latest news   70
from a messenger carrying the olive branch,
and no-one cares if they trample on each other,

so these spirits, blessed though they all were,
jostled for a good view of my face,
distracted from their path towards perfection.   75

Then I saw one of them push right to the front
to hug me with such particular affection
that he inspired me to do the same to him.

Ah shadows, with substance only on the surface!
Three times my arms closed up behind him,   80
and passed straight through him, back on to my chest.

I flushed, embarrassed, I suppose, and then
this shadow pulled backwards with a smile,
and I, following unsupported, nearly fell over.

Gently he told me I must take it easy,   85
and then I knew who it was. I begged of him
to pause a while there and to talk to me.

He answered me 'Just as I liked you when
I'd a living body, freed of it I like you still.
So yes, I'll pause. But you: where are you going?'   90

'Dear Casella, when I've made this journey
I'll be returning back to where I live.
But why have you been robbed of so much time?'

He said to me 'No injustice has been done me   95
if the angel who picks when and whom he pleases
has chosen many times to leave me here:

his action executes the will of justice.
For three months, it is true, he's taken out
without a protest whoever wants to go.   100

I was facing the shore where the Tiber's water
meets the sea and so turns salty, when
I was with mercy gathered in by him.

He has flown just now directly to that harbour
because that is where they all first assemble,   105
those who are not condemned to sink to Hell.'

I said to him 'If this new disposition of things
has not destroyed your memory or your gift
which used to satisfy every desire I had,

Please will you comfort my poor soul with music.   110
It is totally worn out from coming here
encumbered still with my whole earthly body.'

'Love which speaks to me within my mind',
he started then to sing so very sweetly
that the memory of it still echoes deep within me.   115

My guide, myself, and all the people with us
were so enchanted by it that the minds
of all of us had room for nothing else.

We were all taken up with concentration
on his singing, when Cato, inflexibly upright,   120
shouted 'What are you doing, all you idle souls?

What is all this negligence and hanging around?
Hurry to the mountain, to clean off
the filth that stops you seeing the divine.'

And, just like when doves, pecking at wheat or oats,   125
utterly absorbed with their rich pasturing,
calm, without their usual flightiness,

if something comes along that frightens them,
with a sudden whoosh they take off from their eating,
distracted now by a more pressing concern,   130

likewise I saw this new-come assembly
leave the singing and turn towards the hillside,
like people scattering off in all directions.

And Virgil and I were as fast as anyone!

NOTES TO CANTO 2
Nick Havely

1-6. Although this seems a lengthy way of saying that it was about 6 in the morning, like other periphrases in the poem (e.g. *Purg.* 9. 1-9) the passage is not mere rhetoric; it presents time 'not as a private and contingent event, but always as a cosmic process' (*CL* 2: 67).

31-3. As at the end of Canto 1 (130-3), this is another reminder of the disastrous voyage of Dante's Ulysses, whose crew 'made wings of the oars in our wild flight' towards Mount Purgatory (*Inf.* 26. 125).

46. *In exitu Israël de Aegypto* is the first verse of Psalm 114 (113 in the Vulgate). The psalm recalls the Israelites' crossing of the Red Sea and is described by Dante as allegorically representing 'the soul's deliverance

from sin' (*Conv.* 2. 1. 6-7). Here it is the first of many items from the Psalms and the Latin liturgy that are sung in *Purg.* and *Par.* (*DE* 569-71 and 718-19).

70. The olive branch was a sign that the messenger bore good news.

76-104. As l. 91 and the mention of his 'gift' for song in ll. 107-8 make clear, the soul who is eager to meet the pilgrim is a musician called Casella. Little else is known about him: he is named as composer of music for a madrigal in a 13th-century Vatican manuscript and may have been Florentine. Dante's vain attempt to embrace his friend (ll. 80-1) recalls Virgil's Aeneas trying 'three times' to put his arms around the shade of his father Anchises in the underworld (*Aen.* 6. 700-1). Dante's question (l. 93) about the delay between Casella's death and his arrival in Purgatory is not fully answered (l. 97), but it is made clear that the angel who has brought him and the other saved souls is responding to the indulgence granted by Pope Boniface VIII for the Jubilee year of 1300 (*DE* 542-3).

113-23. The *canzone* that Casella begins to sing ('Amor che ne la mente mi ragiona') had appeared in Dante's earlier and unfinished philosophical work, the *Convivio* (at the beginning of the third treatise) and is in praise of Philosophy; see the translation of the whole poem in the Postscript to this volume (no. 2). Cato's apparent harshness towards the souls could be seen as a reflection of the new energy required to move on – to atone for what Dante's Virgil will later call 'not loving good fully' (*Purg.* 17. 85).

CANTO 3
A. E. Stallings

Although their swift and sudden flight
scattered them about the plain
towards the mountain, on which height

justice sorts us, now again
I turned back to my guiding star,   5
without whom I would never gain

the mountain, nor have come so far.
He seemed then stricken with remorse,
for tiny faults pure conscience mar.

And when his feet slowed on their course   10
(as haste undoes all dignity)
my mind, at first restrained in force,

far and wide scanned eagerly:
I turned to face the hill that raised
itself most heavenward from the sea.   15

The red sun that behind me blazed
blocked by my figure, cast a shade
of me before me where I gazed.

Quickly I turned around, afraid
I'd been abandoned, since I spied   20
only the shadow I had made.

And then the comfort at my side
said, turning, 'Does your doubt presume
I am not truly here, your guide?

In Naples, where I have my tomb,   25
it's evening – there my body stays
that, living, cast a shadow's gloom.

Now therefore it should not amaze
I cast none – as spheres in the skies
do not occlude each others' rays.   30

The Power that torments and tries
bodies like these, with chill or burn,
hides its workings from our eyes.

Who thinks his reason can discern
the infinite way of Persons Three   35
in Substance One, has much to learn.

Be satisfied, humanity
with 'since' – were all things in your scope
then Mary's childbirth need not be.

You've seen how fruitlessly some hope,   40
who would have found the things they seek,
left in their endless grief to grope.

It is of Plato that I speak,
Aristotle, others,' then his brow
lowered; he fell silent, bleak.   45

We came to the foot of the mountain now,
a cliff to climb so steep and sheer,
the nimblest legs would not know how.

Compared to this, the most austere
Ligurian cliff-face, in the end,   50
would seem a stairway, easy clear.

'Which side's best – who can apprehend –
to scale it?' Virgil stayed his pace,
'so one with no wings may ascend?'

And while he stood with lowered face,   55
and in his mind, he mulled the way,
I looked around the rocky place,

and on the left, glimpsed an array
of souls who moved with feet so slow
towards us, that they seemed to stay.   60

'Master, lift up your gaze, for lo –
there are some souls who might be heard
on what you search yourself to know.'

He raised his gaze, his spirits stirred:
'Because they are not very fast,   65
let's meet them. Sweet son, rest assured!'

So far they were, that at the last,
we'd gone a thousand paces out,
yet they were still one strong arm's cast

away. They crowded then about   70
the hard rocks and sheer cliff, and stood
stock still, as men delay in doubt.

'O chosen souls, whose ends were good,'
said Virgil, 'by that Peace Sublime
that waits you – as I've understood –   75

tell us the way – how can we climb –
where is the mountain's slope less steep? –
who learns more, less abides lost time.'

And just as, from the fold, come sheep –
first one, then two, then three; the flock   80
stand meek, and faces earthward keep,

and if one walks, the rest will walk;
and when he stops, huddle in place,
meek, mild, not knowing why they balk,

and so a few, with modest face,   85
bellwethers of that happy crew,
approached us at a solemn pace.

When those in front could see I threw
a shadow, rightward in its aim,
to the cliff, and rent the light in two,   90

they hesitated as they came,
and shrank back somewhat, and the rest
not knowing why, did just the same.

'No need to ask – for as you've guessed
a human body cleaves the light   95
upon the ground,' Virgil confessed,

'Trust me, don't wonder at the sight –
he would not seek to scale this wall
were he not backed by Heaven's might.'

'Then turn around,' we heard them call.   100
To us, that worthy caravan,
waving us back, 'And lead us all.'

'Whoever you are,' one soul began,
'turn back to face me as you go,
and recognize me, if you can.'   105

I turned and stared: handsome, just so,
fair-haired, with noble aspect blessed,
but one eyebrow split with a blow.

Humbly, I could not attest
to knowing him. And at my mild   110
denial, he showed, high on his breast,

a wound. 'I'm Manfred,' and he smiled,
'grandson of Empress Constance – please,
when you go back, seek out my child,

fair ancestress of Sicily's   115
and Aragon's pride – see that she knows
the truth, that when these injuries

pierced my flesh with lethal blows,
I gave myself to Him (and cried),
who always willing mercy shows.   120

Dire were my sins, and yet so wide
infinite Goodness's embrace,
that all who seek it fit inside.

Had the priest whom Clement sent to chase
me down not read God's page in vain,   125
my bones might yet rest in their place,

at Benevento's bridge-head lain,
a heavy cairn to hold them tight;
now lashed by wind and washed by rain,

beyond the Kingdom, at a site   130
beside the Greene they lie, that's where
he moved them by quenched candle-light.

Cursed are my bones; yet none, I swear
is so lost they're beyond Love's search
if Hope has any green to spare.   135

It's true: who dies outside the Church,
although they, at the last, repent,
stays on this bank, left in the lurch,

thirty years for each year spent
in stubborn pride, unless devout   140
prayers cut the sentence's extent.

Now bring my happiness about –
tell Constance where I am, explain
how long I must remain locked out:

from those on earth, we here have much to gain.'   145

NOTES TO CANTO 3
Nick Havely

16-24. Virgil's lack of a shadow – like Casella's incorporeality in the previous canto – raises questions about embodiment in the afterlife that will be more fully explored much later, in Canto 25. The recognition of Dante's living physical presence is a reminder both of the exceptional purpose of his journey and of his potential relationship as human intermediary with the astonished souls that he encounters, as in ll. 88-93 (also Canto 5. 4-9, 25-6 and 36-51, below).

27. Virgil died at Brindisi in 19 BCE, and the Emperor Augustus arranged for his body to brought from there and buried in Naples.

34-45. Virgil's account here of the limitations of human 'reason' (ll. 34-6) leads him to some melancholy musing on the examples of the pagan philosophers (Plato, Aristotle) who are his own cohabitants in Limbo (*Inf.* 4. 130-44).

49-51. Purgatory's rocky landscape is at several points compared to mountainous regions with which Dante was familiar during his exile (see, for example the reference to various remote villages and peaks in *Purg.* 4. 25-7). He is known to have been in Liguria, whose steep coast is still subject to landslides, in 1306 / 7 and was in the Casentino at the foot of the Apennines during part of the time when he was composing the *Purgatorio* (see *BGLD* 34-5 and 42-3).

103-20. Manfred of Swabia (1232-66), natural son of the Emperor Frederick II, was associated with the courtly culture of Sicily where he was crowned king in 1258. An opponent of the papacy, the mortally wounded Manfred is the first of many figures in the *Purgatorio* to remind the reader of the conflicts in Dante's Italy: his fatal injuries were inflicted at the Battle of Benevento on February 26, 1266. Manfred's grandparents were Henry VI, Holy Roman Emperor from 1165-1197, and Empress Constance of Sicily (l. 113). He identifies his lineage through his paternal grandmother, whom Dante placed in Paradise (*Par.* 3. 118-20) and not through his father, who was placed with the heretics in the seventh circle of Hell (*Inf.* 10. 119).

Manfred's daughter (ll. 115-17) was also named Constance; she became Queen of Aragon upon her marriage in 1275 to Peter III, the eldest son of King James I. When James I died in 1276, Peter III ascended to the throne with Constance as queen. She was the mother of two kings: James II of Aragon and Frederick of Sicily.

124-32. The Archbishop of Cosenza, acting as the legate of Pope Clement IV, was said to have removed Manfred's body from its initial place of honourable military burial at Benevento to the boundary between the Kingdom of Naples-Sicily and the Papal State, marked by the Garigliano river. The 'quenched candle-light' in his funeral procession, follows the rule that those excommunicated should be buried without cross or lights. The fate of Manfred's exposed body – 'lashed by wind and washed by rain' – recalls that of Palinurus's drowned corpse in *Aen*. 6. 362; and both figures can be seen as similarly doomed 'helmsmen' of the Empire. In line 131, Dante's name for the river (Garigliano) where the Archbishop condemned him to lie is *Verde* (translated here as 'Greene'); this is echoed four lines later by the 'green' (*verde*) of hope.

135. Green was the colour traditionally associated with the theological virtue of hope, as later in *Purg*. 8. 28-9 and 30. 33.

140-5. Manfred's wish that the prayers of his daughter Constance might aid his process of redemption thus concludes the canto by linking divine mercy with human good deeds.

CANTO 4
Mary Jo Bang

When any of the mind's
inherent capacities sense pleasure, or pain,
the soul focuses on that alone.

It seems to ignore the other potentials –
this versus the mistaken claim that one soul   5
above another gets lit up in us.

As a result, when a sight or sound
holds the soul in its grip,
we lose all sense that time is ticking.

The faculty that watches the clock, isn't the one   10
that ties up the mind; the first moves around
while the hands of the other are bound.

I had that actual experience:
while I was listening to that spirit and marvelling,
the sun had climbed a full fifty degrees.   15

I hadn't noticed until we came to a place
where the souls all called out,
'Here's what you were asking about.'

When the late grapes turn brown,
a groundskeeper will often take a garden fork   20
of thorn shrub and plug a larger opening

than the narrow gap that my teacher first,
then I, climbed through – alone now
since the group had gone on without us.

One can make it up to San Leo, or down to Noli,   25
or reach the diadem of snow that crowns Bismantova
on foot, but here one had to fly –

by which I mean with streamlined wings
and feather-light intense desire behind the guide
who gave me hope and lit the way.   30

Where we climbed, the rock was broken open;
the walls, a private hermitage, pressed in on both sides;
the bare ground beneath required both hands and feet.

When we'd reached the highest rim of the precipice,
where it opened out onto a hillside,   35
I asked my teacher, 'Which way?'

'Don't backslide,' he said, 'not even one step.
Just stay behind me and keep gaining ground
until someone arrives who can guide us.'

The summit above soared out of sight;   40
the incline was difficult and much steeper even
than the line that divides a right-angle in half.

Having reached the point of exhaustion, I said,
'You've been a very kind father, but turn and look:
if you don't stop to rest, I'll be left here by myself.'   45

'And you, my son, keep going,' he said, 'just
up to there.' He pointed to a slightly higher ledge
that curved around that side of the mountain.

What he said flipped a switch; as tired as I was,
I forced myself to scramble after him   50
until the narrow beltway was firm beneath my feet.

There we sat to rest, facing east – which was for us
the direction from which we'd begun our ascent.
It helps to see how far one has come.

I first looked down at the shores below,   55
then raised my eyes to the sun,
amazed that its light was striking us from the left.

The poet realized I was totally baffled
by the fact that the sun's aerial car
was cutting a path between us and the North.   60

He said, 'If it were Castor and Pollux
in the company of that big reflecting mirror
that conducts its light in both directions,

you'd see the Zodiac's wheel revolve even closer
to the Bears, unless, that is,   65
it were to suddenly jump its well-worn track.

If you want to understand how this can be,
picture Mount Zion and imagine
both it and this mountain located on Earth

in such a way that they share one horizon   70
but occupy two different hemispheres.
If you consider it closely, you'll see

the path poor Phaeton sadly failed to navigate
must pass this mountain on one side,
when it's passing Zion the other.'   75

'Of course!' I told my teacher,
'Before this, I could never figure it out –
my mind kept missing the point, which I now get:

the mid-circle of celestial motion,
or what's called the equator in some sciences,   80
forever lies between the sun and winter weather,

at the identical angle that – for exactly the reason
you just gave – it once lay for the Hebrews
to the warm-weather South.

But if you don't mind my asking, I'd love to know   85
how much farther we have to go; the mountain rises
higher than I can see with my naked eye.'

'The design of the mountain is such,' he said,
'that when you begin at the base, the climb's harder;
the higher you get the less painful the effort.   90

So, when you seem to be enjoying the ascent,
and the path up feels as effortless as coasting
downstream in a beautiful pea-green boat,

then you will have reached the end
and can hope to rest and catch your breath.   95
Of that much I'm sure. I really can't say more.'

As soon as he'd said those words,
we heard a voice nearby, 'But maybe first...
you'll find you simply have to have a sit-down.'

Hearing that, we both turned   100
and saw on our left a huge boulder,
which neither of us had noticed before.

We went over to the rock and found people
lounging in the shade behind it, as if
they were a bunch of good-for-nothing slackers.   105

One, who seemed quite listless, was sitting
on the ground, arms loosely circling his bent knees.
His lowered head hung between them.

'Whoa, my good lord,' I said, 'take a look
at this one. He's showing more indifference   110
than if laziness were his little sister.' At that,

he slowly turned his head. Resting it on his thigh,
while keeping his eyes fixed on us, he said,
'Fine, Mister Lightning Bolt, you go right on up.'

I now realized who he was.   115
Not even the lingering effects of my recent effort
stopped me from going straight over to him.

When I got there, barely raising his head, he said, 'So,
is your understanding of why the sun drives his chariot
along your left upper arm now complete?'   120

His sluggish manner and curt speech
prompted a slight smile; I said, 'Belacqua,
from now on, I'll no longer worry about you.

But why are you sitting here like this?
Are you waiting for an escort?   125
Or simply going back to your old bad habits?'

'O brother, what's the point of trekking up?
God's feathered messenger in charge of the gate
isn't going to let me in to do my penance.

First, I have to wait outside for as long   130
as in my lifetime the heavens spun around me; this,
because I put off my pious sighs until the very end –

unless, that is, someone whose heart's in a state
of grace helps me out by sending up a few prayers.
What good is anyone, if Heaven can't hear them?'   135

The poet, without waiting for me, had already begun
the climb, calling back: 'Come on now, look
how the sun's crossing the meridian, and at the edge,

the boot of the Western night is about to cover Morocco.'

NOTES TO CANTO 4
Mary Jo Bang & Nick Havely

5-9. Plato maintained that there were 'several souls inside us' (vegetative, sensory, and intellectual), hierarchically resting one atop another (*Timaeus* 69E). Dante follows Aristotle and Aquinas in refuting this idea, arguing that all three "powers"—life, sense, and reason – are integrated in a single soul, and impossible to tease apart. As evidence against the Platonic argument, Dante points out (ll. 7-9) that the rational aspect of the integrated soul can lose track of time when it's totally preoccupied with sensory experiences. If there were three separate souls, the rational soul would continue to track time while the sensory soul was otherwise engaged.

15. If the sun had risen 50 degrees above the horizon, it would be 9.20 am (*CL* 2: 113).

25-6. As in *Purg.* 3. 49-51, Dante here recalls familiar rugged landscapes. San Leo and Noli are towns on steep hilltops in Le Marche and Liguria; whilst the Pietra di Bismantova is an isolated spur of the Apennines in Reggio Emilia with a flat summit and near-perpendicular walls.

57. In the Northern Hemisphere, if someone were looking east, the sun would be on their right and a shadow would be cast to the left. Mount Purgatory, however, is in the Southern Hemisphere; there, the sun would strike a person facing east from the left side and cast a shadow to the right.

61-5. Today is Easter Sunday and the sun is in Aries. If it were later in the year, the sun would be in Gemini (Castor and Pollux) and, thus, farther north and closer to the Bears (Ursa Major and Ursa Minor).

70-71. The medieval Catholic conception of Earth held that Mount Zion was at the centre of the Northern Hemisphere, and that the Southern Hemisphere was covered with water. Dante sets Mount Purgatory, the sole landmass in that vast ocean, antipodal to Mount Zion. The shared horizon is the equator.

73. Phaethon, son of the sun god Helios, insisted, against his father's advice, on driving the sun-chariot across the sky. He lost control and dropped the reins, forcing Jupiter to kill him with a lightning bolt (*Met.* 2). Like the fate of Ulysses (see above, *Purg.* 1. 130-3), Phaethon's story is mentioned in all three parts of the *Commedia* as a myth of human overreaching.

83-84. The sun once passed to the south of Jerusalem to the very same degree that here, in the antipodal Southern Hemisphere, it is now passing to the north of Mount Purgatory.

122. Commentators have identified Belacqua as a Florentine maker of lutes and guitars whom Dante was said to have known. On Samuel Beckett's appropriation of the character, see the Introduction (above, pp. 23-4).

133-5. Here, as at the end of the previous canto (Purg. 3. 140-5) and the beginning of canto 6 (13-27), the value placed on prayers from those in a state of grace in the living Christian community reinforces the human bond with souls in Purgatory.

139. The horizon dividing the Northern and Southern Hemispheres – which Dante sets equidistant from Jerusalem and Mount Purgatory – was thought to extend from the Ganges to Gibraltar. The sun would cross the meridian at noon on Mount Purgatory and 6 pm in Morocco.

CANTO 5
Mary Jo Bang

I'd already left those ghostly shades,
and was following in the footsteps of my guide,
when behind me, one pointed an indicative finger

and shouted, 'Look how there's no sunlight
to the left of the lower one;   5
the way he moves it's like he's alive.'

Hearing that, I turned and saw
how they were staring in awe at me, and only at me,
since it was my body blocking the light.

'What's so captivating,' my teacher asked,   10
'that it's causing you to dawdle?
What do you care what they whisper about here?

Come along behind me, and let people talk.
Stand like a tower of strength, one that won't fall
even if the wind batters it, tower-top to ground.   15

People who allow their thoughts to flit around
soon lose sight of the end-goal;
every new thought splashes cold water on the last.'

What could I possibly say except 'I'm coming'?
As I said it, my face blushed bright red, suggesting   20
I was someone who still might deserve forgiveness.

Meanwhile, just ahead of us, people were coming
across the mountain slope, singing in alternate parts
the verses of *'Have Mercy on Me'*.

When they realized there was no way   25
for the sun's rays to pass through my body,
their song became one long-drawn-out, rasping *Ohhh* – !

Two of them, sent as messengers by the others,
ran over to meet us, insisting,
'Fill us in on your condition.'   30

My teacher said, 'You can go back now
and tell the others who sent you that, yes,
this man's body really is still flesh and blood.

I assume seeing his shadow is what stopped them;
if so, that's all the truth you need to know.   35
They show him respect, it might benefit them.'

I never saw a shooting star slice through
a clear twilight sky,
or lightning rip apart August clouds at sunset,

as fast as those two ran back up. Once there,   40
they and all the others turned and ran back down
like a mob breaching a barricade.

'This crowd pressing in on us,' said the poet,
'they're hoping you'll help them,
but keep walking; you can listen as you go.'   45

They came shouting, 'Soul, on your way seeking bliss
with the same frame you were born with,
please stop here for a while

to see whether you know any of us,
so that you can carry news back to the other side – .   50
Hey! Why are you going? *Hey!* Why don't you stop?

In our past lives, we all died a violent death;
sinners to the end, at our final hour
a perspective pushed through like light from Heaven,

and at that point, penitent and all-forgiving,   55
we abandoned our lives fully-reconciled to God,
our hearts aching with the desire to see him.'

I said: 'I'm carefully examining your faces,
but I don't recognize anyone. But if there's something
you want me to do, you spiritual elite, just say it,   60

and I promise to do it, by the peace
for which I'm searching as I go from world to world
following in the footsteps of this model guide.'

One spoke up: 'Each of us trusts, even without
your swearing it, that you'll do your best for us,   65
unless the power to do as you want suffers a setback.

Speaking first, and only for myself,
if you ever lay eyes on the territory between Romagna
and Naples, where Charles reigns,

I beg you to kindly pray for me in Fano,   70
where through your devout prayers
I might wash away my grievous sins.

I was from there. But the deep wounds, from which
my blood and life force leapt like a fish from a lake,
were delivered in the lap of Antenori land,   75

which was where I thought I'd be safest.
It was Azzo of Este who was out to get me;
his anger toward me was far more than I deserved.

If I'd kept high-tailing it toward La Mira,
instead of stopping off at Oriago, I'd still be back   80
where one breathes and the heart brags *I am.*

Instead, I rode into the marsh, and got so tangled
in the reeds and muck that I stumbled and fell. There,
in the mud, I watched a lake of venous blood gush out.'

Another spoke up: 'To help you get that wish   85
that draws you up the steep mountain,
show some kind pity and help me realize my own.

I was a Montefeltro; I'm Buonconte:
no one cares about me, not even Giovanna.
So, I go around, my head bowed down, with this bunch.　　90

I asked, 'What power or fate led you to wander
so far from Campaldino,
that no one knows where you were buried?'

'Oh, that,' he said. 'The base of the Casentino
Valley is crossed by a stream called the Archiano,　　95
which begins in the Apennines above the Hermitage.

I arrived just where it enters the Arno
and loses its name; stabbed in the throat, fleeing
on foot, making the plain a bleeding piece of earth,

I lost my sight and my voice,　　100
which ended on the name of Mary.
And there I died, and only my flesh was left.

I'll tell you the truth, and you tell it to the living.
An Angel held onto me, as the Hellhound shouted,
"Hey, you from Heaven, why're you taking what's mine?　　105

He shed a little tear, so you're gonna swipe this guy
from me and carry off his eternal part?
Fine, I'll deal in my own way with what's left."

As you're well aware, as soon as moist air rises
and merges with the cold,　　110
the vapour condenses and turns to water.

The evil-one linked his ever-vigilant wickedness
to his intelligence, and using the force
Nature gave him, exploited the wind and fog.

When the day had faded, the entire valley,　　115
from Pratomagno all across the ridge,
was covered in fog; and, just as he intended,

the super-humid air in the sky above
quickly turned to water. The rain fell;
what the ground couldn't absorb filled the ditches   120

and, when those widening streams met, rushed
toward the actual river with such devastating speed
that nothing could hold it back.

The swollen Archiano found my frozen body
at its mouth and swept it into the Arno,   125
undoing the cross my arms had made on my chest

when I'd been overtaken by pain. It rolled me –
on the banks, then along the bed, finally burying me
in a shroud of silt the river had pillaged.'

'When you've gone back to the world,   130
and have rested up from your long time away,'
a third began where the other left off,

'please, remember me, I'm the wishful Pia.
Siena made me, Maremma undid me. As is well known
by the one who ringed me, then did me in,   135

after first having had me with his family jewel.'

NOTES TO CANTO 5
Mary Jo Bang & Nick Havely

4-9. Dante is now headed west, so the sun is to his right. The recognition
of his living physical presence (also in ll. 25-6) is a reminder of both the
exceptional purpose of his journey and his potential relationship with
the astonished souls here (see also ll. 36-51, below).

23-24. Psalm 51 (50 in the Vulgate) is a biblical song of repentance
composed by Ruth for her great-grandson David who murdered Uriah
and committed adultery with Bathsheba. It is known as the *Miserere,*

after the first line of the Latin *Miserere mei, Deus* (Have mercy upon me, O God). The souls are singing a form of monophonic plainsong where two halves of a choir alternate singing verses in unison. This is the first singing to be heard since the arrival of souls in the angelic boat (see *Purg.* 2. 46, above and note).

43-51. On the value placed on prayers from those in a state of grace in the living Christian community, see above, *Purg.* 4. 133-5 and note.

67. It would have been clear to Dante's original readers that the unnamed speaker is Jacopo del Cassero (b. c.1260), a Guelph from Fano who opposed the powerful Azzo VIII d'Este. On his way to Milan in 1298, he was murdered at Oriago, presumably by assassins hired by Azzo.

75. According to legend, the northern city of Padua was established by the Trojan prince Antenor, who plotted with the Greeks to destroy Troy. In the *Inferno* (32. 88), Dante names the second ring of the ninth circle Antenora; there, those who betrayed their political party or their country remain frozen in Lake Cocytus for eternity. That Jacopo del Cassero died in 'Antenori land', gestures to the treachery of those who conspired with Azzo VIII d'Este to murder him.

85-90. Buonconte da Montefeltro (b. 1250/5) was a Ghibelline leader who was killed in a losing battle at Campaldino on June 11, 1289 – a battle in which the 24-year old Dante Alighieri was known to have fought on the side of the Guelphs. Buonconte's body was never located. He was the son of Guido da Montefeltro who has been encountered among the false counsellors in *Inf.* 27. The parallels and contrasts between the two episodes reflect Dante's concern with decisive existential choices: at the very end, the father fails to repent sincerely, whilst the son here does so. Hence, in the first deathbed struggle, the devil wins Guido's soul, whilst in the second (here ll. 103-29) he loses Buonconte's. Giovanna (ll. 89-90) was Buonconte's wife. His progress up the mountain is delayed due to the fact that none of the family members offer prayers for his salvation (see ll. 43-51, above), hence the increased urgency of his plea to the Dante-persona here (ll. 85-7).

96. The 'hermitage' is Camaldoli, located above the Benedictine monastery of the same name below the ridge of the Apennines; it was established in the 11th century by Romualdo, a monk who practised asceticism.

133-136. In Italian, *pia* means pious, with a secondary meaning of innocent or naïve; *pia illusione* is wishful thinking. The speaker refers to herself as *la* Pia. Tradition has it that she was a Sienese noblewoman who, after the death of her first husband, married a second time to someone who was said to have murdered her in order to marry another. The marriage may have consisted only of a declaration of fidelity and the gift of a family ring. There is a clear *double entendre* that implies the consummation of the marriage was an act of deception and that the devout Pia was equally the naïve Pia.

CANTO 6
Bernard O'Donoghue

When a game of dice has reached its end,
the person who has lost stands there alone,
and throws the dice again to see what went wrong,

while the crowd jostles round the winner:
one runs in front, another plucks at his back,   5
a third seeks his attention from the side.

He doesn't stop, nods to this one and that;
whoever he gives a tip to is content,
and so he manages to disengage himself.

So it was with me in that dense throng,   10
turning my face to them, one side, then the other
and escaping from them by my promises.

There was the Aretine who met his death
at the savage hands of Ghin de Tacco
and his countryman who drowned while giving chase. 15

Federico Novello implored me there
with outstretched hands; so did the man of Pisa
who made the good Marzucco show his courage.

I saw Count Orso, and the soul divided
from the body by hate and envy, so they say,   20
and not for any fault committed by him –

by Pierre de la Brosse I mean: and let Mary
of Brabant watch out while she is still alive
that she doesn't end amidst a worse flock.

When I'd got free of the whole lot of them,   25
those shades whose prayer was for the prayers of others
so that their progress to blessedness should speed up,

I began 'O light of mine, it seems
that you expressly deny in a certain passage
that prayer can reverse the decree of Heaven;   30

but these souls pray for precisely this.
Is their hope then fated to be vain?
Or is your meaning not fully clear to me?'

Virgil replied: 'My writing is clear enough,
and their hope is not unfounded either   35
if you attend to it with a sound mind:

because the height of justice is not diminished
if the fire of love fulfils in a single instant
the reparation due from the spirit here.

In the passage where I declared the point,   40
sin could not be atoned by any prayer
because the prayer was disengaged from God.

You absolutely mustn't rest content
in such deep doubt, until she tells you –
she who's the light between truth and intellect.   45

I don't know if you understand: I mean Beatrice;
you'll see her on the summit of this mountain
higher up, smiling in her blessedness.'

I said 'Oh Master, let us then speed up:
I am already less jaded than before.   50
And look now where the hillside casts a shadow.'

'We'll press onwards with this present day',
he answered, 'as long as we are able to;
but things are not quite what you think they are.

Before you get up there, you'll see the sun   55
that now is hidden by the slope turn backwards
so that you no longer blank out its rays.

But see how that spirit, standing there apart,
all on its own, is looking over at us;
it will point out the quickest way to go.'   60

We came up to it. O Lombard spirit,
how remote and disdainful you were standing
and in your eyes' movements noble, unhurried!

It said nothing whatsoever to us,
letting us pass, in the manner of a lion   65
just watching us from where it crouches.

But Virgil drew alongside it, asking
that it show us the best way to climb upwards;
but the spirit just ignored what he requested.

Instead it asked us about our homeland and our lives. 70
And when my gracious guide began his answer
'Mantua...' the spirit was all attention,

and jumped towards him from its previous station,
saying 'Oh Mantuan, I am Sordello
from your country.' And they embraced each other!   75

Oh wretched Italy, homeground of misery,
ship with no pilot in a mighty storm,
no queen of your provinces, but a whorehouse!

That noble spirit was as quick as that,
just at the sweet sound of his homeland's name,   80
to give his fellow-citizen such greeting.

And now in you your live inhabitants
can't live without war, and one gnaws at another
though enclosed within the same boundary wall.

Search, wretched land, all round the shores   85
of your sea-coasts, and then say from your heart
if any part of you can boast of peace.

What good is it for Justinian to fit the bridle
if the saddle's riderless? Except for that,
it wouldn't be quite so disgraceful. 90

Oh people who should be law-abiding
and leave Caesar to sit up in the saddle,
if you understand rightly the word of God,

note how this wild beast has become vicious
because of not being mastered by the spurs 95
since you took the reins in your own hands.

Albert of Germany, you who're abandoning
the mare which has become lawless and savage,
though you ought to bestride her saddle-bows,

may fitting judgement fall down from the stars 100
upon your blood-line – new and manifest
so your successor will live in dread of it.

You and your father, hampered back there
by a life of avarice, have allowed
the garden of the Empire to be laid waste. 105

Regardless as you are, observe the Montagues
and Capulets, the Monaldi and Filippeschi,
those already mourning and these in dread.

Come, cruel man, come and see the oppression
of your nobles: tend their injuries, 110
and you will see how safe it is at Santafiora.

Come and see your Rome itself which weeps,
widowed and bereft and calling day and night:
'My Emperor, why do you not accompany me?'

Come and see how the people love each other. 115
And if you are not moved by any pity for us,
come out of shame at your own reputation.

And if I'm allowed to ask, Jove on high
who on the Earth was crucified for us,
are your just eyes turned somewhere else?   120

Or is this some preparation you are making
in the depths of your wisdom for some good
that is totally shut off from our perception?

For the cities of Italy are all full
of tyrants, and every backwoodsman   125
who plays the nationalist is a Marcellus.

Oh my Florence! You can indeed feel happy
about this digression which doesn't touch you
of course since your people are so reasonable.

Many have justice in their hearts but release it   130
slowly because it doesn't come instinctive to the bow.
But your people have it always on their tongues.

Many refuse public responsibility;
but your people don't wait until they are asked
but shout out eagerly 'I am ready for it.'   135

So now rejoice, because you have good reason:
so prosperous, so peaceable, so wise you are.
If I am right, the facts will bear me out.

Athens and Sparta, who made the ancient laws
and were so civic-minded in their customs,   140
give only the merest hint at life well lived

compared to you who make such good provision
for the winter that what you spin in October
hardly lasts to the middle of November.

How often in the time still in your memory   145
have you changed laws, currency, offices
and practices, and replaced the leadership.

And if you remember and still see any light,
you will see how you resemble that sick woman
who can't find any comfort in her bed   150

but tries to ease her pain by tossing and turning.

NOTES TO CANTO 6
Nick Havely

13-27. The crowd of those seeking 'the prayers of others' (l. 26) includes
contemporary victims of vendetta (13-14 and 19), civic faction (15-18)
and envy (19-23). Mary of Brabant (22-4) was the queen of Philip III
of France and is warned here to repent for having accused the King's
chamberlain (Pierre de la Brosse) of treason.

28-30. The 'passage' in Virgil that Dante refers to here is the speech
of the Sibyl rejecting the plea of Palinurus (Aeneas's dead helmsman),
who has appealed to Aeneas to speed his journey over the Acheron
(*Aen.* 6. 363-76).

46-8 and 55. Virgil points forward to Dante's meeting in the Earthly
Paradise on the summit of Mount Purgatory (cantos 30-3) with Beatrice
who is named here for the first time since the beginning of the journey
(*Inf.* 2. 70, 103).

58-75. The 'remote and disdainful' Lombard soul is named at the
end of this passage as the poet Sordello (d. 1269), who was born near
Virgil's birthplace, Mantua and wrote entirely in Provençal (*DE*, 794-
5). In Dante's treatise on the vernacular he is described as a writer
'of unusual eloquence' (*DVE* 1.15.2): his most famous poem – and a
reason for giving him the role of guide in the next two cantos – was
a 'complaint' about the inadequacy of European rulers, written on the
death of a Provençal nobleman which is translated in the Postscript to
this volume (no. 3).

88. The 'bridle' is a metaphor for the code of law (*Corpus iuris civilis*),
instituted by the Roman Emperor Justinian (527-65), who also
reconquered parts of the Empire and rebuilt Constantinople (*DE* 550).
Dante's commitment to the ideal of world monarchy leads him to quote
from Justinian's laws (e.g., *Conv.* 1. 10. 3 and 4. 19. 4) and to make him
the voice of the Christian Empire in *Par.* 6. 97-105.

97-102. In contrast to Justinian, Albert I of Austria, Holy Roman Emperor from 1298 to 1308 is here – together with his father Rudolph of Habsburg (l. 103) – said to have betrayed the Imperial ideal, and Italy in particular, through avarice and neglect. The 'fitting judgment' prophesied in line 100 refers to the assassination of Albert in 1308. A few years later (1311-13), around the time of the *Purgatorio*'s composition, Dante hoped in vain that a new Holy Roman Emperor (Henry VII) might restore Imperial rule in Italy and much of the *Commedia* reflects his sense of that failure (*BGLD* 38-43).

103-26. Dante's apostrophe now portrays various forms of division and decay in Italian cities: conflict between families in towns such as Verona, Cremona and Orvieto (ll. 106-8); the decline of noble families such as the Aldobrandeschi counts of Santafiora (109-11; see also note on canto 11. 58-72, below); and the desolation of Rome (112-14). Opponents of the wider Imperial ideal in Italy are seen here as petty tyrants (124-6), and leaders of civic factions are ironically compared to the Roman Claudius Marcellus, an energetic opponent of Julius Caesar (*DBC* 1. 313).

127-51. The ironic tone intensifies in the canto's final address to Dante's native city, Florence, which was active in opposing Henry VII and frequently exemplifies civic decadence and disorder in the *Commedia* (e.g., *Inf.* 6. 60-75, 15. 61-78, 26.1-12).

CANTO 7
Bernard O'Donoghue

After the noble and happy greetings had been repeated
three and four times, Sordello drew him aside
and said 'So who exactly are you?'

'Before the spirits worthy to ascend to God
were turned towards this mountain, my bones   5
already had been buried by Octavian.

I am Virgil. And for no other failing
did I lose Heaven than not having faith.'
That is what my leader answered then.

Like somebody who sees something before him   10
suddenly and is astounded by it
so he believes in it and doesn't, saying 'It is! It isn't!'

– so Sordello seemed. He bowed down his head,
and humbly turned back again towards him
and embraced him down where the inferior does.   15

'Oh Glory of the Latins', he said 'through whom
our language showed what it was capable of;
Oh praise for ever of the place from which I come,

what deserving or what grace shows you to me?
If I am worthy at all to hear your words,   20
tell me if you come from Hell, and from what cloister?'

'Through all the circles of that sorrowful kingdom,'
Virgil answered, 'I have come here. A power
from Heaven urged me, and with it I came.

Not for doing but for not doing I have lost   25
the vision of the high Sun that you desire
and that was recognized too late by me.

Down there is a place not pained by torture
but just by darkness, where the lamentations
don't resound as screams, only as sighs.   30

There I remain with the little innocents
bitten by the teeth of death before
they were exempted from original sin.

There I remain amongst those who were not dressed
with the three cardinal virtues, yet knew   35
the others and observed them fully without sin.

But if you know it and are able, please give us
some direction by which we can come most quickly
to where Purgatory proper has its start.'

He answered: 'There is no fixed place for us   40
I am allowed to go up and around.
For as far as I can go, I'll be your guide.

But see how the day is already declining;
and since it isn't possible to go upward at night
it would be good to think of a fitting resting-place. 45

There are some spirits off here to the right.
If you are agreeable, I'll bring you to them,
and not without joy they will be known to you.'

'Why is this?' asked Virgil. 'If somebody
wanted to go up at night, would he be stopped   50
by someone else, or just because he couldn't?'

And the good Sordello drew his finger
along the ground, saying: 'Look, even this line
you couldn't cross after the sun's gone down;

It's not that anything except the shade   55
of night prevents the movement upward:
that's what depletes the will with lack of power.

It's possible of course to go back down at night
and wander aimlessly around the hillside
for as long as the horizon holds the day closed off.' 60

Then my leader said, as if in wonderment,
'Lead us then, to where you say
it's possible to delay in happiness.'

We had not travelled far on from there
when I saw that the mountain had hollows   65
in the way that valleys are scooped out with us.

'There,' said that spirit, 'we will make our way
where the mountainside forms a kind of breast
and there we will wait for the new day.'

There was a slanting path, neither steep nor level, 70
which led us to the downside of that valley
where the ridge's slope falls more than half its height.

Not gold or refined silver, cochineal,
white lead or bright polished Indian wood,
nor fresh emerald at the instant of its splitting   75

could match in colour the grass and flowers
set within that glade, just as anything lesser
is outclassed by its superior.

Not only had Nature been the artist there,
but out of the sweetness of a thousand scents   80
it had made one, unfamiliar and unique.

There, seated on the grass amid the flowers
singing the '*Hail, Holy Queen*' I saw spirits
which because of the slope were not visible outside.

'Before the fading sun sinks now to rest,'   85
began the Mantuan who had led us aside,
'don't wish that I should guide you in amongst them.

From this terrace you will know the actions
and faces of them all more clearly
than you'd gather from that hollow in their midst.   90

The one sitting highest up who has the air
of having neglected what he should have done
and doesn't move his lips with the others' songs,

was the Emperor Ridolfo who could have cured
the wounds that killed off Italy with the result   95
that now it's too late for anyone to save her.

That other one, who seems to be consoling him,
ruled the land where the water rises up
which the Moldau leads to the Elbe, the Elbe to the sea.

Ottocar was his name, and in his cradle   100
he was worth more than his bearded son,
Wenceslaus, consumed by lust and sloth.

And him with the little nose who seems to be
advising the man with such a genial face
died as he fled, disgracing the fleur-de-lys.   105

See how he is still beating his breast.
And look at that other one who, sighing,
has made his palm a bed to rest his cheek.

They are the father and son-in-law of France's scourge;
they know about his vicious and repellent life –   110
hence comes the sorrow that torments them.

The one who seems so sturdy, and who sings
along with the one with the Roman nose,
wore round his waist the belt of every quality.

And if the young man who is sitting there behind him   115
had stayed as king in succession to him,
that quality would duly have passed from one cup to the next –

which can't be said about the other heirs.
James and Frederick have those kingdoms now.
And neither of them has the better heritage.   120

Rarely does human virtue rise through the branches.
And He who gives it wants it to be so,
in order that it should be prayed for from Him.

Also, my words are directed to the big-nosed one,
no less than to the other, Peter, who sings along   125
because Apulia and Provence are mourning now.

So far has the plant declined from its first roots
that, even more than Beatrice and Margaret,
Constance still boasts about her husband.

Look where the king of the simple life is sitting,   130
Henry of England, on his own. He
has had better fruit out of his branches.

That one who abases himself amongst them,
looking downward, is the Marquis Guglielmo
because of whom Alessandria and its war   135

causes Montferrato and the Canovese to weep.'

NOTES TO CANTO 7
Nick Havely

25-36. Virgil emphasises the difference between himself and his fellow Mantuan poet (Sordello), and recalls the description of the pagan poets heroes and philosophers, along with unbaptised children (ll. 31-3), in Limbo on the edge of Hell (Inf. 4). The noble pagans are said (36) to have exercised moral and intellectual virtues, such as courage, temperance, prudence and justice (*DE* 866-7), but their ignorance of the Christian virtues of faith, hope, charity (34-5) excludes them from salvation – an issue that Dante continues to wrestle with, e.g., in *Par.* 19. 67-78.

82-3. *Salve regina, mater misericordiae* ('Hail, Queen, Mother of Mercy') is an antiphon addressed to the Virgin Mary that was traditionally sung at the end of the evening Office of Compline; on such songs see also *Purg.* 2. 46 and note, above.

91-102. From this point on in the canto, Dante's Sordello presents a modern version of the historical Sordello's 'complaint' about the princes of western Europe (see note on *Purg.* 6. 58-75 above). It begins with Rudolph I of Habsburg, elected ruler of Germany and Italy from 1273 to 1291, whose neglect of Italy helped to make Henry VII's campaign in 1311-13 come 'too late' (ll. 91-6; see note on *Purg.* 6. 97-102, above).

103-27. As the lines on virtue rarely being passed down through generations suggest (ll. 121-3), several of the princes portrayed here were followed by less worthy successors: Ottakar II of Bohemia (1253-78) by Wenceslas II (1278-1305); Philip III of France (1270-85) by Philip IV (1285-1314); Peter III of Aragon, King of Sicily (1282-85) by his sons James and Frederick. Peter's rival (with whom he now sings in harmony), Charles of Anjou, ruler of Provence and the Kingdom of Naples and Sicily (1266-85), was succeeded by his son, Charles II (1285-1309), whom Dante claims to have misgoverned both Provence and Puglia.

128-9. Beatrice and Margaret were the first and second wives of Charles I (Charles of Anjou), whilst Constance was the daughter of Manfred (see above, *Purg.* 3. 115-16) and married Peter III of Aragon.

130-6. In this closing passage the sole exception to the pattern of decline is Henry III of England (1216-72), whose son, the future Edward I, enabled him to regain the throne in 1265. Sordello's survey ends with an Italian example of failure and desolation: Marquis Guglielmo VII was a prominent Ghibelline leader in northern Italy and ruler of Montferrato and Canavese in Piedmont who was captured by his enemies and died in prison (1292); whilst his son Giovanni laid waste to the two regions of his inheritance.

CANTO 8
Jamie McKendrick

It was already the hour at which seafarers
turn tenderly towards the vanished shore
and the dear friends who bade them farewell;

the hour the novice pilgrim feels heart-stricken
to hear far off the rolling clang of bells   5
that seem to mourn the day's decline,

when my ears began to close their portals
as I stared at one of the souls who had risen
to call for quiet. Had he something to tell?

He joined together and lifted both his palms,   10
but his eyes were on the East, as if to say
'Why should I care for any light but Yours'.

So devotedly and with such sweet notes
did *Te lucis ante* rise from his throat
that I lost all sense of self and my senses reeled   15

while the others as sweetly and devotedly
accompanied that soul through every verse
keeping their eyes fixed on the wheeling stars.

Now, reader, sharpen your gaze for here
truth's covering is thin as gauze,   20
so to pass beyond will ask for little force.

I saw that silent wan and august company
stand fixing their eyes upon the sky
poised between hope and expectancy,

and I saw two angels swooping downward –   25
each brandished a flaming sword,
its end blunted, instead of being pointed.

Their raiments, the green of bright new leaves,
fanned by the wind of their green wings,
rippled and fluted in folds behind their flight.   30

One of the pair alighted just above us,
the other opposite, so that effectively
all the souls between them were protected.

Their blond hair could be clearly seen
but the eye recoiled from their countenance   35
confused by all that radiance.

'From the Virgin's lap, they've made their descent'
Sordello said, 'to guard this valley from
the serpent whose arrival's imminent.'

At that, not knowing whence it would appear,   40
I looked all round and, chilled with fear,
huddled close beside my trusted guide.

Then said Sordello: 'Let's go down to the valley
to speak with the great souls who will surely
welcome you both with great acclaim.'   45

I'd only descended a few paces
when I noticed a figure staring as if unsure
I could really be who he thought I was.

It was already dusk though not so dark
that what distance had hid from us before   50
was not now undeniable and clear.

In unison we approached each other:
noble Judge Nin how relieved I was to find
you there, not cast among the evildoers!

Our greeting was prolonged and heartfelt.   55
Finally he asked: 'How long since you crossed
the far water to the mountain's foot?'

'Oh,' I replied, 'it was only this morning that I left
the place of sorrow, and I'm still in the first life.
This journey I'm on prepares me for the next.'   60

When Sordello and the soul beside him
heard my reply, they started and shrank back
as though the fact amazed them.

The one turned to Virgil, and the other to
a nearby seated figure, crying, 'Get up, Currado,   65
come see what marvel God's will has brought about.'

Then, turning to me: 'By that great blessing
granted you by Him whose purposes are hid
so far beyond the human mind's imagining,

when you are back across the wide water   70
ask my daughter Giovanna to seek the altar
where innocence's pleas are heeded

to pray for me. I doubt her mother still has any flame
alight for me. She set aside her white widow's weeds,
and soon, poor woman, will wish she'd kept them.   75

You see in her how fleeting is the blaze
of women's love, how soon extinguished
when unrekindled by frequent touch or gaze.

The viper on Milan's banner will afford her
a far poorer tomb than had she held fast   80
to the Galluran rooster on my crest.'

This was what Nino said, but whatever
strong emotion flamed within his heart
his features kept their usual composure.

My avid eyes were trained upon that lower   85
reach of sky where the stars are fewer and, like spokes
close to the hub, seem to move slower.

My guide wondered what I was gazing at,
and I replied: 'Those three beacons all ablaze
that spread their fire across the southern pole.'   90

Then he explained: 'The four stars which shone there
this morning have now dipped below the horizon
and these three have taken up their station.'

While Virgil spoke, Sordello drew him over
and pointing where our gazes followed said: 95
'Look where our enemy has broken cover!'

At the open verge of the shallow valley
a serpent was sidling in, perhaps the very
one who offered the bitter fruit to Eve.

That foul stripe slunk between the grass and the flowers,   100
occasionally raising its wedge-head to lick
its sinuous back as if to make it slick.

I didn't witness – so it's not for me to say –
how the heavenly hawks took to the air
but I saw the fell and rapid way they flew.   105

Hearing their green wings whir, the serpent
fled, and the angels then wheeled upwards to alight
just as they were, each on their own vantage-point.

The shade who at the judge's call had drawn
close to him, throughout that aerial affray,   110
had kept his eyes on me unwaveringly.

'May the lamp that guides you ever upwards find
in your determination ample fuel
to reach the enamelled peak on high,'

he began, 'if you have any reliable news   115
of Valdimagra or the lands nearby
I once was lord of, tell me now.

My name was Currado Malaspina,
not the original one, but of his stock.
Here the love I bear my family is refined.'   120

Although' I replied, 'I've never visited your lands,
nowhere in all of Europe would you find
a region where your name does not resound.

The fame your family has is rightly honoured
by town and country, rich and poor,   125
and known to those who never once set foot there;

and by the hope I have to reach my goal I swear
your house has lost none of its former glory,
is still preeminent in purse and sword.

Though habit and nature have twisted the earth   130
awry in the sway of a wicked ruler, yours
at least have kept to virtue's narrow path.'

And he: 'Enough of that, and yet the sun won't
return seven times to settle on the bed
where the four starry feet of Aries are planted   135

before your generous judgment will be nailed
more firmly in the middle of your head
than it ever was by talk you may have heard

unless God's decree has somehow been annulled.'

NOTES TO CANTO 8
Nick Havely

13. The hymn *Te lucis ante terminum / rerum creator poscimus* ('Before the ending of the day we beseech you, creator of all things') is, like *Salve regina*, sung at the Office of Compline; it appeals for protection against the dangers of the coming night (see also *Purg.* 7. 82-3 and note, above).

19-30. A number of direct addresses alert the reader to significant moments of transition, symbolism or wonder throughout the *Commedia*. This is the first in the *Purgatorio* and draws attention to the role of the guardian angels (ll. 22-39) who later (ll. 95-108) will defend the souls against their 'enemy': the serpent who had tempted Eve but is now powerless to harm them. 'Truth's covering' or 'veil' was a common metaphor for allegory; it appears in one of Dante's earlier addresses to the reader (*Inf.* 9. 61-3), where the meaning of the 'strange verses' is more challenging. Here, the significance of the angels' swords being 'blunted' (l. 27) is not entirely clear; perhaps, following Christ's atonement, Satan can be vanquished merely by a token sword (*CL* 2: 237); but other features, such as their green wings and clothing (ll. 28-9), obviously symbolize hope. For Dante's views on allegory as 'a truth hidden under a beautiful lie', see *Conv.* 2. 1. 2-15.

53. Ugolino (Nino) Visconti (d. 1296) was a nobleman from Sardinia, involved in the tortuous politics of Pisa (see *Inf.* 32-3) and probably became friendly with Dante around 1290, when he was leader of the Pisan Guelfs (see *DE* 873-4).

65. Currado / Corrado Malaspina (d. c.1294) was the grandson of the 'original' Currado (ll. 118-19) who founded the powerful family who ruled over much of NW Tuscany and S Liguria in the mid to late thirteenth century; on Dante's association with them, see below, ll. 118-39 and note.

67-9. Acknowledgement of the unfathomable depth of these 'hidden purposes' 'emphasizes the incomprehensibility of the ways of divine grace, in this case bestowed upon a man [Dante] lacking the particular qualities that might justify it; compare *Inf.* 2. 31-3' (*CL* 2: 243).

70-81. Judge Nino's daughter Giovanna (c.1291-1339) is seen as more likely to remember him and offer the prayers that souls in Purgatory need (see above, *Purg.* 6. 26) than is her mother, Beatrice d'Este, who married Galeazzo Visconti, ruler of Milan, a few years after Nino's death. According to *CL* (2: 245), it's possible that Beatrice might have taken notice of what Dante says here, since on her own death in 1334 her tomb would bear the emblems of both Galeazzo (the 'viper') and Nino (the 'rooster').

85-93. Dante looks towards the South Pole where he had earlier seen the stars representing the four 'cardinal' virtues (*Purg.* 1. 22-7) and finds now that they are replaced by ones signifying the three 'theological' virtues of faith, hope and charity (as defined by St Paul in 1 Thessalonians 3 and 1 Corinthians 13:13).

114. Currado is referring to the 'enamelled' greenery of the Earthly Paradise (on the summit of Mount Purgatory) which Dante will indeed enter at the beginning of canto 28.

115-39. The two voices – of the Dante-persona and of Currado Malaspina, who has first been named in l. 65 (above) – end the canto by celebrating a family with a power base in the Val di Magra on the western slopes of the Apuan Alps (l. 116) whom Dante came to know well during his exile. The founder of the dynasty, Currado il Vecchio (d. 1254), was 'famed' as a patron of poets. Dante is known to have been hosted by his grandson Franceschino, to have acted as a negotiator on behalf of the family in 1306 (i.e. less than seven years after the fictional date of the *Comedy*, as lines 133-8 suggest) and to have sent one of his poems to another powerful member of the clan, Moroello Malaspina (see *Inf.* 24, 145-50; *DE* 628-9 and *BGLD* 34-5). In contrast to this noble family's adherence to the 'narrow path' of virtue, the political ambitions of the Papacy are said to have led the world astray (ll. 130-2; compare *Purg.* 16. 97-114 and 127-9, below).

CANTO 9
Angela Leighton

Dawn, the mistress of Tithonus ever old,
already paling on the eastern border,
had slipped the arms of her sweet lover.

Her forehead glittered with gemstones, shaped
like the starry Scorpion, that cruel-cold beast   5
that lashes everyone with stinging tail.

The night that comes on hour by hour
had climbed the first two steps where we stood,
a third was already shadowed by its wing,

when I, my old-Adam's nature upon me,   10
overcome by sleep, sank down on the grass
just where all five of us had come to sit.

At the hour near daybreak, when the swallow starts
her sad twitterings, perhaps in memory
of all Philomela's ancient woes –   15

the hour when the wandering, peregrine mind,
no longer flesh-bound, caught up in thought,
reaches to visions almost divine –

I seemed to see in dream, suspended,
a sky-borne eagle, golden-feathered,   20
with open wings intent to swoop;

and it seemed I might have soared to where
Ganymede once, abandoning his friends,
was snatched by Jove to the gods' high halls.

I thought to myself: 'Perhaps just here,   25
nowhere else so apt, is where he'd come
to catch us up to the heavens in his claws.'

Then it seemed to me, after circling a while,
he shot like a bolt of lightning down
and snatched me into the realms of fire.   30

There, he and I seemed to burn in flames.
And if the imaginary blaze did sear,
it certainly ripped through my sleep's safe-cover.

Just so, Achilles once woke with a start,
his wide-open eyes casting all about   35
to know where on earth he might have landed

when his mother, fleeing from Chiron to Scyros,
carried him sleeping in her arms to where
the Greeks would one day lure him away.

So I – shocked through as the dreaming sleep   40
slid from my features – lay dead to the world,
like a man who freezes in terror at what he sees.

At my side, Virgil, sole comfort, was steadfast;
and the sun had already risen two hours
while my face stayed turned to that surrounding sea.   45

'Don't be afraid!' my master declared.
'Be assured, we have found a good spot on the way.
Don't slack, but gather up all your powers!

For see, you've reached Purgatory after all.
Look, there's the rock that circles it round.   50
And look, the entrance where the rock is breached.

Just now, at dawn which heralds the day
when your spirit was sleeping deep within you
on flowers that brighten the place below,

a Lady came who said: "I'm Lucy.   55
Come, let me take this sleepy fellow.
I'll ease his way along the road he must go."

Sordello hung back with the other princely shades,
but you she lifted, and as the day grew clear
carried you hither; and I followed after.   60

Here she laid you. But first, her beautifully
lucent eyes showed the door wide open.
Then quick, both she and sleep slipped away.'

Like one reassured after deepest doubt,
who exchanges terror for consolation   65
in finding the truth revealed to his eyes,

so was I changed. And when my leader
saw me free of care, he advanced to the ramparts,
I, close behind, making for the heights.

Reader, take note how my theme reaches high.   70
And yet, do not be amazed if I,
with greater art, must raise it higher.

So we approached, and came to the place
where I seemed to have seen a break or fissure,
as if a wall had been riven apart,   75

and I spied a door, and below, three steps
leading up to it, in various colours,
then a porter who uttered no word as yet.

And as my eyes opened wider, high up
on the topmost step I saw one sit   80
whose face was such I could not bear to look,

for in his hand a naked sword
sent such reflected rays into my eyes
I failed to trace the expression on his face.

'Stop there! So, what the hell do you want?'   85
he challenged for a start. 'Who's your escort?
Mind that you come to no harm up here!'

'A Lady from heaven, expert in such things,'
my master replied, 'just now commanded:
"Go right ahead now; there's the door – "'   90

'And may she guide your way to the good,'
that courteous porter quickly replied.
'Now come. Approach the stairs before you.'

So we ventured near, and the initial step
was of such white marble, such a glossy sheen,   95
I was mirrored in it exactly as I might seem.

The second was coloured blacker than black,
a roughened rock, parched and dry,
deeply scored both lengthwise and across.

The third, of porphyry, massing above,   100
appeared to me like crimson flame,
like blood that suddenly spurts from a vein.

On this, the angel of the Lord had placed
two feet, sitting square astride that threshold
hard as diamond, adamantine stone.   105

Up these three steps my leader drew me,
wishing me well. 'Now pray,' he urged,
'in all humility that the lock dissolve.'

Devoutly I fell before the holy feet;
and begged an opening for pity's sake,   110
beating my breast three times in remorse.

Then on my brow, with the point of his sword,
seven P's were inscribed. And: 'Once inside,
be sure to wash away these wounds,' he advised.

His garments were the colour of ash or clay   115
when dried and dug well out of the ground.
From deep within them he drew two keys.

One was of gold, the other silver;
first with the white and then the golden
that door eased open to my delight.   120

'If one or other of these keys should stick
and fail to slide straight into its slot,
the way wouldn't open,' he explained to us.

'One is more precious, but the other requires
greater art and skill to work the lock,   125
for that's the one to loosen the knot.

From Peter I have them, who urged me to err
in opening up, not in keeping shut,
so long as folk bow, repenting, to the ground.'

Then he heaved open the great holy door,   130
saying: 'Enter; but mind that, once inside,
you never look back or you're out for good.'

And when the pivots of that sacred gate
turned on their hinges, ringing aloud
in their strongly forged metal grooves,   135

no roar was greater, harsher, not even
the Tarpeian door when good Metellus
was dragged away, leaving it agape.

I quickly looked up on hearing the first noise,
and seemed to catch a *Te Deum* sung   140
by mixed-voice choirs to the sweetest tune.

That image in the ear then seemed to render
all that I heard as mere snatched sense,
as when you hear singing by an organ drowned;

the words, now audible, now lost in sound.   145

NOTES TO CANTO 9
Nick Havely

1-6. The description here is probably of sunrise back in Italy; whilst in Purgatory it is still the 'third hour' of the night (9 pm; see ll. 7-9). Dawn (Eos / Aurora) in classical myth is personified as the lover of the Trojan prince Tithonus, to whom the gods gave eternal life but not eternal youth.

15. The tragic and gruesome 'ancient woes' of the sisters Procne and Philomela and their transformations into birds are portrayed in Ovid, *Met.* 6. 412-674. Ovid describes how one of them was changed into a swallow and the other into a nightingale, and the traditions of commentary and etymology associate Philomela with the latter. But, as his reference to the myth later (in *Purg.* 17. 19-21) indicates, Dante appears to have been following a version in which Procne becomes the nightingale and Philomela the swallow.

23. The story of Jupiter transforming himself into an eagle to carry off Ganymede is in Ovid, *Met.* 10. 155-61.

34-8. Achilles's mother, to prevent him going to the Trojan War, removed him from the care of Chiron the centaur and hid him at the court of Lycomedes on Skyros.

55. Lucy is the patron saint of sight and is associated in the poem with illumination and vision (*DE* 576-7). Virgil has also described how she intervened earlier on Dante's behalf (*Inf.* 2. 97-108).

94-102. The three differently coloured steps may represent aspects or stages of confession: recognition of sin; contrition; desire to do better.

112-17. The 'seven P's' represent the seven sins (*peccati* in Italian, *peccata* in Latin) that will be dramatized and expiated on the terraces of Purgatory; whilst the ashy or earthy grey of the angel's garments reinforces the association with penitence.

117-29. The two keys indicate the divine sanctioning of penitence (gold) and the priesthood's guidance of the process (silver).

136-8. According to Lucan's poem on the Roman Civil War (*DBC* 3. 153-5), the Roman tribune Metellus abandoned the defence of the city's treasury, allowing Julius Caesar to take control of it.

CANTO 10
Angela Leighton

Then as we made our way through that door
which the soul's unwise, earthly desires
disable quite, so a wrong path seems right,

I heard it clang resonantly shut.
If then I'd turned to look back in regret   5
what could have excused my disobedient heart?

We climbed up higher through a stony fissure
that rocked first one way, then another,
like a wave concussing in ebb and flow.

'Here we must employ a modicum of art,'   10
my leader began, 'in edging close,
this way or that, by the side which rolls.'

And so we went with such cautious steps
that not before the waning moon
had snuggled down in her darkening bed   15

did we clear the gap in that needle's-eye pass.
But once we were out and free of danger,
up where the mountain levelled to a plain,

I, quite exhausted, and both of us still
uncertain where to step, we rested on the flat –   20
a road lonelier than any desert track.

And from that edge which gives onto nothingness
to the foot of the rise that rises higher still,
the measure was just three lengths of a man;

though as far as my eye could see to scan   25
either by the left side or the right,
that circling plateau stretched an equal span.

We'd not yet started to trudge uphill
when I perceived that, all around,
the bank rose sheer, abrupt and pathless,   30

and the Parian marble was adorned with reliefs
that might have outdone, not only Polyclitus'
chiselled art, but nature's own.

The angel, who came to earth with news
decreeing the age-long, wept-for peace,   35
unlocking the sky's old barrier to heaven,

appeared so lifelike beside us there,
and sculpted with such a graceful sweep,
it seemed an image about to speak.

One might have sworn he cried: 'Ave!'   40
For there, imaginatively carved, was the one
who turned the key, unlocking God's love.

Her very stance seemed to tell the tale:
'Behold the handmaid of the Lord'– just so
an imprint sets its seal in wax.   45

'Don't let your mind fixate on one thing,'
my gentle master warned, and drew me
round to the other, heart-side of his shade.

Yet something made me look again to see,
behind the Virgin, on the side where he,   50
my motive force and guide, now stood,

another story etched on the rock-side.
Slinking round Virgil, I approached quite near
to observe the thing displayed before my eyes:

for carved in relief in the very marble there,   55
cart and oxen dragged the Holy Ark,
in awe of which unsanctioned deeds are shunned.

Before it a crowd, divided in seven choirs,
seemed to baffle my ears and eyes as if
the one claimed 'no'; the other, 'yes, they sing.'   60

Likewise, in the thickening mist of incense
so imaginatively carved, both eyes and nose
quarrelled to perceive – was it yes, or no?

And there, preceding the Holy Ark,
the lowly psalmist lifted dancing feet.   65
Both more and less than a king he seemed.

Opposite, Michal, his spouse, looked out
from a grand palace – contemptuous and sad
to see him thus cavorting in the street.

But I shifted away from the place where I stood   70
to observe more closely the story behind,
dazzling my eyes with its blinding white.

This was the tale of that Roman emperor's
glorious deed, whose goodness moved
Gregory to win the very heavens over.   75

I speak of Trajan, that magnanimous ruler,
and the poor widow who, tearful, grieving,
rushed before to grab his horse's reins.

Trampling cavalry and a surging throng
pressed all round, while gold-carved eagles   80
hovering above seemed to glide in the wind.

The poor little widow in all that crowd
still appeared to be calling: 'Lord, avenge
my dear son dead, or my heart will break!'

and he to reply: 'Now wait till I   85
return.' But she, as one whom grief
spurs on, insisted: 'Suppose, my Lord,

you never return?' 'The one who takes
my place will act.' 'What good's another,
if *you* forget the duty you owe?'   90

At last he agreed: 'Take comfort. You're right.
Duty must be done before I depart.
Justice commands me, compassion constrains.'

So He, for whom nothing's new under the sun,
produced this strangely speaking picture   95
unlike any earthly art that's known.

And while I lingered to trace the lines
of such imaginings, such humbling designs,
admiring the priceless skill of the Artist,

my poet was murmuring: 'Look over there;   100
so many, and passing with such slow steps –
these will lead us to the upper stairs.'

My eyes, always full of wonder and desire,
eager for novelties, for sights unseen,
were quick to turn in the direction marked.   105

But reader, I'd not have you turn in dismay
from good resolutions, when you come to hear
how God ensures the debt is paid.

Don't dwell too much on the sufferers' pains.
Think what's to come; think that, at the worst,   110
nothing can outlast the Judgement Day.

'Master,' I began, 'the thing that I see
creeping towards us seems less than human.
What, I know not. Do my eyes deceive me?'

And he to me: 'The grim conditions   115
of their heavy torment so bows them to the ground
that, at first, my eyes also doubted what I found.

But look closely there, and disentangle
the human forms underneath the stones.
Soon you'll notice how they beat their breasts.'   120

O Christians proud, wretched and so tired,
infirm of purpose, blinkered in your sights,
thinking you progress when in fact you backslide,

don't you know we're all as worms down here,
born to be transformed in angelic butterflies   125
that will fly, unhampered, to the justice of the skies.

As sometimes, propping up a roof or arch,
a bent caryatid presents a grotesque
with knees doubled up against the chest,

from which is born, in those who can discern,   130
some true fellow-feeling for fictional untruth –
so did I *sense* their pain, just seeing it.

The truth is, each was hunched beneath
the weight now carried, whether more or less;
while even the most patient, in what he bore,   136

wept, as if to say: 'I can bear no more.'

NOTES TO CANTO 10
Nick Havely

32. Polyclitus was a Greek sculptor of the late 5th century BCE and stands here for supreme human artistry.

34-42. The scene is that of the angel's annunciation to the Virgin Mary, initiating ('opening') the process of humanity's redemption (Luke 1: 26-38).

55-69. 1 Chronicles 13-15 tells how King David brought the Ark of the Covenant (which had been recovered from the Philistines) back to Jerusalem. During the journey, an Israelite (Uzzah) reached out to steady it and was struck down by Yahweh for daring to touch the sacred vessel (1 Chronicles 13: 9-11). When the Ark eventually entered Jerusalem, David celebrated its arrival with music and dancing, much to Michal's disapproval (1. 15: 25-9).

73-92. The medieval legend of the justice and compassion of the Roman emperor Trajan (98-117 CE) developed in the 8th and 9th centuries, and it came to be believed that the prayers of Pope Gregory the Great (c.540-604) had enabled this pagan ruler to gain salvation (*DE*, 823-4). Dante thus places him in the Heaven of Just Rulers (*Par.* 20. 43-8) and at the centre of a debate about the status of virtuous pagans.

CANTO 11
Angela Leighton

'Our Father, who dwells in the heavens,
uncircumscribed, but full of love
for the first creations that surround you there;

hallowed your name by every creature,
and the power it bears; for it is most fitting   5
to render thanks to your sweet spirit!

Grant us here the peace of your kingdom
which we, by our own will, by all our art,
can never attain unless it comes from above.

Just as your angels sacrifice   10
their wills to yours and sing Hosanna,
so may your will be done among men.

Give us this day our daily bread
without which, wandering in this barren desert,
we slip ever back at each step taken.   15

And as we forgive every evil suffered
at the hands of others, so, benign one,
forgive us our sins, don't calculate our worth.

Of our strength, so easily, lightly overcome,
do not make trial with the ancient adversary,   20
but deliver us from him, who tempts us ever.

This final prayer, O dearest Lord,
is not for ourselves who have no need,
but for those who remain on earth, behind.'

Thus wishing well for themselves and for us,   25
those shadows went praying under such loads
as sometimes weigh on us, deep in dream,

while round and about the first terrace they went,
each in his own way tormented, exhausted,
yet purging the evil vapours of the world.   30

If they, in that place, always speak for our good,
how much more should we, from the depths of goodwill,
do the same for them, as far as we are able?

Indeed, we should help them wash off the stains
they bring with them, so that lightened, purified,   35
they'd rise and emerge among the starry spheres.

'So now, if justice and mercy might ease
your loads, according to your hearts' desires,
and you go lighter, soon to take wing,

show us the shortest way by the stairs,   40
to the left or the right; if more than one,
teach us to find the least strenuous ascent;

because this fellow who accompanies me here,
burdened by his old-Adam's dress of flesh,
is slow to climb, however willing his spirit.'   45

In answer to the words of him I followed,
this was the sense that seemed to emerge
from somewhere nowhere, very hard to place;

and this was the gist: 'Come along with us
to the right by the bank, and you'll find the path   50
even a living person might ascend.

And if I were not impeded by this rock
which subdues the haughty pride of my neck
so I go bowed, face-down to the ground,

I'd look up to see if I know this man   55
who's still alive but remains unnamed,
and gain his pity for my burdened state.

I was Italian, Tuscan-born.
Guglielmo Aldobrandesco, my father,
I wonder, did you ever hear the name?   60

My great forbears' aristocratic blood
and noble heritage made me arrogant,
so that, forgetting our common mother Earth

and holding all men in such contempt,
I met my death, as the Sienese know   65
along with every child in Campagnatico.

I am Omberto, and not only I
but all my kin were ruined by my pride,
dragged down by that same fateful fault.

And so I'm forced to carry this weight   70
till God is satisfied. Burdens I never
bore among the living, I bear among the dead.'

I stayed still, listening, and bowed my head.
Then one of the company, not he who spoke,
twisted round under his heavy load,   75

and saw me, and knew me, and called out loud,
keeping his eyes with difficulty fixed
on mine, who skulked, bent double, alongside.

'Why now, aren't you Oderisi?' I asked,
'Glory of Gubbio, and glory of that art   80
known in Paris as *illumination*?'

'Brother', he answered, 'the pages penned
by Franco the Bolognese must please far more.
The glory's all his, mine a tiny part.

Yet while I lived I'd not have given   85
such generous praise. My heart was set
only on furthering my own ambition.

For such high arrogance the price must be paid.
I'd not even be here, had I not once
while still a sinner turned again to God.   90

Oh what vainglory lies in human power!
How short-lived the green shoot of fame, even when
not followed by a time of decline and fall.

In painting Cimabue believed that he
would hold the field; now Giotto's all the rage,   95
his fame obscuring the other's art.

So too, in verse, a second Guido steals
glory from the first; and perhaps another's
born already to oust both from the nest.

The roar of earthly fame's no more   100
than a breath of wind blowing this way and that,
changing quarters as it changes the names.

What fame would be yours if, instead of growing
old in body, you'd died before
you'd finished lisping *Da-Da* or *doo-doo*,   105

and a thousand years had passed? That time's
to the length of eternity, as the twitch of an eyebrow
to the slowest, starry spheres of the skies.

He who walks with such slow strides
ahead of me there, once famous in Tuscany,   110
is now barely mentioned, even in Siena.

He was lord of that city at the time he put down
the fury of Florence – as proud in those days
as now she's supine, lazy as a slut.

Your own pre-eminence is as the colour of grass   115
which comes and goes. What makes it flourish
when young in the earth, makes it fade and pass.'

I replied: 'True words which speak to the heart
of wise humility, and prick my self-worth.
But who's the person you mentioned just now?'   120

'That was', he replied, 'Provenzan Salvani.
He's here because he was too presumptuous
in annexing Siena all for himself.

So he walks and walks without repose
ever since his death; repaying in kind,   125
like all who are guilty of earthly pride.'

'If, as I know, any human spirit, slow
to repent fully before the end of life,
must stay below, forbidden to ascend

unless prayers offered for his soul can help,   130
must stay confined the length of time he was alive,
how did it happen that he came through the gate?'

'When in the fullness of his glory,' came reply,
'he went out freely, putting shame aside,
and stood there begging in the Campo di Siena   135

in order to save his friend, who was due
to be punished in the prison of Charles d'Anjou –
an act which made him tremble in every limb.

I can say no more. I speak dark things.
But the time will come when you'll unlock their sense,   140
when those near you will think on similar lines.

This good deed freed him from those first confines.'

NOTES TO CANTO 11
Nick Havely

1-24. The souls of the proud recite the Paternoster (Matthew 6: 9-13), on behalf not of themselves but of others. In the original, *manna* in l. 13 (here translated as 'bread'), has the dual sense of physical and spiritual sustenance.

58-72. The speaker is Omberto Aldobrandesco (d. 1254), Count of Santafiora near Grosseto. He and his family serve here as an example both of pride in nobility of rank and of declining fortunes, since his arrogance led to defeat and death at the hands of the Sienese leader Provenzan Salvani (see below, note on ll. 109-14 and 120-42). Campagnatico (l. 66) in Sienese territory was one of the Aldobrandeschi castles.

79-90. Oderisi of Gubbio (d. 1299) and Franco Bolognese (l. 83) were famous as illuminators of manuscripts in Dante's time. Not much is now known about either of them, but Oderisi (*DE* 658) worked in Bologna and Rome, and Franco (who may have been his pupil) is referred to in Vasari's *Lives of the Artists* (*DE* 419).

82. Oderisi's addressing Dante as 'brother' (*frate*) reflects the wider sense of community in Purgatory, not only between artists and poets but also between friends and fellow Christians; see above, *Purg.* 4. 127, and below, 13. 94, 16. 65, 19. 133, 21. 13 & 131, 23. 97 & 112, 24. 55, 26. 115, 29. 15, and 33. 23.

94-6. The references to Cimabue (1240- c.1300) and Giotto (1266-1337) reflect Dante's interest not only in fame but also in innovation in the visual arts.

97-9. Guido Guinizelli of Bologna (1230?-76) and Dante's Florentine friend and contemporary Guido Cavalcanti (1250/5?-1300) were influential practitioners of the 'sweet new style' of love-poetry (see *Purg.* 24. 57), and both are referred to a number of times in Dante's work: see, e.g., *Purg.* 26. 73-135; *BGLD* 115-21; and examples of both poets' lyrics in the 'Postscript' to this volume (nos 4b, 7a, 9 and 11). The unnamed figure who will supplant both Guidos is probably Dante himself (with the implied proviso that he too may yield to another).

108. The slowest moving of the concentric spheres of the medieval cosmos was the eighth and outermost one: the sphere of fixed stars.

109-14 and 120-42. Provenzan Salvani was leader of the Sienese Ghibellines who defeated the Florentines at the battle of Montaperti in 1260 but was in turn defeated and killed by them at Colle Valdelsa in 1269 (referred to below in *Purg.* 13. 115). His act of humility in publicly begging money for his friend's ransom, rather than extorting it (ll.

133-9) is the reason for placing him on this terrace of Purgatory, rather than 'below' (l. 129) among those who delayed repentance, and his portrayal reflects the 'political evenhandedness' of the canto (*DE*, 718).

140. The 'time' that Oderisi sombrely speaks of is that of Dante's exile (1302 onwards).

CANTO 12
Lorna Goodison

Evenly yoked like bull-cows of the same size
the poor soul and me, step in step, side by side
for as long as my good teacher allowed it.

But when he said, 'Forward up yourself and leave
him, for like sea men who set out for the quays,   5
each must proceed by paddling their own canoe,'

I raise up myself and stand to my full height
so that I could walk tall, dignified and upright,
although my thoughts still did bend down low.

I moved on and was following most obediently   10
in my master's footsteps. We were already
picking up pace, when he checked me, said:

'Lower your gaze, in order to see your way clear,
you need to sight up what is on this walkway where
you are lifting up and putting down your feet.'   15

Just as how in some church floors, tombs are inlaid
underfoot so the details of a life lived are engraved
never to be forgotten, always preserved,

and a memorial to the departed remains to gaze on
when their dear ones go there as pity brings tears on   20
when the tenderhearted are pierced by memory;

so, to one side I saw a depiction of that same one, he
created more handsome than any star-boy matinee
idol, reeling down like lightning from the skies.

On the other side I saw Bra-irus, who scammed us   25
struck by a lightning bolt, and lying down comatose,
cramp and cold-up in the ground.

I see those: Tim B, his Pal, and Mars, gunmen all,
bearing arms, gazing at the scattered body parts
of their father Joe, and other big time gangsters.   30

Nimrod I saw, demented under his mighty works,
confused and dazed, looking in vain to his followers
spangled in bling and glitter in the land of Shinar.

O Niobe! I see your eyes running with khol water.
That is how I see you, representing on that pathway.   35
Betwixt your seven and seven dead pickney.
.
And what a subject for a lament, you were king Saul,
Stabbed by your own sword on top of mount Gilboa
Where neither rain nor dew-water will hereafter fall.

O trickify Anansi! It is just so I see you there so: 40
half a spider, full a grief, unfriended on the threads
of your mischief works spun on the web.

O Rehoboam, now you can no longer be a menace
to us with your hard face; for see, a chariot racing
to come haul away your overbearing statue.   45

And seen too on that stony path was the ultimate
highest price Al C made his own mother pay
after she betrayed his father for jewellery.

And there also, I beheld, a sequence of Sennacherib,
being shot up in the temple by the young assassins   50
he'd trained, who then exited and left him for dead.

It showed the troubles, the endless cycle of violence
strife and riots that Miss T set off, when she opened
her mouth and bragged to Mass Cyrus:

'O, is blood you want? Well, is blood I will full you up of."   55

It showed how the Assyrian ran like bolt from the rout
after Holofernes' death, and in the graphic images,
we saw the corpse of the slaughtered Don himself.

I saw Troy the city, once green, it fell to ashes, ruins!
O ill-clad man how you were pictured in those scenes: 60
Reduced, reduced, reduced.

What skilled master artists did light and shade
that chiaroscuro? Those features, who was it made
them appear so impressive to *bona fide* art lovers?

Take it as I tell you: The dead look dead for true.   65
The ones supposed to be alive? look like me and you.
Any eye-witness to those events as they happened

could not see any more than me when I trod on
the scenes upon that pavement. So, exalt yourself,
go on, push out your chest, you children of Eve.   70

Do not bother to look under your feet, next thing
you go and see the evil path you're trodding.

So by now we'd passed farther round the mountain
leaving more of the sun behind, than I, who certainly
not paying much mind, had been taking notice of,   75

when he – who always walked in front, on the lookout –
gave out: 'Heads up. Do not be looking idly about.
This is how you must proceed, eyes forward, be attentive.

See an angel is now preparing to come this way,
behold how the sixth servant girl of the day   80
is coming back from service with all due respect?

Get you ready O, and set yourself right, so the seraph
will consent to be our guide as we take the upward path.
Hold this thought: This day will never dawn again.'

As I was now used to his warnings not to waste time   85
he never again needed to lecture me and remind
me about this, because by then I fully overstood.

The divine being approached us robed all in white.
That countenance resembled the morning star, bright
and suffused with trembling radiance.   90

Extending angel arms, flexing feathered pinions,
the said seraph said: 'Come, here the stairway opens,
from now on you will be able to climb it with ease.

Not many mortals respond to this call to come.
O human race born to lift up on wings and soar,   95
why do you fall back because of a little breeze-blow?'

The bright-soul led us to where the rock was split,
then smote me with those wings on my forehead
and promised that we would have safe passage.

And like when you climb the hill on the right hand   100
side, to reach that church which seems to overhang
that well-ordered little town above Rock Hall,

and the sharp gradient is then lessened somewhat
by stairways that were made back in the time that
right and proper building standards were kept   105

and so that steep steep incline is made easy and nice
when it cut across sudden from that other cornice
that brushes by the high cliffs situated on either side.

As we were turning to go up the stairs, *Beati Pauperis*
Spiritu – Blessed are the poor in spirit, to you – this   110
was being sung in dulcet tones so ethereal, so delicate

that ordinary tongue could not describe it.

O my, what a complete difference between this site
and hell. Up here, you come in accompanied by high
praise songs, below, it is so-so savage lamentations.   115

We were already on the treads of the holy stair
when it felt to me that my entire being was lighter
than I had seemed when I was down on the plains.

'Master,' I asked him, 'What kind of heavy weight
has been taken off of me, so that I can now barely   120
feel exhaustion or fatigue as I proceed on my way?'

He answered: 'When the P's that still remain on
your forehead – though they are now almost gone
like this first one – are erased,

then your steps will be cushioned by compassion   125
and you will no longer feel any exhaustion.
Instead, you will go upwards singing like the poor

people of our country who do not notice that they
still bear the weight of slavery days on their heads,
except when some passing scholar mentions it,   130

and that is when they reach up a hand and touch
and feel it, and so they remind themselves: I can not
always put my finger on why I still carry this load.

Like this.' I spread my fingers and found that only six
of the P's the Keyman had marked on my brow   135
remained. When he saw this, my noble guide smiled.

NOTES TO CANTO 12
Nick Havely

22-61. What Virgil in the next canto (*Purg.* 13. 40-2) will call the 'bit' or 'bridle' of images warning against pride includes twelve main examples (over 13 tercets) which alternate Christian with pagan material and reflect various forms of overweening pride and braggartry that in myth and legend met with disastrous consequences. They are:
(1) the fall of Lucifer (Isaiah 14: 12-15);
(2) the defeat of the Giants who had challenged Jupiter and the Gods at the hands of Pallas Athene and Mars (*Theb.* 2. 595-601 and *Inf.* 31. 97-9);
(3) Nimrod, traditionally associated with the building of the Tower of Babel (Genesis 11: 1-9) – a key example of human over-reaching – who appears in all three parts of the *Commedia* (see also *Inf.* 31. 46-81 and *Par.* 26. 124-9);
(4) Niobe, Queen of Thebes, who set herself up against Latona (mother of Apollo and Diana), as in *Met.* 6. 146-312 and as a result lost her seven sons and seven daughters;
(5) Saul, first King of Israel, who killed himself after his defeat by the Philistines on Mount Gilboa (1 Samuel 31: 1-6);
(6) Arachne, the spinner and weaver who challenged Athene to a contest and was as a result turned into a spider (*Met.* 6. 5-145). Ovid's story highlights her artistic skill, and similarly the spider god Anansi (as in the translation here) features in West African and Caribbean myth as an accomplished spinner of tales;
(7) Rehoboam was the tyrannical successor to his father, King Solomon, and was humiliated by a rebellion of his subjects (1 Kings 12: 14-19);
(8) Alcmeon (here 'Al C') of Thebes killed his mother who had betrayed his father in exchange for a necklace forged by Vulcan (*Met.* 9. 406-12);
(9) On Sennacherib, King of Assyria, and the disastrous end of his campaign against Hezekiah, King of Judah, see 2 Kings 19: 35-7;
(10) How Thamyris, Queen of the Scythians (here 'Miss T') avenged the death of her son by beheading Cyrus II, King of the Persians is one of many stories Dante takes from the *Historia adversus paganos* by Paulus Orosius (see *DE* 662-3);
(11) The beheading of the proud Assyrian general Holofernes by the Israelite heroine Judith – a prelude to the defeat of the former's army (Judith 13: 6-10);
(12) The fall of Troy (described as 'proud Ilium' in *Aen.* 3. 2-3) ending the sequence.
    In the original (ll. 25-63), Dante repeats the letters V, O and M each four times at the beginning of the tercets, thus forming in an acrostic pattern the Italian word for 'Man': UOM ('u' being interchangeable with 'v') and further emphasising pride as the key human flaw.

62-70. Praise of the work of the 'skilled master' here recalls the celebration of divine artistry reflected in the earlier images of humility (*Purg.* 10. 94-9).

80. The 'sixth servant girl of the day' refers to the sixth hour after dawn – i.e., mid day.

89. Comparing the guardian angel to 'the morning star' suggests a deliberate contrast to the 'day star', Lucifer, whose fall from heaven has been mentioned (ll. 22-4) as the first warning against pride.

101-2. In the original, the church on the hill is San Miniato al Monte, above the Rubaconte bridge in Florence. Here the equivalent is the church above the hillside community of Rock Hall, north-west of Kingston, Jamaica.

109-10. 'Blessed are the poor in spirit, for the Kingdom of Heaven is theirs' (Matthew 5:3) is the first of seven beatitudes from Christ's Sermon on the Mount through which Dante celebrates the virtues opposing the seven sins expiated in the *Purgatorio* (see *DE* 89).

CANTO 13
Steve Ellis

Here we find, coming to the top,
    this mountain's second cutting
    that cleanses us as it climbs,
with a terrace there that circles
    round, just like the one below,   5
    only with a circuit more sharp.
There's no image or carving here,
    the ground and bank are all bare,
    the colour only that of raw rock.
'If we waited to ask people now,'   10
    the poet was saying, 'I worry
    we'll delay going on too much.'
Then he fixed his eyes on the sun,
    swivelling on his right-hand side
    and bringing his left side round.   15
'O sweet light in which we trust,
    be guide to us in this new zone,'
    he says, 'as guidance is needed.
Warmer of the world, illuminator,
    unless other reason says contrary   20
    your rays should always lead us.'
As on earth you'd reckon a mile
    we'd already gone from this spot
    in little time, our intention keen,
when flying towards us we heard   25
    – but didn't see – speaking spirits
    inviting us to the feast of love.
The first of these airborne voices
    shouts out, 'They have no wine,'
    and goes off away repeating it,   30
and before it gets out of range
    we hear another, 'I am Orestes'
    shouting as it goes, without halt.
'Gosh father,' I say, 'what's this?'
    and just as I ask, there's a third   35
    crying, 'Bless them that curse you.'

And my good master: 'This circle
   gives lashes for the sin of envy,
   and the whip is plaited with love.
The bit will be opposite voices   40
   which I presume you should hear
   before reaching the pass of pardon.
But look closely now, up ahead,
   you'll see people sitting down,
   all of them leant against the slope.'   45
So now I really sharpen my eyes
   and see in front souls in cloaks
   exactly the same colour as the rock.
And when we'd got a bit nearer
   I hear a shout: 'Mary, pray for us!'   50
   and 'Michael', 'Peter', 'All saints'.
I doubt there's anybody on earth
   so unfeeling, as not to be stung
   to the heart, by what I saw next,
because, when I got near enough   55
   to be sure of what their state was
   grief was milked from my eyes.
Their clothes were coarse sacking,
   and everyone shoulder to shoulder,
   all of them backed by the rock: 60
exactly like the sightless beggars
   who cry their needs on holy days,
   heads leaning against each other
to prompt the pity of passers-by,
   not only with the noise they make   65
   but no less with the look of them.
And like the blind gain no benefit
   from the sun, so the spirits here,
   not gifted by the light of heaven,
because their eyes are all sewn up   70
   with wire thread, like wild hawks
   are treated, to make them tame.
For me it seemed a discourtesy
   to go by seeing, not being seen,
   so I turn to that fount of wisdom   75

who realised what my silence said:
    there's no need for any question,
    but 'Ask,' he says, 'and to the point.'
Virgil was beside me on that side
    you could fall from, off the edge,   80
    since there's no curb going round;
and on my other side the spirits,
    their cheeks wet with devout tears
    seeping through the ugly stitches.
I turned towards them and began: 85
    'O people sure to see light on high
    which now is your only concern,
so that grace speedily defogs
    your conscience, and flows down
    into your mind like a pure river,   90
say as an act of kindness to me
    whether any soul here is Italian;
    it might profit him to be known.'
'O brother, all here are citizens
    of a true city – what you mean is,   95
    did any live in Italy as a pilgrim.'
It seemed that I heard this reply
    a bit onward from where I stood,
    so I concentrate in that direction.
There I see a soul waiting facially,   100
    and if anybody asks me, 'How?'
    like blind people lift their chins.
'Spirit submitting, in order to rise,'
    I say, 'if it's you who answered
    give me either your name or origin.'   105
'I'm Sienese,' she replies, 'with these
    polishing up here my rusted life,
    crying to Him to reveal Himself.
Wise I wasn't, even if called Wise,
    more happy in the harm of others   110
    than in any advantage of my own.
And to show you I'm not kidding,
    listen to me confess my stupidity,
    even in my more mature years.

My townsfolk were beside Colle,   115
    met in the field with their enemy
    whose victory I prayed from God;
when they broke in the bitter rout
    of flight, I watched their reverse
    with a joy never equalled before,   120
so that I lifted up my flushed face
    to cry at God, "Now do your worst!"
    like the blackbird in a spell of sun.
At the very last, I wanted peace
    with Him, but all my repentance   125
    wouldn't have paid what I owed,
if it hadn't been for Pier Pettinaio
    recording me in his holy prayer,
    increasing my charity dividend.
But who are you, busying yourself   130
    with our condition, with open eyes,
    as I guess, breathing as you talk?'
'My eyes will be denied me here,'
    I said, 'but not long, since envy
    isn't a sin blinding them much.   135
My mind is much more bothered
    with worry of the torment below,
    so that I feel its burden already.'
She asks, 'But who's brought you
    up to us, if you go down again?'   140
    And I: 'This one quiet beside me;
and I am alive, so don't hold back,
    you saved soul, if you'd like me
    to mobilise mortals on your behalf.'
'O, this is such wonder,' she replies,   145
    'it's a certain sign God loves you,
    so let your prayers help me some.
And I ask, by that you most desire,
    if you ever tread on Tuscan land
    report me well to my own people,   150
residing among those hapless folk
    who put their trust in Talamone,
    more waste of hopes than finding
the Diana, more loss of personnel.'

NOTES TO CANTO 13
Steve Ellis

32. The words are spoken by Pylades in impersonating his friend Orestes, in order to undergo the latter's death-sentence for avenging his father Agamemnon (see Cicero, *De amicitia*, 7. 24).

36. Christ's words from the Sermon on the Mount (Matthew 5: 44, Luke 6: 28).

39. The stimulus to the virtue opposed to each vice is expressed in terms of governing a horse, as is the reining in from the sin itself ('the bit', l. 40), where the examples of envy we are given in the following canto, before Dante exits from the terrace, are anticipated (ll. 41-2).

109. The speaker is Sapia (meaning Wise in Italian), who died before 1289, the aunt of Provenzan Salvani, for whose defeat at the battle of Colle di Valdelsa (l. 115) see the note to canto 11. 109-14, above. We are dependent on this passage from Dante for knowledge of her implacability towards her own people.

127. Pier Pettinaio was a hermit and holy man of Siena, who died in 1289 and was celebrated after his death by an annual feast in his honour.

137. The 'worry' is about the punishment on the terrace of pride. That Dante was proud (e.g., of his poetic achievements) is regularly attested by his own writings and those of his contemporaries, including Boccaccio in his *Life of Dante*.

152. The Sienese acquired the small port of Talamone in 1303, but attempts to develop a maritime trade to rival that of Genoa or Venice failed, as did the search for the river Diana, reputed to flow under Siena, in the hope of supplementing the city's scarce water supply.

CANTO 14
Steve Ellis

'Who is it, rounding our mountain
    before death has flown him up,
    who can open and shut his eyes?'
'I've no idea, but he's not alone:
    you're nearer to them, you ask,   5
    but do it nicely, so he'll speak.'
So two souls were talking of me
    leant on each other on my right;
    then raising their faces to speak
one said: 'O soul bound for heaven   10
    but still going fixed in your flesh,
    for charity's sake, please tell us
who you are, where you're from;
    your state of grace amazes us,
    as a thing never heard of must.'   15
And I: 'Through middle Tuscany
    a stream uncoils from Falterona,
    a hundred-plus miles in length.
From beside it I bring this body:
    there's no point saying my name   20
    since so far it's not much known.'
'If I can flesh out your meaning
    by my understanding,' he replies,
    'it's the Arno you're referring to.'
The other asks: 'Why did he hide   25
    the name of that river, like a man
    concealing something horrible?'
And the soul who was asked this
    replies, 'I don't know; it's good,
    though, this valley is blotted out;   30
because from its head, in that part
    that's densest of the mountain-chain
    that Pelorus was broken off from,
to where it finally gets to restore
    what the sky absorbs from the sea,   35
    from where each river has its load,

virtue is seen as an enemy, fled
    by all like a snake, by some curse
    on the place or by bad practice;
and their natures have so changed,   40
    the people of that woeful valley,
    it's as if they have Circe as pastor.
Among filthy pigs, whose feeding
    should be acorns, not human food,
    it begins its miserable meanders.   45
Coming down, it meets curs next,
    full of snarling, empty of power,
    and turns its snout away in scorn.
It runs on down; and as it swells,
    that accursed and luckless ditch,   50
    it finds all the dogs become wolves,
and then on through its deep gorges
    it meets such a set of crafty foxes
    they don't fear any trap being set.
I don't care that others hear me;   55
    and good for this man, if he notes
    what a true spirit discloses to me.
I see your grandson, now hunter
    of those wolves, terrorising them
    on the bank of that bloody river.   60
He sells their flesh as it still lives,
    then butchers them like old meat,
    annulling life and his own honour.
In blood, he exits that dire wood,
    left so that in a thousand years   65
    it'll never re-seed itself the same.'
Like people hearing awful news
    show woeful faces as they listen,
    wherever the threats come from,
so I saw the other soul, attentive,   70
    getting disturbed and distressed
    as he grasped what was spoken.
The words of one, the other's look
    made me eager for their names
    so I asked, pleading with them.   75

The one who'd first spoke to me
    began: 'You want me to behave
    to you, as you wouldn't do to me.
But since God wants to use you
    as such a showcase for his grace,   80
    I agree; so, I was Guido del Duca.
My blood burned so with envy
    that if I saw anyone's happiness
    you'd see my face getting livid.
I reap straw from such seed here: 85
    O human race, setting your heart
    where brotherhood is excluded!
This is Rinier, prize and honour
    of the house of Calboli, but now
    no-one is the heir of his valour.   90
And not only is his blood shorn
    of the good and graces of living:
    from shore to shore, from the Po
to the mountains, is a wasteland
    of poisonous twigs, so too late   95
    it is, now, for any garden to grow.
Where's good Lizio, Harry Mainardi,
    Pier Traversaro, Guido di Carpigna?
    O Romagnesi, all degenerates now!
In Bologna, where's Fabbro's line?   100
    Or Bernardin di Fosco's in Faenza,
    noble offshoot of a modest stem?
Don't be amazed, Tuscan, if I cry,
    recalling men like Guido da Prata
    or Ugolino d'Azzo, one of ours,   105
Federigo Tignoso and his circle,
    the Traversara and Anastagi family
    (both of them with no successors),
knights, ladies, and all the deeds
    sparked by our love and courtesy,   110
    where now all hearts are brutish.
O Bertinoro, why not vanish away,
    since your family's one of many
    to die out, to avoid contamination?

Bagnacaval does well not to breed,   115
    and bad Castrocaro, worse Conio,
    spawning such a problem brood.
The Pagani should call a halt too
    after that devil dies, even though
    their reputation is gone for good.   120
O Ugolin de' Fantolin, you're ok,
    since no more are expected now
    to darken or to derail your line.
But go now, Tuscan: all I desire
    is to weep, rather than say more,   125
    our talk has made me so glum.'
We knew that those dear spirits
    heard us go, so by not speaking
    they led us to trust in our way.
After we'd walked further alone,   130
    lightning seemed to split the air
    and a voice hurling these words
at us: 'Everyone that findeth me
    shall slay me,' growing fainter
    as thunder when a cloud bursts.   135
Our hearing was just recovering
    when there's another such fracas
    like thunderclap on thunderclap:
'I'm Aglauros, turned into stone.'
    At this, to get closer to the poet,   140
    I step to the right, not forwards.
And now everywhere was quiet;
    he says: 'That was the harsh bit
    that should keep humans in line.
But you eat the bait on the hook   145
    of the old enemy, who nets you,
    so reins or rewards are little use.
Heaven calls you, circling above,
    showing off its eternal beauties
    and you look only at the ground;   150
so he afflicts you, who sees all.'

NOTES TO CANTO 14
Steve Ellis

24. The Arno rises below Falterona (l. 17), a peak in the densest part of the Apennines (l. 32) and flows through Tuscany on its way to the sea (ll. 34-5), passing through Dante's native city Florence (l. 19).

33. Pelorus is the mountain at the extreme north-east point of Sicily, supposedly broken off from the Apennine chain by some geological upheaval.

58. Guido del Duca (see below, l. 81) now turns to prophesying the shame of Rinier's grandson, not caring that he does this to Rinier himself (l. 55; see below, l. 88). Fulcieri da Calboli was *podestà* (Governor) of Florence in 1303 and was ferocious in his actions against the White Guelphs on behalf of the Blacks, Dante maintaining the image of the wolf-hunt in the wood (l. 64) to describe the political actions in Florence. In return for 'selling' (l. 61) the flesh of the Whites, Fulcieri was able to extend his governorship beyond its due term.

81. Guido del Duca was a well-connected individual from Ravenna who acted as judge in various cities in the Romagna, still living in 1249. Of his disposition towards envy we have only Dante's testimony in this canto. His remarks on 'brotherhood' (ll. 86-7) which puzzle Dante will be explained in the next canto.

88. Rinier da Calboli was governor of various cities in the Romagna between 1247-92 and was heavily involved in various military feuds which led to his eventual death in battle.

104. Guido da Prata is recorded in documents between 1184-1228; Ugolino d'Azzo (l. 105), a member of the noble Tuscan family of the Ubaldini, spending the greater part of his life in his castles in the Romagna, died 1293.

112. Bertinoro is a castle in the Romagna near Forlì, birthplace and former haunt of Guido del Duca (see l. 81) and his circle. The counts of Bertinoro were extinguished by 1177 (ll. 113-14).

115. The Malvicini family, counts of Bagnacavallo, had no male heirs by 1300, in contrast to the counts of Castrocaro and Conio, whose corrupt lines continue (ll. 116-17). The Pagani (l. 118) were lords of Faenza, whose present representative, Maghinardo da Susinana ('that devil', l. 119), is also castigated in *Inf.* 27, 49-51. Ugolin de' Fantolin (l. 121) was a noble of Faenza whose two sons had died without male issue by 1300 (ll. 122-3).

133. The words of Cain after murdering his brother Abel (Genesis 4: 14).

139. Aglauros was daughter of Cecrops, king of Athens, turned into stone on account of her envy of Mercury's love for her sister Herse (Ovid, *Met.* 2. 708-832). This instance and that of Cain comprise the 'harsh bit' (l. 143) restraining envy (see note on *Purg.* 13. 39, above).

CANTO 15
Rob A. Mackenzie

As much as appears, from daybreak
till the third hour, of the sun's
rise and spiral between the tropics
with a child's playfulness – so much
remained in view of the sun's course: 5
vespers in Purgatory, midnight in Italy.
The beams struck us full in the face
as we had turned around the mountain
to head directly northwest
but I felt my forehead burdened   10
by splendour far greater than before;
the cause, unfathomable, left me dazed.
I raised my hands to shield my eyes
from such excess in plain sight.
A beam rebounds from water or mirror,   15
rising at the same angle it descended,
each at equal distance from a plumb line
as revealed by experiment and science –
so such light reflected ahead
seemed to strike at my vision;   20
I wished for speed to escape it.
'What is this, dear father?' I said.
'I can barely shield my face from it
and it seems to be moving towards us.'
'Don't be astonished if the heavenly clan   25
still dazzles you,' he replied. 'A messenger
has come with an invitation to climb.
Seeing such things will soon not be hard
but will bring as much delight as nature
enables you to feel.' When we arrived,   30
the blessed angel said, cheerfully,
'Enter here. The stairway is far less steep
than the others.' We left that place
and were climbing when, behind us,
we heard sung *Blessed are the merciful!*   35
and *Rejoice, you conquerors!*

My master and I pressed on upwards,
just the two of us, and I was thinking
how I might profit from his words;
I turned to him and asked,   40
'What did the spirit from Romagna mean
by "prohibition" and "companionship"?'
He said to me: 'He understands the cost
of his greatest fault; don't then be surprised
if he scolds us for it, hoping for less   45
to sadden him. Because your desires
are pinned on notions that partnership
means a shared loss for each partner,
envy makes your lungs sigh like bellows.
But if the supreme realm of love   50
were to drag your desires upward,
this theme would not play in your chest;
the more people say "ours", the more
good each person possesses, and the more
charity flares in that community.'   55
'I hunger more for contentment and more
doubts crowd my mind than if I had
been silent before. How can a good
shared between many make more rich
than if shared between few?' He replied: 60
'Because your mind dwells on earthly things,
you gather darkness even from light.
The infinite good above, beyond
all description, speeds to love
as a sunbeam to a bright form.   65
The more it gives of itself, the more love
it finds; the greater the spread of charity,
so much it gains in eternal value.
The more people above love
each another, the more there is   70
to love well and love more;
each renders to the other as in a mirror.
If my argument does not bring relief
from hunger, you will see Beatrice
deliver you from this and all such yearning.   75
Persevere, that your five wounds are soon

erased, just as two already have been;
healing will come through their pain.'
I planned to say, 'You have satisfied me!'
when I realized I had come upon   80
the terrace above and my eager eyes
made me silent; it seemed to me
they were drawn suddenly into
an ecstatic vision: I saw a temple
full of people and, at the entrance,   85
a woman of sweet, maternal disposition,
who said, 'My son, why do you act
like this towards us? Your father and I
have been in distress, searching for you.'
She then fell silent and what had just   90
formed, dispersed. A second woman
appeared with tears running down
her cheeks, grief distilled and rising
to great spite against another, and said:
'Pisistratus, if you are ruler over   95
the city whose name the gods disputed,
from where all knowledge radiates,
take revenge on those brazen arms
that dared embrace our daughter.'
The ruler himself appeared to me,   100
genial and mild, and replied to her
with tranquil disposition: 'What ought
we do to those who wish us evil,
if we condemn those who love us?'
Then I saw, kindled by the fire of anger,   105
a crowd stoning a youth to death,
crying loudly to each other, 'Kill! Kill!'
I saw him slump to the ground, already
heavy with death, but always his eyes
were fixed on the gates of heaven.   110
Under this fierce assault, he prayed to
the Lord on high to forgive his persecutors
with a disposition fit to unbind compassion.
When my mind returned to the truths
outside itself, I remembered those apparitions   115
were as much truths. My guide, who

could see me act as if still freeing
myself from slumber, said: 'What's wrong
that you can't hold yourself upright
and have walked more than half a league   120
with veiled eyes and stumbling feet
like one overcome by wine or sleep?'
'My dear father, if you listen, I will tell
what appeared when my bodily senses
were removed.' And he said: 'If a hundred   125
masks covered your face, your thoughts,
however faint, would not be closed to me.
What you saw was so that you'll always
open your heart to the waters of peace
that spring from the eternal fountain.   130
I did not ask "What's wrong?" as one
who looks with unseeing eyes on a body
stretched out and lifeless, but I asked
to give strength to your feet; the lazy
need a prod, lest they are slow to use   135
their faculties when these return.'
We walked through the evening,
looking as far ahead as possible
into the sunset's bright rays
and, little by little, smoke inched   140
towards us; smoke dark as night
with no possible escape anywhere.
It stole both sight and the fresh air.

NOTES TO CANTO 15
Nick Havely

2. The 'third hour' is 9 in the morning.

35-6. *Blessed are the merciful* is the fifth Beatitude (Matthew 5: 7) and the second to be heard in *Purg.* Marking the ascent out of the terrace of the envious, the praise of the merciful identifies the opposite virtue: concern for others (*misericordia*). On the Beatitudes and their appropriateness to the sins expiated in Purgatory, see the note on *Purg.* 12. 110, above. The source of *Rejoice you conquerors* is less certain: it may derive from the phrase *gaudete et exultate* at the end of the Beatitudes, Matthew 5: 12, (as suggested by *CL* 2: 444), and it probably refers to the envious soul's conquest over itself.

41. 'The spirit from Romagna' is Guido del Duca in the previous canto, and the pilgrim is puzzled by Guido's reference to brotherhood and exclusion in *Purg.* 14. 87, above.

63-75. With their emphasis on love as brightness and reflection, these lines anticipate 'the brilliant theological language' of the *Paradiso* (*CL* 2: 447); hence at the end of the passage Virgil points forward to Beatrice.

84-113. Mary's gentleness when rebuking Jesus in the Temple (Luke 2: 41-6), the clemency of the Athenian Pisistratus (Valerius Maximus, *Facta et dicta memorabilia* 5. 1, ext. 2), and St Stephen's forgiveness of the mob stoning him to death (Acts 7: 54-60) are the third set of positive examples which Virgil has described as the 'whip' towards the appropriate virtue on each of the terraces (*Purg.* 13. 37-9). As before, they combine biblical and classical narratives, and in this case they have become more internalized: the examples in *Purg.* 10 were images in stone; in 13 (ll. 28-36) they were voices; whilst here they are formed by the Dante-persona's own 'ecstatic vision' (l. 84).

CANTO 16
Steve Ellis

The darkness of hell, or of night
    devoid of any star in a blank sky,
    or coped in the densest of cloud,
this was never a veil to my eyes
    like that smoke, over us there,   5
    nor so rough and acid to the sight.
You couldn't keep your eyes open;
    so that my wise and faithful guide
    came to me, to offer his shoulder.
As a blind man behind his helper   10
    avoids getting lost, or a collision
    that could harm or even kill him,
so I go on in that bitter, filthy air,
    listening to my leader as he says
    repeatedly, 'Hold on tight to me.'   15
I heard voices seeming to pray
    for mercy to the Lamb of God
    that takes away sin, and for peace,
'*Agnus Dei*' their one beginning,
    all in the same note and manner   20
    as if together in total harmony.
'Are these souls, master, I hear?'
    I ask – 'That's right,' he replies,
    'ones untying the knot of anger.'
'Who are you, cleaving our fog,   25
    speaking of us as if the calendar
    still governs your sense of time?'
So one of these voices spoke out;
    my master says, 'Reply to him,
    and ask if we climb hereabouts.'   30
And I: 'O soul polishing yourself
    to return lovely to your maker,
    follow me, to listen to marvels.'
'I'll follow as far as I'm able to,'
    he says, 'and if eyes can't see   35
    our ears can couple us instead.'

So I begin: 'Inside the wrapping
    that death dissolves I climb up,
    coming here via hell's torment.
And if God gives me such grace   40
    that he receives me into his court
    in a way unknown to these days,
then don't conceal who you were
    in life, and if the pass is at hand;
    so your words will be our guide.'   45
'I was a Lombard, called Marco:
    a man of sagacity and the virtue
    that no-one aims at any longer.
This is the right way to go aloft.'
    So his reply, adding, 'I pray you   50
    to pray for me when you're up.'
I reply to him: 'I swear I'll do
    what you ask, but I'm bursting
    with a doubt I have to clear up,
one reinforced by what you say,   55
    confirming me of its relevance
    to something I heard elsewhere.
The world absolutely is a desert
    of all virtues, as you indicate,
    and a garden rampant with evil;   60
but I pray you to tell me why,
    so I know and can inform others:
    is it us or heaven to be blamed?'
His deep sigh changes to a moan
    to begin with; 'Brother,' he says,   65
    'the world is blind, you're of it,
one of the living who suggest all
    is caused by heaven's motions
    alone, determined by necessity.
If this was so, free will in you   70
    would be null, and any justice
    in heaven or hell's joy or pain.
The heavens start your impulses –
    not all of them – but even if all
    you have a light to discern evil   75

from good, as well as free will;
    if this tires in battling the stars
    at first, it wins if guided well.
Free subjects of greater powers
    you are, and of a higher kind,   80
    creating mind in you, beyond
the stars' reach. So if earth errs,
    the reasons must lie with you,
    and now I'll tell it you straight.
From his hands who adores it   85
    even before it is, like a child
    at play, laughing, crying, exits
the simple little soul, who knows
    nothing, only that made in joy
    it turns willingly to the joyful.   90
It finds it in lesser goods first;
    here it strays in chasing these,
    its love without guide or reins.
For such reins laws are needed,
    plus a king who can make out   95
    the true city's tower at least.
Law exists, but who directs it?
    No-one, because the head priest
    may chew the cud, but his hoof
isn't cloven: his flock watch him   100
    lusting only for the same goods
    as they do, their only ambition.
So you see that rubbish guidance
    is the cause of the world's evil,
    not nature's corruption in you.   105
Rome, that made the earth good,
    once had two suns, illuminating
    two paths, the world's and God's;
one's eclipsed the other, crozier
    and sword are melted together,   110
    so naturally they proceed badly
because there's no mutual fear:
    if you doubt me, see the crop,
    plants are known by their fruit.

Adige and Po once watered lands   115
   known for courtesy and valour
   before the struggles of Frederick:
now anyone feeling too ashamed
   by the company or conversation
   of good men, can go safely there.   120
True, there are still three seniors
   making the old shame the new,
   restless for a better life in God:
good Gherardo, Currado da Palazzo
   and Guido da Castel, better named,   125
   as in France, the honest Lombard.
So you see how the Roman church
   in its duplicity falls in the mud,
   and fouls itself and its functions.'
'O my Marco,' I say, 'this is good;   130
   now I see why the sons of Levi
   were excluded from inheritance.
But what Gherardo is it, you say,
   a reminder of the lost generation
   and reproof to this wicked age?'   135
'Either you're teasing me,' he says,
   'or I don't follow, if as a Tuscan
   you're unaware of good Gherardo.
I identify him by no other name,
   plus the fact of his daughter Gaia.   140
   God be with you, here I stop.
There's the dawn, getting brighter
   through the smoke; I have to go
   before the angel there sees me.'
He turned, hearing me no more.   145

NOTES TO CANTO 16
Steve Ellis

16-21. Those punished on this terrace for the sin of anger pray for the
opposite qualities of mercy and peace, praying to Christ, the 'Lamb of

God' (John 1: 29, 36), as embodying the qualities opposed to anger (ll. 17-18). They sing the liturgical prayer of the *Agnus Dei* (l. 19) – O Lamb of God … have mercy upon us …' – in harmony (l. 21), in opposition to the divisive effects of anger on earth.

46. According to contemporary chroniclers, Marco Lombardo, belonging to a generation previous to Dante, was a man of court and experienced in politics, with a reputation for justice and generosity and fearless in reproving leaders who did not live up to his ideals.

70-2. Marco rejects the idea of astral determinism, because this would deny the freedom of the will and make a nonsense of divine justice.

85. Having established that humans are responsible for their own moral choices, Marco now goes into the second part of his discourse, explaining why the world has gone to the bad. The soul, created directly by God 'in joy' (l. 89), is instinctively drawn to what promises it joy, and 'like a child' (86) finds this in material and imperfect things unless wisely guided by the 'reins' of law (91-4).

98. The pope does not possess both characteristics of the beasts designated as clean in Leviticus 11: 1-8: chewing the cud and having the hoof cloven. Allegorically, the former represents spiritual meditation which the head priest practises, and the latter the discrimination between good and evil, which has been lost in the 'lusting' after temporal and political power (101).

106. Imperial Rome is a model of the secular state for Dante, so much so that God chose this moment to have his son redeem the sins of mankind under its legitimate justice (*Mon.* 2. 10. 4 - 2. 11. 7). Thus the emperor and pope are Rome's 'two suns' (l. 107), working in mutual cooperation and respect to illuminate the proper paths of civic and religious life respectively (108).

115. The third part of Marco's speech castigates Lombardy particularly – location of the two rivers mentioned – as exemplifying the dire state of things, dating from the Emperor Frederick II's political struggles with the Church (l. 117).

124. The three exceptions to the decadence of Lombardy are Gherardo da Camino, lord of Treviso from 1283 till his death in 1306, and, although an adversary of the imperial cause, also saluted by Dante in *Conv.* 4. 14. 12-13; Currado da Palazzo, a Guelph who among other offices was governor of Piacenza in 1288; and Guido da Castel (l. 125), born 1235, still alive in 1315, renowned for his hospitality to the French forces in Reggio Emilia (l. 126) and also saluted in *Conv.* (4. 16. 6).

131. The 'sons of Levi' are excluded because of their sacerdotal function from the inheritance of earthly goods (Numbers 18: 20-4).

CANTO 17
Steve Ellis

Reader, think if in the mountains
    you were ever cut off by cloud,
    blind as a mole with furred eyes,
and then, the damp, thick vapour
    starting to thin, you see the sun   5
    through it, showing a faint orb;
so you'll easily be able to picture
    how I saw the sun again, at first,
    which was now close to setting.
So, steps matching the trusty step   10
    of my master, I exited the smog
    to light already gone from below.
O imagination, that steals from us,
    at times, outward things, so a man
    might be unaware of a brass band,   15
what fuels you, if our senses don't?
    It must be a light, born in heaven
    directly, or willed down to earth.
The evil of her who was changed
    to that bird that loves above all   20
    to sing, this came to my mind;
and this absorbed my imagination
    so much, that from the outside
    there was nothing able to enter.
Then my high fantasy was fired   25
    by someone crucified, scornful
    and cruel-looking, dying such
with great Ahasuerus around him,
    his wife Esther and that just man,
    Mordecai, true in word and deed.   30
When this imagining all by itself
    popped, like a bubble in water
    rises to where the water ceases,
there rose into my visions a girl
    shrieking and speaking: 'O queen,   35
    why wish extinction in your fury,

killing yourself not to lose Lavinia?
  Lost me you have! For your loss
  I grieve, mother, above anyone's.'
Just like sleep goes if, all at once,   40
  a new light hits your closed eyes,
  though it wavers before going fully;
so my imaginations ebbed away
  as soon as a light struck my face
  far brighter than any usual light.   45
I gazed round to see where I was
  when a voice spoke 'Climb here,'
  which occupied all my attention;
and it made my desire so strong
  to see who it was who spoke it,   50
  it couldn't rest, without seeing.
But like the sun dazzles our sight
  and veils himself in his brightness,
  so my powers couldn't manage it.
'This is a divine spirit, telling us,   55
  before being asked, where we go,
  and hiding in his own luminosity.
He treats his neighbour as himself:
  to wait for a needy man's request
  is already to maliciously deny it.   60
So, let's suit our feet to his offer
  and hurry to climb before dark,
  because then it's vetoed till day.'
So said my leader; the two of us
  turn our feet towards the stairs,   65
  and just as I reach the first step
I feel near as if a brush of wings,
  air on my face, a voice: '*Blessed*
  are the peacemakers, rejecting
evil anger!' Above, the last rays   70
  were already followed by night,
  and stars appearing on all sides.
'O my powers, why do you fail?'
  I asked myself, already feeling
  the strength in my legs on hold.   75

We'd got to where the staircase
    doesn't go up any further, stuck,
    just like a ship beached on shore.
I waited a while, to see if I heard
    any sound from the new terrace;   80
    then I turn to my master, to ask
'What crime is it, sweet father,
    that's purged here, in this circle?
    Feet may stop, but not your talk.'
And he: 'Not loving good fully –   85
    so here the shortfall is topped up;
    here the lazy rower works his oar.
But so you understand me clearly,
    attend to me now, and our delay
    will result in good fruit for you.'   90
He began: 'Son, neither creature
    nor creator was ever minus love,
    as you know, natural or chosen.
The natural is always guiltless,
    but the other can err in its target   95
    or if it's too powerful or feeble.
While it's fixed on the key good
    and measured in secondary goods
    then its pleasures can't be corrupt;
but turning to the bad, or to good   100
    with too much or too little desire,
    means man at work against maker.
So you can see how it has to be
    that love is the seed of all virtue
    in you, but also of all your vices.   105
Now, since from his own interest
    someone's love can never deviate,
    all beings are safe from self-hate;
and because no being can be seen
    separate from Being, self-standing,   110
    that also is excluded from hatred.
What's left, if I'm being logical,
    is wanting evils for other people,
    a trio of love in the mire of men.

There's him who to beat everyone   115
    wants to excel, agonising for this,
    hoping others fall off the ladder;
there's him scared of losing fame,
    power, honour, luck, if it means
    others get them, so he's in love   120
with the opposite result; and him
    who, hurt, is so bent on revenge
    he's always ready to hurt others.
This triple love is lamented below
    our feet; now I want you to know   125
    the other, aimed at good wrongly.
All men confusedly sense a good
    to quiet the soul, and long for it,
    everyone striving to arrive there.
If feeble love deflects the vision   130
    or stops it being won, this circle,
    after due repentance, hurts you.
No other goods can give felicity,
    true felicity that is, the essence
    of the harvest, its root and crop.   135
But love that puts trust in these
    is wept for in the terraces above,
    but I don't say how this divides
in three, to spur your own search.'

NOTES TO CANTO 17
Steve Ellis

19. The first of Dante's visions of anger is Procne, who revenged herself on her husband Tereus, after his rape of her sister Philomela, by killing their son Itys and serving the body to Tereus in a meal. See further the note to *Purg.* 9. 15, above.

26-30. The person 'crucified' is Haman, minister of the Persian king Ahasuerus and 'full of wrath' (Esther 3: 5) against Mordecai, who refused to reverence him. His wish for revenge was foiled by Esther, Ahasuerus's wife (see Esther 3-7).

34. The 'girl' is Lavinia, lamenting her mother Amata's killing herself in the belief that her daughter had already been given as a spoil of war to Aeneas, after his defeating in battle her fiancé Turnus (*Aen.* 12. 595-607).

58. 'He treats his neighbour as himself': see Christ's commandment in Matthew 22: 39 and Mark 12: 31.

63. The 'veto' is explained above in *Purg.* 7. 44-60.

68-70. The seventh Beatitude (Matthew 5: 9) and the third to be pronounced in *Purg.*. 'Evil anger' (l. 70) is distinguished from just anger or zeal.

91-105. Virgil first enunciates that all sins are occasioned by a love in the individual to which the will assents, which is either misdirected, feeble or excessive (ll. 95-6), in the latter case towards the 'secondary goods' (l. 98) that must be loved in proportion.

106-11. Virgil now explains that the love which 'err[s] in its target' (above, l. 95) is the love of harm to others (l. 113), since creatures cannot logically love self-hatred (ll. 106-8) or hatred towards the divine creator from whom being derives (ll. 109-11).

112-23. The love of 'evils for other people' (l. 113) is now identified with the three sins expiated on the terraces below: pride (115-17), envy (118-21) and anger (121-3).

125-39. The other type of love, 'aimed at good wrongly' derives from the innate longing to return to the source of good (ll. 127-9), as explained in the previous canto (*Purg.* 16. 85-93). 'Feeble' love for this source (i.e., sloth) is expiated in the present circle (130-2), whilst in the remaining three terraces above this one excessive love of secondary goods is expiated (133-9).

CANTO 18
Jonathan Galassi

The great teacher had ended his discourse
and he stared deep into my eyes
to see if I looked satisfied;

and I, already spurred by a new thirst,
was quiet outwardly but said inside: 5
'Maybe my asking too much troubles him.'

But that true father, who perceived
the timid wish that I had not expressed,
since he spoke, encouraged me to speak.

So I said: 'Master, my insight is so   10
enlivened by your light that I see clearly
all your teaching posits or describes.

Therefore I ask you, dear kind father,
to explicate love, which you call the source
of all good action and its opposite.'   15

'Turn the sharp eyes of your intellect
on me,' he said, 'and you will understand
the error of the blind who act like guides.

The mind, which is conceived to love at once,
responds to everything that pleases it   20
the minute pleasure rouses it to act.

Your perception takes an image from
a real thing and in you elaborates it,
so that the mind turns to it;

and, once turned, if it inclines toward it,   25
that inclination is natural love,
which binds itself to you anew through pleasure.

Then, in the same way that fire moves higher
according to its essence, which is born to rise
where its substance will survive the longest,   30

so the mind, enthralled, enters into desire,
a movement of the spirit, and won't rest
until the thing it loves affords it joy.

Now you can see how much the truth
is hidden from those persons who assert   35
that every love is worthy in itself;

for though its matter may seem always good,
not every seal is good
although the wax is.'

'Your words, and my meditating on them,'   40
I answered him, 'have revealed love to me,
but this has made me more beset by doubt;

for if love is given to us from elsewhere
and the soul takes no other step alone,
if it goes right or wrong is not its doing.'   45

And he to me: 'I can tell you everything
that reason understands here; to go further
wait for Beatrice: it involves faith.

Every substantial form, which is distinct
from matter yet conjoined with it,   50
has a specific power in itself,

which goes unperceived except in action,
and doesn't show itself but by effect,
as life does in the green leaves of a plant.

Which means that man is ignorant of where   55
our understanding of first things comes from,
or our attraction to our first desires,

which are within you like the bee's instinct
for making honey; and this primal wish
has no relevance to praise or blame.   60

So that all other wills conform with this one,
the faculty of reason is inborn in you,
to stand watch at the threshold of assent.

This is the principle by which
you determine what is virtuous,   65
sorting and sifting good and guilty loves.

Those who thought about it most profoundly
understood this innate liberty;
and they bequeathed ethics to the world.

Let us posit then that every love   70
which burns in you comes of necessity;
yet to restrain it is within your power.

Beatrice understands this noble virtue
as free will; take care you remember it,
if she should ever speak of it to you.'   75

Though it was nearing midnight, the late moon
was still glowing like a fiery bucket,
making the stars seem more diffuse to us;

it moved against the sky along the ways
the sun enflames when one in Rome observes it   80
setting between Sardinians and Corsicans.

And that gentle shade because of whom
Pietola is the best-known Mantuan town,
had freed me of the burden I'd imposed;

though I, who had been offered plain and open   85
reasoning about my questioning
remained like one who wanders in his sleep.

But my drowsiness was interrupted
all of a sudden by a group approaching
who'd come around behind our backs to meet us.   90

And much as the Ismeus and Asopus
saw a raging throng along their banks
on those nights when the Thebans turned to Bacchus,

so those in the coming crowd whom I saw
driven by good will and righteous love   95
cut across that circle like a scythe.

Soon they were on us,
for the whole huge multitude was running,
two of them shouting in the vanguard, weeping:

'Mary hurried to the mountains;   100
and Caesar, out to conquer Lerida,
attacked Marseille and then ran off to Spain.'

'Hurry, hurry, let us not lose time
for lack of love,' the others with them cried,
'for wanting to do good turns mercy green again.'   105

'O people, whose sharp fervour now may make amends
for the negligence and tardiness
of your past lethargy in doing good,

this man, who is alive – and I don't lie –
wants to go up when the sun returns;   110
so tell us where the nearest opening is.'

These were my guide's words;
and one of the spirits answered:
'Come after us, and you will find the gap.

We are so full of the desire to go   115
that we can't stay; and so please forgive us
if our penance strikes you as ill-mannered.

I was the abbot of San Zeno in Verona
under the rule of the good Barbarossa,
whom Milan still talks about with sorrow.   120

And someone there has one foot in the grave
who will soon regret that monastery,
and lament that he held power there;

for he installed his son, unsound of body,
worse in mind, and ill-born to boot,   125
instead of its true pastor.'

I don't know if he said more or was still,
he had moved on so far from us; but this
is what I heard and still wish to remember.

And he who answered to my every need   130
said: 'Now turn around: and you will see
two who come nipping at sloth.'

They were following the others, crying:
'The people whom the Red Sea parted for
died before the Jordan saw their offspring.   135

And those who didn't make the ultimate
sacrifice beside Anchises' son
went on to live a life that lacked for glory.'

Then, once those shades were gone so far from us
that they no longer could be seen,   140
a new idea was planted in me,

out of which many other ones were born;
and I flitted so from one thought to the other
that my eyes closed in my wandering   145
and I made my thoughts into a dream.

NOTES TO CANTO 18
Nick Havely

18. Behind Virgil's warning about 'the blind who act like guides' is the now proverbial description of the Pharisees (as 'the blind leading the blind') in Matthew 15: 14. In Dante's case the inadequate guides would perhaps include earlier poets who had addressed the nature of love without full understanding, such as Guittone d'Arezzo and Guido Guinizelli (both mentioned later, in *Purg.* 24 and 26; see also the latter's poem about love in the Postscript, no. 8).

Virgil's own extended discourse about love in this canto (ll. 19-75) focuses on distinctions between its nature as 'primal wish' or early instinct (59-60) and as governed by 'free will' (61-3), and he acknowledges that his own guidance will be subject to confirmation by Dante's later guide, Beatrice (146-8 and 73-5).

28-30. Fire is the lightest of the four 'elements' of which matter was believed to be composed. Each of the four was thought to be naturally drawn towards its 'sphere', and in the geocentric universe, fire would rise to the highest of these, next to the sphere of the Moon, as Dante also notes in *Conv.* 3.3.2.

49. 'Substantial' denotes what is essential or 'core' to a thing or being's nature, as opposed to what is 'accidental', such as colour or shape.

59-60. One of Dante's 14th-century commentators, Francesco da Buti notes that such instincts do not attract praise or blame because 'the Philosopher [Aristotle] says that they are not within our power'.

67-9. Those who 'bequeathed ethics to the world' would in Dante's book have included Aristotle in his *Ethics* which was commented on by, among others, Thomas Aquinas.

73-5. Free will does indeed continue to be an issue addressed by Beatrice in Dante's *Paradiso* (e.g., *Par.* 5. 19-24). On debates about the subject in medieval philosophy and elsewhere in Dante (e.g., *Mon.* 1. 12. 2-5), see *DE* 425-7.

79-81. The Moon is thus said to be moving against the apparent west-east motion of the sky and is now in the constellation of Sagittarius (the sign seen at sunset from Rome in November). Once again – as in *Purg.* 2. 1-6 – the passing of time is marked in wider cosmic terms.

83. Pietola, near Mantua, was the birthplace of Virgil.

91-3. The frenzied actions of the cult of Dionysus / Bacchus beside these rivers in Boeotia is described by Statius in *Theb.* 9. 434-6. The allusion creates a striking convergence between the Christian and the pagan: the approaching souls of those expiating the sin of sloth are momentarily metamorphosed into maenads.

100-2. The Virgin Mary's haste to visit Elizabeth in the mountains of Hebron is referred to in Luke 1: 39; and Julius Caesar's swift and energetic campaigns in southern Gaul and the Iberian peninsula are described by Lucan in *DBC* 3. 453-5 and 4. 11ff. Voicing these two examples of promptitude in such a brisk and brief form seems an appropriate task for the souls expiating sloth.

118-26. Dante's son Pietro noted in his early commentary on the poem that laziness is a monastic vice. Dante may have heard about the Abbot of San Zeno during his first stay in Verona (see *BGLD* 28-30). The passage also reflects Dante's concern with government and the separation of secular and ecclesiastical power. Hence the reference in l. 119 to the 'good Barbarossa' (Emperor Frederick I) and the concern about the mistaken action of one who 'held power' in Verona: the ruler who made his illegitimate and unworthy son abbot of the monastery (ll. 121-6). The oblique reference is to Alberto della Scala, who was also father of Dante's later patron, Cangrande della Scala (see *DE* 136-7).

134-8. Two further examples are delivered by these souls as the 'bridle' or warning against sloth: the Israelites who gave up on the journey to the Promised Land (Numbers 14: 1-37); and the Trojan followers of Aeneas who failed to reach Latium and remained behind in Sicily (*Aen.* 5. 711-71).

CANTO 19
Colin Donati

That hour when earth, with Saturn's aid,
defeats what latent heat remains
to check the bitter lunar chill,

and geomancers before dawn
mark in the east their Great Spae rise   5
by soon to be extinguished paths,

a stammering woman in my dream
came cross-eyed, on camshauchled feet,
with hands but stumps, and ashen face.

I watched her, and, as sun revives   10
the leaden limbs a cold night locks,
so did my looking serve to loose

her tongue, duly set straight her frame
entire, and to that wasted face,
as love desires it, granted colour.   15

Thus mended, she began to sing
such that my will was sorely tried
to turn from her: 'It's I,' she sang –

'It's I, a sweet siren, whose song
lures mariners mid-sea astray,   20
so deep it pierces them. I drew

Ulysses from his doubtful course.
Completely gratified, the one
at ease with me seldom wins free...'

The mouth was barely closed before   25
a saintly woman, keen to quash
this other, stood now at my side.

'Virgil, O Virgil, who is this?'
She spoke with force; he, stepping up,
with eyes fixed on that honest one,   30

then seized the other, tore in two
her mantle and exposed the kyte:
the reek which issued wakened me –

My eyes lit on the gentle master:
'I called you thrice,' he said. 'Look sharp!   35
Let's find your traverse up.' I rose.

Broad light of day by now struck all
the sacred mountain's terraced heights.
And on we walked, sun in our nears…

Trailing behind, with head as one   40
so bowed by care his figure makes
the part arch of a bridge half built,

I heard: *this way; your pass is here* –
a sound so kind and softly voiced,
like none known in our mortal realms.   45

The one who spoke then pointed up
with swan-like wings to where between
two walls of hard rock rose our road.

A waft from those extended wings
affirmed *Qui lugent* – blesséd those   50
who weep; their souls have solacing.

'Why do you glower so at the ground?'
my guide began once we had cleared
some height not far above the angel;

and my reply: 'I go in qualms   55
at that last vision which so grips
my thoughts it can't be shaken off.'

'You've seen,' he said, 'the age-old carline;
up there there's none else left to weep for;
you've seen how one wins free from her.   60

Enough! Press on! The lure you need
to fix on now is spun with the
eternal King's great wheels above.'

Just as the falcon, head down at first,
turns at the cry, then stretches itself out,   65
craving the meat that brought it there:

so I; and so, for the whole course
the cleft lifted our road around the rockface,
I mounted up to the next ledge.

Out on the fifth circle, I saw   70
at large there, everywhere, people in tears,
all sprawled out, face-down on the earth.

'My soul is stuck fast to this floor'
I heard them chant with such great sighs
the words could barely be made out.   75

'All you whom God chose to endure
what's easier borne with justice and hope:
direct us on to our higher path.'

'If you come safe from being held flat
and have no eye but for your road,   80
your short way round is right side out.'

The poet thus asked; and the reply
came near at hand, by which I marked
that hidden other from the speech,

and caught the eye of my good lord   85
who offered back his glad assent
to what my look had asked of him.

Free then to act by my own lights,
I stepped in through to stand above
this creature sensed through words alone   90

and said: 'Spirit, whose tears mature
that without which none could face God,
pause for a moment your great care.

Tell me, who were you, why you're all
face-down, and if there's aught I might   95
beseech for you from where I come, still living?'

And he to me: 'You'll hear soon why our backs
spurn heaven here; but first *know me for one*
who has succeeded in the line of Peter.   99

Between Sestri and Chiavari
the bonny river rolls which gives
the highest title of my clan.

For just six weeks I tried the weight
of those great robes we hain from glaur:
all other weight seems as light as down.   105

I was, alas, converted late;
but I, as pastor-elect of Rome,
saw all too soon life's tricks and frauds;

saw nothing there could soothe the heart;
saw nowhere higher to advance: 110
thus, love for this new life was born.

Till then, through avarice, I'd been
a wretched soul, estranged from God:
see now my punishment for that;

see in this penance of souls turned   115
arse up what avarice has done.
The mountain bears no harsher pain.

For since our eyes had never once
sought higher things, so justice here
seals them down fast onto this earth.   120

And as our clutching snuffed out love
for all that's good – freedom the price –
so justice clamps us to this floor

pinned hand and foot; and, for so long
as our just Lord is pleased to keep us,   125
so long we'll be bound prostrate here.'

As I, now kneeling, made to speak,
he, from the tone alone, could sense
my reverence. 'And what,' he said,

'bends *you* to earth?' 'The guilt that I   130
beside your dignity,' I said,
'stayed on my feet.' 'Brother, unbend

those legs and lift yourself back up!
Make no mistake: I serve, like you,
and all these souls, one single Power.   135

If from the Gospel you have heard
that holy sound – *We marry none*,
you'll see at once my line of thought.

Away with you: I'll not allow
another word to check these tears   140
which shall mature as you described.

My niece, Alagia – a good soul,
so long as she stands firm against
the baleful influence of our house –   144

she's all that's left for me back there.'

NOTES TO CANTO 19
Nick Havely

1-3. Saturn, the most distant planet in the medieval cosmos, was associated with both the 'cold, dry' humour of melancholy and with misfortune; its presence thus adds a touch of foreboding to the pilgrim's ensuing dream.

4-6. Geomancers were diviners who based their predictions upon patterns (originally of scattered earth or sand). The pattern of stars they referred to as *Fortuna major* (here in Scots, 'Great Spae') comprises parts of the constellations of Aquarius and Pisces. Its appearance in the east, on a path 'soon to be extinguished' by the light of dawn, indicates (again by marking time in cosmic terms) that it is around 4 am, a time of day – morning – when dreams were believed to convey truth.

7-33. This is the second of the three dreams marking transitions in the Dante-persona's journey through Purgatory; the others are at the start of canto 9 and the end of canto 27. Here, his vision of the deformed 'stammering woman' on 'camshauchled [Scots for 'lame, shambling'] feet' who turns into a 'sweet siren' under his gaze may represent the 'illusive images of good' which he later confesses to following (*Purg.* 30. 131 and 31. 34-5) and which Beatrice will describe as 'sirens' (*Purg.* 31. 45). The siren's resemblance here to Circe who turned Ulysses's followers into beasts (ll. 23-4) suggests that she may be associated with the sins expiated on the next three terraces: avarice, gluttony and lust. The 'saintly woman' (26) who urges Virgil to unmask the siren by exposing her belly (Scots 'kyte' here in l. 32) is unidentified but may have affinities with St Lucy – who has already acted as guide in canto 9 – and with divine grace to overcome temptation.

41. *nears* (Scots for 'kidneys') stands for the back, as *reni* does in Dante's Italian.

50. 'Blessèd those who weep' (Matthew 5: 5) is the fourth of the seven Beatitudes from Christ's Sermon on the Mount to be quoted in *Purg.*. Its connection to the expiation of sloth (the sin of the terrace now being left) is not very clear, but it may reflect the passion for repentance that the souls here have shown (e.g., in *Purg.* 18. 103-8).

58. *carline/ carling* in Scots can mean 'witch'; Dante's original describes the siren similarly as *strega*.

61-6. The simile of the falcon trained to come to its lure paradoxically portrays the pilgrim as a ravenous bird whose greed is exploited by God ('the eternal King', l. 63) who acts through the spheres of Paradise (the 'great wheels'). The image of flight as mental or spiritual progress is recurrent in the *Commedia* and is particularly striking in the later stages of the *Purgatorio,* as the pilgrim's upward progress accelerates (e.g., *Purg.* 24. 64-6; 25. 10-15; 26. 43-5; 27. 121-3; 31. 55-63).

73. 'My soul is stuck fast to this floor' is part of verse 25 from Psalm 119 (118 in the Vulgate) and is the motto of the souls expiating avarice on this terrace.

79-82. The 'reply' from the souls to Virgil's request for direction shows that they, with their 'faces down to the earth' (l. 72), think that he and Dante must be exempted from the sin of avarice.

97-105. The soul who has begun to speak in l. 79 now identifies himself as one of the very few redeemed popes to appear in the *Commedia*: the words in italics describing him as *one / who has succeeded in the line of Peter* (ll. 98-9) are in the original in the Church's formal language, Latin. Hadrian V reigned for little more than a month (July 11 to August 18 1276); he was of the noble Fieschi family who held lands in Liguria (l. 100). There does not seem to be specific evidence for his avarice, but he probably here represents more broadly the temporal wealth of the Church with which Dante is concerned throughout the *Commedia* and in Book 3 of *Mon.*, as does the metaphor of the [papal] 'robes we hain from glaur' – Scots for 'shield from the mud' – in l. 104.

127-45 By addressing the pilgrim as 'brother' (l. 132) and as fellow-servant of God (134), and by quoting Christ's words in Matthew 27: 29-33 about the irrelevance of earthly status in Heaven (where 'We marry none'), Hadrian forcefully rejects the trappings of papal office, focusing solely (like Manfred and Nino Visconti in *Purg.* 3. 46 and 8.71) upon the value of prayers from a member of his family: Alagia dei Fieschi (142-5), whom – as she was the wife of a patron – Dante knew personally.

CANTO 20
Colin Donati

Against a better will will strives in vain;
and so against my pleasure, to please him,
I drew the sponge out from the water dry

and made my way. Out on the rocky ledge
my guide was moving in the unclaimed space   5
like one constrained to tread high parapets

since this people, who smelt down through their eyes,
drop by slow drop, that world-consuming vice,
were crowding too close to the outer edge.

You ancient wolfine, damnably accursed,   10
of all beasts the most ravenous for prey
to slake the deathless chasm of your want!

O sky, whose great rotations we believe
can change the state of things down here,
when does he come who drives her out?   15

We picked a slow and cautious way forward,
I watching all the time those shades I heard
so pitiably weeping and lamenting,

and quite by chance I caught 'O sweet Maria!'
called out from up ahead so like the cry   20
made by the woman who is giving birth;

and it continued: 'Just how poor you were
is seen from the low refuge where you stooped
to lay your sacred burden down.'

Then could be heard: 'O good Fabrizio,   25
who elected to keep honest poverty,
not live iniquitously in great wealth.'

I felt so overjoyed to hear these words
that I stepped in about to find and meet
the spirit I could sense was speaking them.   30

It now was telling of the open gifts
made to the maiden girls by Nicholas
to guide the honour of their youth.

'O soul that speaks so highly of the good,
tell me, who were you, and why you alone   35
repeat all these deserving praises: your words

will not,' I said, 'deny you mercy if,
along the road I'm travelling, I return
to live this fleeting life out to its end.'

And he: 'I answer not for any salve   40
from there which I might hope to win, but for
that light you emanate while you yet live.

I was the taproot of that evil tree
which overshadows all our Christian earth
so that the fruit it yields is seldom good.   45

But if Douai and Lille and Ghent and Bruges
had power, their vengeance would be swift:
I pray the judge of all might grant it!

My name back there was Hugh Capet:
those Lewises and Philips which have since   50
ruled over France all trace their line from me,

and I, a Paris butcher's son; for when
those in the ancient line of kings were all
no more (save one who donned the coarse black cloth)

I found my fingers held those reins that guide   55
the governance of kingdoms, and with such power
so newly won, and all its many friends,

saw soon enough how to that widowed crown
was lifted my son's head. With *his* began
the sacred bones of all the rest of them.   60

Though with the great endowment of Provence
the rudeness of my blood was not toned down,
so small its worth, it yet did little harm.

There with force and fraud began the plunder
and the rape; and then, to make amends, Pointhieu   65
and Normandy were seized; then Gascony.

Charles then in Italy, to make amends,
saw Conradin despatched for sacrifice, then
sent Thomas heavenward – to make amends.

I see a time – one coming very soon –   70
that brings another Charles from out of France
to win a greater name for him and his.

He comes unarmed, with nothing but the lance
which Judas carried to the ploy – but *his* point
is aimed to burst the underside of Florence.   75

From this, in consequence, he wins not ground,
but sin and shame; and all the worse for him
the more he tries to make light of those ills.

Another – the one once captured out at sea –
I see sell his own daughter and strike the bargain   80
just as the corsair does for his other slaves.

O avarice, what greater can you do
now that you draw this blood of mine so far
it has no thought for one of its own flesh?

To outshine all those past and future crimes   85
the *fleur-de-lys* then comes into Anagni:
Christ in His earthly vicar I see seized;

I see a second time when He is mocked;
I see afresh the vinegar and wormwood;
amid our living thieves He dies again.   90

I see the new Pilate, one now so vicious
such things are not enough, but, without leave,
he turns his sails of greed upon the Temple.

O my great Lord, when will I have the joy
to see the vengeance which mysteriously   95
makes sweet your anger in your secret depths?

That which I said about the sole bride of
the Holy Spirit which prompted you to turn
and hear from me an exposition – this much

is taken up in all our prayers   100
so long as day lasts; but, at length, when night falls –
that's when we raise a very different clamour.

We then recite the case against Pygmalion,
that thief, that traitor and that parricide,
all through his gluttony for gold;   105

also the bitter grief of greedy Midas
which came of his demand for ceaseless goods –
something for which he earns unending laughter.

We each of us remember foolish Achan,
how he ransacked the spoils, so that the wrath   110
of Joshua again seems here to gnaw him.

Sapphira with her husband we denounce;
we laud the hoof-kicks Heliodorus earned himself;
and, for his crimes, reel off around the mountain,

the Polymnestor who felled Polidorus.   115
To top it all, we cry: "Crassus, pray tell –
for you well know – the *flavour* that the gold had."

There's one whiles speaks aloud, another soft,
according to what moves us at the time,
goaded to greater or to less degree,   120

but just now, in that praise by day of good,
it was not I myself alone: rather,
no others nearby spoke in a raised voice.'

We had already left him, pressing on,
striving the best we could to make headway   125
along such of the path as would allow,

when like a thing that drops, I felt the mountain
tremble and quake – which gripped me with a chill
such as might take one on the verge of death.

Delos, for sure, was not shaking so hard   130
ahead of when Latona built the nest
in which she hatched the two eyes of the heavens.

A great roar now rose up on every side
so that the master drew me close to him
saying: 'No fear while I am guiding you.'   135

'*Gloria* everywhere *in excelsis*
Deo,' so far as I could tell from those
close by, whose words thus could be heard, rang out.

We stood there motionless and in suspense,
just like the shepherds who first heard that song,   140
until the quaking and the singing both

were done; then we resumed our sacred way,
watching those shades pressed to the earth return
already to their more accustomed weeping.

No ignorance had ever had me so   145
at war in my desire to understand,
if memory here is not deceiving me,

as just then, in my mind, I seemed to be,
neither, for haste, daring to ask the cause,
nor able there, myself, to grasp the thing: 150

so I walked on, head bowed and wondering.

NOTES TO CANTO 20
Nick Havely

10-15. Traditionally an emblem of avarice, the hungry wolf who blocks the traveller's way in the first canto of the *Inferno* (*Inf.* 1. 49-54 and 94-9) also shows aspects of this sin. The pervasiveness of greed is a key concern in Dante's work and here, as in *Inf.* 1 (101-11), the poem looks to some form of divine intervention as a remedy.

19-27. Examples of 'honest poverty' are those of the Virgin Mary, giving birth in a stable, and the life of Gaius Fabricius Luscinus (Roman consul in 282 and 280 BCE), whose austerity is praised by Dante in *Conv.* 4.5.3 and *Mon.* 2.5.11.

32-4. St Nicholas of Bari is the third positive example here, opposing avarice with generosity (*larghezza*). He was said to have provided dowries for three girls to save them from being sold into prostitution.

44-96. In the central passage of the canto, Hugh, the first king of the French Capetian dynasty, takes responsibility for his family of 'Lewises and Philips which have since / ruled over France' (ll. 50-1). He portrays their record in the thirteenth and early fourteenth centuries as one of progressively more avaricious 'plunder' (65 and 82-4): the acquisition of further French provinces (65-6); the Angevin expansion into Italy in 1265-6 and the alleged murder of Thomas Aquinas in 1274 (67-9); Charles of Valois's takeover of Florence for the Papacy in 1301, leading to Dante's exile (70-8); the humiliation of Charles II of Anjou in a sea-battle and his 'selling' of his daughter to gain influence in northern Italy (79-81); and finally, 'to outshine all those past and future crimes', the kidnapping of the pope by agents of the French King Philip IV in 1307, leading to the former's death (85-93). The divine vengeance that Hugh Capet expects (94-6) at the fictional date of Dante's journey (1300) would take place, during the time of the *Purgatorio*'s composition (1314), when Philip died as the result of a hunting accident.

97-9. 'The sole bride of / the Holy Spirit' refers back to the Virgin Mary (ll. 19-24), as in Matthew 1: 20 and Luke 1: 38.

103-17. Cautionary 'bridles' or examples of avarice here are: Pygmalion, King of Tyre, who killed his uncle for his wealth (*Aen.* 1. 346-52); Midas (Ovid, *Met.* 11. 100-45); Achan, who stole booty from the sack of Jericho (Joshua 7: 1-26); Sapphira, wife of Ananias who attempted to bribe the Apostles (Acts 5: 1-11); Heliodorus, the Syrian punished for seeking to appropriate the treasures of the Temple at Jerusalem (2 Maccabees 3: 7-40); Polymnestor, who robbed and murdered his young brother-in-law Polydorus (*Aen.* 3. 49-57); and the rapacious Roman consul Crassus, defeated and killed in 53 BCE by the Parthians, who then mockingly poured molten gold into his mouth (Cicero, *De Officiis* 1. 30).

130-2. Delos was said to be a floating island on which Latona / Leto gave birth to Apollo and Diana, gods associated with the 'two eyes of the heavens' (the sun and moon).

135-4. 'Glory to God in the highest' is, in Luke 2: 9, the angels' song of rejoicing, announcing the birth of Christ to the shepherds – here marking a human rebirth.

CANTO 21
Michael O'Neill

The thirst our natures feel which nothing slakes
    except the water which the poor woman
    of Samaria asked for, that is, grace,

tormented me, and haste urged me on down
    the jostling path behind my leader,   5
    and the just punishments made me feel pain.

And, look – even as Luke is our recorder
    that Christ met two travellers to Emmaus
    when newly risen from the sepulchre –

a shade appeared, and came behind us,   10
    gazing at the crowd that lay prone;
    not that, until it spoke, we saw what it was.

When it said, 'God give you peace, brothers of mine,'
    we turned swiftly and Virgil,
    greeting him with the appropriate sign   15

began: 'That blessed council
    – may the true court bring you to it,
    the court that has sentenced me to eternal exile.'

'So,' the other said, while we quickened our stride,
    'if you are shades whom God does not favour,   20
    who has led you up his stairs like an escort?'

And my teacher: 'If you examine the insignia
    which this man displays and the angel's set,
    you'll see he's destined for the highest honour.

But since she who spins by day and by night   25
    had not yet run off the full length of thread
    which Clotho allots each of us and winds tight,

his soul, with which ours are united,
    would not have had the strength to climb alone,
    because our mode of sight is denied it –   30

which is the reason I was drawn through the open
    jaws of hell to be his guide, and I'll pace
    onwards with him, lead him as far as my school can.

But tell me, if you know, why our ears
    still ring with the mountain's shaking when all shouted 35
    with a single voice down to its yielding base.'

In asking this he was able to thread
    the needle's eye of my desire; the hope he gave me
    was the sole means by which my thirst was reduced.

The other began: 'The holy   40
    rule of the mountain allows nothing to happen
    here that is unaccustomed or unruly.

This place is free from any alteration;
    that of which Heaven is the end and origin
    is the only force here to have a causal function.   45

Therefore, neither hail, nor snow, nor rain,
    nor dew, nor frost can fall any higher
    than the short stairway the three steps design.

Clouds, dense or tenuous, do not appear,
    nor do lightning flashes, nor Thaumas's daughter   50
    who often shifts her station over there.

Dry air does not evaporate
    above the top of those three steps I spoke about
    where Peter's vicar sets his feet.

The quaking below may be little or great,   55
    but because of the wind which the earth conceals,
    I don't know how, it's never shaken at this height.

There's a tremor here when a soul feels
    itself purged, so that it quickens and is moved
    to climb, and a greeting shout stirs the pulse.   60

It is the will that gives proof
    of such purging; the soul's free to change its chamber,
    stunned by what it's now capable of.

Yes, it willed, but its central desire
    one with divine justice, stood in the way,   65
    intent on torment as on sin before.

And so I, who have endured this penalty
    for five hundred years or more, only now
    felt my free will long for a loftier sky.

Therefore you felt the earthquake and that's why   70
    you heard the pious spirits around the mountain
    praise the Lord – may he soon let them move on high!'

So he spoke to us; and since the pleasure that's in
    a drink matches the greatness of our thirsting
    the good he did to me defeats expression.   75

And the wise leader: 'Now I see the traps sprung
    for you here, and how they can be broken through,
    why it shakes here and why you joyfully sing.

Now I hope you'll tell me who
    you are, and why you have stayed put   80
    so many ages; let your words instruct me.'

'When the good Titus with the support
    of the Highest King avenged the wounds
    through which trickled the blood that Judas bartered,

owning the name that most resounds   85
    with honour,' answered that shade, 'I lived yonder,
    famous, but without the faith that grounds.

So sweet was the sound I left on the air
    that Rome drew me from Toulouse,
    and placed a crown of myrtle on my hair.   90

People there still call me Statius;
    I sang of Thebes, then of the mighty Achilles,
    but fell by the way, the sequel too much.

The sparks of my poetic fire, its seeds
    and lit essence, came from the divine flame   95
    that's inspired countless creators of words.

I mean the *Aeneid*, which was like a mama
    to me and nourished my poetry-making;
    without it, I'd not weigh a gram.

And to have lived there, while Virgil was living,   100
    I would spend an extra year in exile
    here than was required by my wrong.'

These words made Virgil swivel
    a face to me that mutely said, 'Be mute.'
    But the power of the will is not total;   105

for laughter and tears give such hot pursuit
    to the feeling from which each springs
    that they're least subduable in the truest.

I only smiled, like one who slightly winks:
    at this the shade fell silent and looked me   110
    in the eyes, where the soul most belongs.

'In the hope your great work ends successfully,'
    he said, 'tell me why your face this instant
    shone with a look of near-frivolity?'

Between the two of them I'm in a bind: 115
    one orders me to say nothing, the other
    entreats me to speak; my master understands

my sigh, and says to me, 'Don't have a fear
    of speaking; just speak, and give him
    an answer to what he asks with such desire.'   120

So I: 'Perhaps you're marvelling,
    classical spirit, at the smile I gave,
    but you should wonder at a greater thing.

The one who guides me towards what lies above
    is the same Virgil as he from whom you   125
    drew strength to sing of men and gods so bravely.

If you entertained the thought my smile grew
    from any other cause, dismiss it as untrue;
    trust it was the words that came from you.'

He was already stooping to kiss the shoe   130
    of my teacher, but the latter said, 'Brother,
    don't; you're a shade and a shade is what you see.'

And he, rising: 'You can discern the sheer
    love which drives me towards you
    by the way I forget our lack of power,   135

endowing shades with physicality.'

NOTES TO CANTO 21
Nick Havely

1-3. The encounter between Christ and the Samaritan woman beside Jacob's Well at Sychar is in the biblical source (John 4: 5-29) already fraught with symbolism, harking back to the Old Testament, where spring-water signified God-given life and spirit 'imparted by divine Wisdom and the Law' (*JB* 1751). Identification of the water here with grace which alone can satisfy human demand for knowledge 'marks a central moment in Dante's entire intellectual development' (*CL* 2: 615).

7-9. The comparison of the newly arrived shade's appearance with that of the 'newly risen' Christ meeting the two apostles on the road to Emmaus (Luke 24: 13-32) foreshadows the mystery and drama of the subsequent encounter in this canto, whilst also highlighting the theme of the soul's resurrection and ascension, which are the subjects of both Luke 24 and the *Purgatorio*.

13. 'Peace be with you' is Christ's greeting to the apostles when appearing to them after the Resurrection (Luke 24: 36 and John 20: 19 and 26). Dante's version here also recalls the fraternal greeting of the early Franciscans, whilst the reference to Dante and Virgil as 'brothers' reflects the sense of religious community in *Purgatorio*.

22. The 'insignia' that the pilgrim 'displays' are the Ps marked on his forehead by the angel at the end of *Purg.* 9.

25-7. Virgil portrays the span of Dante's life in terms of the thread spun by the Fate Clotho and measured out by her sister Lachesis – as in *Purg.* 25. 79.

46-54. Normal effects of weather are thus imagined occurring only as far as the gate of Purgatory: the 'three steps' (l. 53) that are more fully described in *Purg.* 9. 94-102. The 'daughter of Thaumas [the Titan]' (50) was Iris, goddess of the rainbow.

82-102. Like Virgil in *Inf.* 1. 68-72, the Roman poet Statius (c.45-96 CE) now identifies himself: first through the time of his birth, under the Emperor Titus (79-81 CE) who sacked Jerusalem and destroyed the Temple; and then through the place of his birth (wrongly identified as 'Toulouse', through confusion with another Statius). Author of the *Thebaid* (a work highly influential on Dante and other medieval poets) and the incomplete *Achilleid* (ll. 92-3 here), Statius's deep indebtedness to Virgil is acknowledged (94-102), as Dante's was at his first meeting with the latter in *Inf.* 1. 79-87.

CANTO 22
Michael O'Neill

The angel was already behind us,
the angel who'd led us to the sixth circle,
who'd erased a scar from my face,

and who'd told us that those to whom justice beckons
are blessed, a blessing he enacted when he   5
said *sitiunt* (they thirst) all on its own.

Lighter here than in the previous circuits,
I moved in such a way that without effort
I caught the rapidly ascending spirits

and Virgil's opening sally: 'Love, lit   10
by virtue, has always ignited love
the moment that its flame shone out.

As a result, from the time Juvenal
told me of your affection
when he came down to our limbo in Hell,   15

my feelings for you out-compare
any displayed towards someone unseen –
I'll make quick work now of these stairs.

Tell me, though, and pardon if as a friend
I show too little concern for the bridle,   20
and speak with me candidly, as with a friend,

how could avarice root itself in you,
given that wisdom flooded your being,
thanks to your absorption in study?'

At first these words made Statius smile   25
a little; then he replied: 'Each utterance
of yours composes love's dear symbol.

Truly it's often the case appearances
provide false grounds for doubt
when there's no sign of the real reasons.   30

Your question shows me your conviction
I was covetous in that other life,
maybe because of the circle you found me in.

You need to know that avarice was too
distant from me, that it was lack of moderation   35
which was punished during thousands of moons;

and if I hadn't righted my direction,
having attended to the place where you cry out,
as though human nature aroused your derision,

"What part of the longings of mortals   40
do you not rule, sacrilegious hunger for gold?",
I'd roll and suffer Hell's brute wrestling hold.

Then I saw that profligate hands might be wings
too widely spread and I repented of that error
along with other sinful things.   45

How many will display the prodigals' shaved hair
through unawareness, which checks repentance
of sin when alive and at the last hour!

Know, too, that any fault, which counters a sin
as its straight opposite, shares in its fate here,   50
helping to wither its luxuriant green.

If you found me among those who feel pain
for avarice, I received such punishment
as sinning in a contrary way to their transgression.'

'Now when you rehearsed the hideous plot   55
of Jocasta's doubled tragedy,'
said the *Eclogues'* poet,

'to judge by Clio's inspiration there,
faith seems not to have made you faithful,
without which good deeds are so much hot air.   60

If that is so, what was the sun or candle
which drove away the dark and prompted your
voyage towards the Fisherman with re-fitted sail?'

And he to him: 'You first called me towards Parnassus
to drink in its shaded places and you then   65
lit the path for me towards the Logos.

Yours was the way of one who walks through dark,
bearing the light behind him, not aiding himself,
but making wise those who move in his wake,

when you wrote: "The age is born again;   70
justice comes back and the first human prime,
and a new generation descends from heaven."

Through you I was a poet, through you a Christian;
but, to put the matter less tersely,
I'll add some colour to that sketched outline.   75

The whole world was already giving birth
to the true creed, after the seeds had been sown
by the messengers of the eternal throne;

and your words, touched on above, rhymed
so musically with those of the new teachers,   80
I got into the practice of visiting them.

They then appeared so holy in my eyes
that, when Domitian persecuted them,
laments of mine were chorus to their cries.

And while, down there, I drew breath   85
I helped them, and their good ways
made me feel contempt for any other faith;

and before, as a poet, I brought to
Thebes' rivers the Greeks, I was baptized;
fear made me a closet Christian, though,   90

paganism my over-long disguise;
and this timidity meant that I lapped
the fourth circle for more than four centuries.

You, therefore, who have lifted the cover
which hid from me the good of which I speak,   95
while our climb gives us the leisure,

tell me, where is our Terence, of such renown,
Caecilius, Plautus and Varro, too, if you know;
tell me, are they damned and in which dungeon?'

'They, Persius, I, and many others,'   100
my leader responded, 'are with that Greek
to whom the Muses showed the greatest favours,

in the first circle of the blind prison.
We often talk of the mountain
where our foster-mothers live for ever.   105

Euripides is with us, and Antiphon,
Simonides, Agathon and many more Greeks,
who once bound their brows with the laurel-crown.

Of those you breathed life into you can find
Antigone, Deiphyle and Argia   110
and Ismene, still the most saddened.

There, too, is she who showed them Langia;
also the daughter of Tiresias, and Thetis,
and, with her sisters, Deidamia.'

Now both poets fell silent, newly keen   115
on taking in what lay to hand,
set free from the walls and the ascent;

and four handmaidens of the day were already
behind us, and the fifth at the helm guided
the sun's chariot as its tip burned ardently,   120

when my leader: 'I think it would be best to turn
our right shoulders to the furthest edge,
circling the mountain as our practice has been.'

Thus usage served for our instruction there,
and we embarked on the route with less doubt   125
because of the approval of that exemplar.

They went ahead and I, solitary,
followed, and listened to their talk
which gave me ideas for poetry.

But soon that fine conversation was interrupted   130
by a tree we came on in mid-road,
with fruit whose scent was delightful and good.

And as a fir-tree slims towards the top
from bough to bough, so did this towards the foot,
in order, I think, that no one might climb up.   135

On the side where our way was blocked,
a clear spring tumbled from the high rock
and broadened its spray over the leaves.

The two poets approached the tree;
and a voice from inside the leafage   140
cried: 'You'll know this food by its scarcity.'

Then said: 'Mary thought more how
Cana's wedding might be the source of honour
than of her mouth, which now entreats for you.

And in antique days Roman women   145
were content with water for their drink,
Daniel, despising food, discovered wisdom.

The first age was as beautiful as gold;
it gave an appetising savour to acorns
and streams quenched thirst like nectar as they rolled,   150

Locusts and honey were the meat
which fed the Baptist in the wilderness;
therefore he achieved glory and is great

as, through the Gospel story, is revealed to you.'

NOTES TO CANTO 22
Nick Havely

1-9. The rapidity of the transition from the fifth to the sixth terrace is matched by the abbreviated Beatitude pronounced by the angel ('Blessed are they who thirst [after righteousness]', Matthew 5: 6) and by the pilgrim's increased ease of movement (ll. 7-9), as had been foretold by Virgil in *Purg.* 4. 88-95, above.

13-15. The Roman satirist Juvenal – who is here imagined bringing news of Statius to Virgil in Limbo – died around 130 CE.

37-75. Statius attributes his religious and poetic re-direction partly to Virgil's denunciation of the 'sacrilegious hunger for gold' (ll. 40-1, re-working *Aen.* 3. 56-7) and partly to the earlier poet's prophecy of a renewed Golden Age (lines 70-2 translate the first three verses of Virgil's fourth *Eclogue*). It is also envisaged as a voyage following the boat of St Peter ('the Fisherman' of l. 63), i.e. the Church, and as progression from 'Parnassus' (mountain of the Muses) to God (64-6).

76-93. Statius explains that because of his fears during the persecutions by the Emperor Domitian (81-96 CE), he failed to declare himself as a Christian and hence has had to expiate the sin of sloth in the 'fourth circle' of Purgatory (l. 93).

100-14. In response to Statius's question about the fate in the afterlife of contemporary Roman writers, Virgil recalls the poem's earlier description of encounters in Limbo, 'the first circle of the blind prison' (l. 103, see *Inf.* 4. 118-44), and in ll. 106-14 he now adds other noble figures from Greek antiquity to the list, including some who feature in Statius's own works: e.g., Antigone and Ismene (in his *Thebaid*) and Deidamia (in the *Achilleid*).

118-20. The 'handmaidens of the day' are the hours (as in *Purg.* 12. 81), so the time is now between 10 and 11 in the morning.

130-54. Giving the first indication that the terrace now reached is that of gluttony, the voice within the fruit-laden tree speaks of the food that the penitent souls now yearn for, and (as the 'whip' towards the opposing virtue) ends the canto by alternating biblical and classical examples of temperance: the Virgin Mary's conduct during the Marriage at Cana (John 2: 1-5); the abstemiousness of early Roman women (Valerius Maximus, *Facta et dicta memorabilia* 2. 1. 5); the prophet Daniel's refusal of food from Nebuchadnezzar's table (Daniel 1: 8-16); the austere diet of humanity in the classical myth of the Golden Age (*Met.* 1. 103-6); and the food of John the Baptist in the desert (Matthew 3: 4 and Mark 1: 6).

CANTO 23
Andrew Fitzsimons

With my eyes fixed on those verdant leaves,
as lost in looking as one whose life is run
in wait for tiny game birds, forgetting to live,

my more than father said to me, 'Son,
enough of that, the time that's allowed us   5
ought to be more profitably spent. Come on.'

So I returned my face and my footsteps to those
wise ancients, to follow them and their talk
that made the hard going seem so easy.

But then such crying and singing broke   10
upon us, of *'Labia mea, Domine'*,
that in us grew both delight and heartbreak.

'O sweet father, what is this orison?'
I began, and he: 'Spirits who work to free
as they go, perhaps, the knot of their sin.'   15

Just as with pilgrims who encounter
an unknown face and, filled with thought,
turn but a moment to look and do not linger,

so, from behind us, with looks full of doubt,
they came and they passed, moving briskly,   20
a troop of souls, silent and devout.

Dark and hollowed out were their eyes,
pallid their faces, and with bodies so wasted
the skin seemed to form itself from their bones.

Not even Erysichthon reached so wretched   25
a state, I believe, not even when his hunger
could no longer be feared and on himself he fed.

I murmured to myself, thinking: 'So here
I see the people who lost Jerusalem
when Mary, daughter of Eleazar, gnawed at her   30

son.' They were as finger-rings without gems:
those who read in human faces 'O-M-O'
would in theirs have easily made out the 'M'.

Who is it could believe, not knowing how,
that the scent of fruit, the presence of water   35
could bring such desire and bring them so low?

I was transfixed by the idea
of the as yet unshown to me cause
of their ravaged and scaly squalor,

when behold, from out of the depths of his face,   40
a shade turned his eyes to me and stared,
then cried: 'What grace granted me is this?'

By his face I wouldn't have known him, but I heard
that voice of his and in it could recognize
all that had been turned into a grim regard.   45

The spoken spark re-kindled at once
memories of that now altered visage
and I saw once more him that I'd known as Forese.

'Bah, don't concern yourself with the savage
scabs that plague me', he pleaded, 'nor my skin,   50
my want of flesh nor my body's damage.

Tell me all about you; who are those twin
souls that are your companions through this place?
Please don't leave me without making your tale known.'

'Your face, which I grieved over when you had just   55
passed on, in this moment grieves me no less,'
I answered, 'now I see its form so debased.

In God's name, tell me why your body undoes
itself so, don't make me speak while I am numbed.
He speaks ill whose mind is filled and at a loss.'   60

And then he to me: 'From the Eternal Wisdom
power descends into that water and that plant
behind you, and my body's flensing is the same.

All of these people, crying as they chant,
who in life, beyond all measure, valued their gullets,   65
are re-made now in hunger and thirst and want.

The desire that grows in us to drink and to eat
arises from the aromas of fruit and spring
that upwardly yon tree disseminates.

And not just for one time, this revolving   70
space replenishes our punishment:
I say punishment, but better an up-lifting,

for the desire that leads us to those branches
led Christ in joy to exclaim *"Eli"*
when he liberated us with his veins.'   75

Then I said to him: 'Forese, from that day
you exchanged our world for the better life
no more than five years have passed till now.

If the possibility of further sin had ceased
in you before you reached the succour   80
of the sweet pain that reconciles us with God,

how is it that you are already here?
I had thought to find you there below
where by waiting lost time is restored.'

And he replied: 'I was conveyed here so   85
quickly, to drink the martyrs' sweet wormwood,
by the tears poured by my dearest Nella.

Because of her pious prayers and devoted
sighs I was raised from that slope where souls wait,
and from other turns too I was liberated.   90

So much dearer and delighted of God
is my bereaved widow, who I love so well,
for the loneliness she takes on in doing good;

even Sardinia's Barbagia is full
of women more chaste than the Barbagia   95
where I left her and where she still dwells.

O sweet brother, what do you want me to say?
I foresee a future, a time from which
the present will seem not so very far,

in which the pulpit will prohibit   100
brazen Florentine women from parading
the streets touting to the whole city their tits.

Was there ever barbarian, ever Saracen
that to get them to cover up needed the law,
a spiritual or some other form of discipline?   105

But if these shameless hussies only knew
what the swift heavens had in store for them
now for screaming they would have opened their maws;

and if this foresight is not fooling me
they'll surely be grieving before the bum fluff   110
grows on him now listening to nursery rhymes.

Well, brother, you've kept it from me long enough!
Now look at how not just me, but all these people
stare at the ground where by you the sun's blocked off.'

And so I said to him: 'Should you recall   115
what in youth I was to you and you to me
remembering here now must be unbearable.

From the life of the world I was taken, the day
before yesterday, by the one there who precedes
me, when that one's sister was round in the sky,'   120

I pointed to the sun, 'he brought me through the deep
darkness of the truly dead and accursed,
even though I still bore this true flesh that he leads.

Then by his guidance I have been hoisted
in the climbing and circling of this mountain,   125
which straightens you whom the world has twisted.

He says that he shall be my companion
until I am there where Beatrice is;
and from that point without him I'll go on.

Virgil it is, the one who tells me all this,'   130
I pointed to him; 'and this other is that shade
for whom your mountain, every terrace

trembled just now, to release his soul's weight.'

NOTES TO CANTO 23
Nick Havely

10-15. 'Lord, you shall open my lips, and my mouth will speak out your praise' (*Domine, labia mea aperies, et os meum annuntiabit laudem tuam*) is a verse in the middle of the penitential *Miserere* Psalm (51: 15; 50: 17 in the Vulgate); the imagery seems appropriate in the mouths of the penitent gluttons. For other appropriate prayers, hymns and verses from the Psalms in Purgatory, see *DE* 570.

25-7. Erysichthon scorned the gods and cut down a sacred oak in the grove of Ceres, who sent for Famine to afflict him with such hunger that in the end he fed upon himself (*Met.* 8. 738-878).

28-31. The act of parental cannibalism during the Roman siege of Jerusalem by the Roman Emperor Titus in 70 CE (see *Purg.* 21. 82-4 and note) was described in Book 6 of the contemporary *History of the Jewish War* by Flavius Josephus and is referred to by several early medieval sources.

32-3. OMO (*uomo*) in medieval Italian means 'man'. The bone-structure of the human eyebrows, together with the nose and eye sockets is thus said to resemble the rounded 'm' in uncial script, with two 'o's on either side of the middle downstroke. The shrunken faces of the gluttons thus make the 'm' outline of bones much more visible.

48. Forese Donati (c.1260-before 1296) was a member of a powerful Florentine family and a friend and kinsman of Dante, who had married a cousin of his. The two had also exchanged six insulting sonnets; in one of them Dante speaks of his friend as glutton and spendthrift and in another as a scarfaced desperado.

70-1. 'It seems that there may be a number of such trees to be encountered around this terrace' (*CL* 2: 682).

74. The crucified Christ's words, 'My God [*Eli*], why have you forsaken me' (Matthew 27: 46) echo the cry of despair at the beginning of Psalm 22, but they are 'followed in the Psalm by an expression of joyful confidence in final victory' (*JB* 1657, note s). Hence they are said to reflect ultimate 'joy' through suffering, as sought by the souls here.

79-81. In other words, Forese's final illness had deprived him of the ability to sin before he reached the stage of repentance (paradoxically described as 'sweet pain').

85-90. Nothing is known about Forese's wife (and widow) Nella, but her presence here gains 'extraordinary prominence' as a deliberate contrast to the contempt with which she had been treated in the exchange of poems between Forese and Dante (*CL*, 2: 684; and above, note to l. 48). Once again the closeness of the connections between the human world and that of Purgatory is emphasized by the penitent soul's need for the prayers of those still alive; see above, e.g., *Purg.* 6. 26 and 8. 70-81. It is thus the prayers of his widow that have freed Forese from delay in Antepurgatory and speeded him through the previous five terraces.

94-6. Barbagia was a remote region of central Sardinia which seems to have been a byword for licentiousness.

97-111. Forese here denounces Florentine morals in similar tones to those used on occasion in the *Inferno* (e.g. 6, 15, 16) and later in the *Paradiso* (e.g., 16). His prophecy of vengeance upon Florence echoes the language of similar predictions, for example in *Inf.* 26. 7-12. Several of Dante's public letters in 1311 call for the Imperial invader, Henry VII, to deal severely with Florence's opposition to his authority, so the prophecy that a baby now (in 1300) new born will witness that punishment before he begins to grow a beard (ll. 109-11) may refer to the Emperor's campaign in 1311-13, around the time when Dante may have been composing this part of the *Purg.* (see *BGLD* 38-43). On Forese's use of the term 'brother' (*frate*) here in l. 97 and in l. 112, see above, *Purg.* 11. 82 and note.

120-1. The goddess associated with the moon was Diana, sister of Apollo, god of the sun. Their father was Jupiter and their mother Latona (see *Met.* 6. 184-381).

131. The 'other' companion Dante points to is the Roman poet Statius (see *Purg.* 21. 82-93, above) who will continue to accompany Dante to the summit of the mountain and the end of the *Purgatorio*. The 'trembling' of the mountain (ll. 132-3) signalled his release from the terrace of the Avaricious (above, *Purg.* 20. 127-41 and 21. 40-72).

CANTO 24
Andrew Fitzsimons

Neither talk the going nor going the talk
slackened, but speaking on we pushed ahead,
like a boat gathered to a favourable tack;

and those shades, seeming as things twice dead,
out the sunken pits of their eyes in wonder   5
looked upon me, perceiving the life I still had.

And I, still speaking with this friend and brother,
said: 'Statius journeys upward more slow
than otherwise he would because of another.

Now tell me, where is Piccarda, if you know?   10
And tell me if there's someone to be noted
among these people who regard me so.'

'My sister, who, whether "beautiful" is suited
better or "good," I know not, now triumphs
in highest Olympus and wears her coronet.'   15

So first he spoke, and then: 'Here no forbiddance
disallows anyone to be called by name,
since our diet has so hollowed our semblance.

This,' said he pointing, 'is Bonagiunta, him
of the town of Lucca, and that other face   20
beyond him there, scrawnier than all of them,

had all the Holy Church in his embrace;
of Tours he was, and purges now by this fast
Bolsena's eels, and rivers of vernaccia.'

And one by one he named others of that cast,   25
and to be named there all seemed so content
that not one dark look across any brow passed.

I saw out of hunger snapping at the vacant
air, Ubaldin da la Pila, and Boniface,
who pastured many with his crozier's battlement.   30

I saw Sir Marquis who had far more space
to drink his draughts at Forlì, and with less drought,
for he was one whose thirst was bottomless.

But like he who glances then singles out
more one than another, so I with the Lucchese,   35
who to know of me seemed keenest of that crowd.

He was murmuring; something the likes
of 'Gentucca' I heard there where he felt the wounds
of justice upon him, there where pain latches.

'O spirit,' I said, 'who seems so much to want   40
to speak to me, let me know what it is
you intend, appease us both with your spoken words.'

'A woman is born, not yet adult in dress,'
he began, 'who will make my native city
please you, castigated though it be by most.   45

You will go from here with this prophecy:
if due to my murmurings at a loss you leave,
true things will bring in time their clarities.

But tell me if, before me here, I see him move
who drew forth those new rhymes beginning   50
"Ladies who have some insight into love"?'

And said I to him, 'I am but one who, when
inspired by Love, takes note, and out of what
has been dictated within make meaning.'

'O Brother, now I see,' he said, 'the knot   55
that held back the Notary, Guittone and me
from getting to that style so new so sweet.

Now I see so well how your poets' plumes
fly by following straight Love's dictates,
no such thing ever happened in our themes,   60

and whosoever sets to teasing it out
will find no more between one and the other style,'
and then he was quiet, as if content with that.

Like as the birds that winter by the river Nile
at times will form a flock upon the air   65
then in quickening flight stretch out in file,

in that same way those people gathered there
turning their faces, quickened their step,
light-footed all from leanness and desire.

And like that man who, tired of keeping up,   70
lets his companions go on ahead and walks
more slowly till the beating in his chest lets up,

so Forese permitted that holy flock
to pass him by, and coming up behind me
said, 'When will it be I see you come back?'   75

'I don't know,' I replied, 'how long my life will be,
but my return could never be soon enough,
longing would have me on this shore already,

for the place where I was given to live
is day by day ever more drained of the good   80
and to sad ruin ever more willing to drive.'

'Know this,' said he, 'the one who bears most guilt
I see dragged at heel by the tail of a beast
towards that ditch where sin's never purged.

With each step the beast rampages faster,   85
its momentum growing until the blows leave
him a body broken, mangled and smashed.

Those wheels there have not much more to revolve,'
he raised his eyes to the sky, 'before
it will be clear to you what my words can't reveal.   90

Remain as you are, for time is precious here
in this realm and far too much I lose
moving along with you pacing as a pair.'

Sometimes one knight will gallop forth from a close-
packed troop, leave his companions behind   95
to claim the honour of the battle's first clash,

so thus he parted from us with longer stride,
and I remained on the path with those two shades,
such great marshals of the world at one time.

And when he had gone so far ahead my eyes   100
strained and could no more follow him than
my mind could follow those words of his,

there appeared to me the branches, laden
with fruit and verdant, of another tree
close by, near where we had made our turn.   105

I saw beneath the tree people raising their
hands and to the branches crying I know not what,
like needy little children who in vain try

begging but the one begged from responds not,
rather to render their longing even more keen   110
does not hide the thing they desire but holds it aloft.

They departed then as if disillusioned,
and so we came to that great tree now
that so many prayers and tears disdains.

'Pass on by, you, without drawing too near: 115
further on high is the tree eaten from by Eve
and from that this offshoot was grown as new.'

A voice unknown spoke thus through the leaves;
and Virgil and Statius and I, pressing close,
continued to edge our way along the cliff.   120

'Remember the accursed ones,' said the voice,
'formed of the clouds, centaurs drunk and engorged,
their doubled chests battled against by Theseus,

and those Hebrews on drinking so engaged
that Gideon refused them as companions   125
when down the hills on Midian he charged.'

So, clinging to one side of the verge's margins
we passed along, hearing sins of the gullet
followed now by their miserable earnings.

Then, spreading out upon the lonely path,   130
a thousand steps and more brought us on,
each one of us wordless, lost in thought.

'You three, why so pensively walking alone?'
a voice suddenly said, at which I started
like an animal frighted where it had lain.   135

To see who'd spoken I raised my head;
never was seen in any furnace glass
or metal glowing so radiantly red

as the one I saw who said: 'If you wish
to ascend, here's the place you must turn,   140
this the path for those in search of peace.'

His countenance had robbed me of vision
so that I moved now in behind my two teachers
like one who by what he hears stumbles on.

And as when the May breeze, that harbinger   145
of the whitening dawn, fragrantly flows,
filled with the aroma of grass and flowers,

so now I sensed in the middle of my brow
a wind, and sensed clearly a wing's flight
that suffused the air with ambrosia.   150

And these words I sensed: 'Blessed are those the light
of grace illumines so that the love of taste
within their breast does not enflame appetite,

hungering always for the measured and just!'

NOTES TO CANTO 24
Nick Havely

9. The 'other' because of whom Statius is going more slowly is his
master Virgil, with whom he wants to spend more time. This brief
reminder of the bond between the fellow Latin poets prefigures the
canto's emphasis on Dante's relationships with poetic predecessors
(Bonagiunta *et al.*) and his fellow Florentine (Forese).

10-15. Forese's sister Piccarda will be encountered thus 'crowned' in the
first sphere of Paradise (*Par.* 3. 34-120).

19-20. Bonagiunta Orbicciani of Lucca (referred to in documents
between 1242 and 1247) is the first of several Italian vernacular poets to
be mentioned in this canto.

21-33. Pope Martin IV (1281-5) was, according to one of Dante's
fourteenth-century commentators, 'greatly given to gluttony [...] he
had eels taken from the Lake of Bolsena [near the papal residence
at Viterbo], had them drowned in vernaccia [white wine], then ate
them roasted', and the eels were said to have rejoiced when he died.
Other later fourteenth-century figures here – a Tuscan nobleman, an
archbishop of Ravenna, a dipsomaniac marquis from the Romagna –
all seem to have had a popular reputation for gourmandizing.

37-45. The indirect reference to Bonagiunta's mouth (ll. 38-9) highlights
the functions of eating and speaking – both significant here. His
mentioning of one 'Gentucca' – as a young woman who will make
Lucca 'please' Dante (38 and 43-50) – suggests she may have helped
him in some way while he was in the region during his exile, and the

implication of affection between them anticipates the discussion of love poetry in the following passage.

49-63. The exchange between the Dante-persona and that of Bonagiunta, though quite brief, touches upon key features of the *Purgatorio*'s poetics. The historical Bonagiunta was a follower of the older Tuscan school, regarding the 'new style' of Guinizelli as unduly academic; see the exchange of sonnets between the two poets in the Postscript to this volume (nos. 4a-b). Dante here places his work within a tradition of Italian vernacular lyric that includes Sicilians like Jacopo da Lentini ('the Notary' in l. 56) and their Tuscan successors such as Bonagiunta himself and Guittone d'Arezzo (56). Earlier, (in *DVE* 1. 13.1), Dante had spoken of Bonagiunta among those whose poetry is 'fitted not for a court but at best for a city council'. For further examples of these Tuscan and Sicilian poets' work, see the Postscript (nos. 6 and 7b). Whilst acknowledging that tradition, however, Dante contrasts his own new understanding of love – exemplified by Virgil's discourse on its nature in *Purg.* 18 – with the limitations (55-7) evident in the work of writers such as Bonagiunta and Guittone. Bonagiunta is thus made to pay tribute to the groundbreaking effect of Dante's key poem in praise of Beatrice, the canzone *Donne ch'avete intelletto d'amore* (in *VN* 19); which is translated here in the Postscript (no. 5). *Donne ch'avete* was widely circulated in the poet's lifetime, whilst the Dante-persona offers the older poet a somewhat offhand explanation of his 'new style' (52-4). Awareness of the poets' common goal, however, is reflected in Bonagiunta's addressing Dante in his reply as 'Brother' (55).

64-6. The migratory 'birds' are cranes: the purposefulness of their flight (and the renewed movement of the souls) harks back to Bonagiunta's portrayal of the 'plumes / pens' of the soaring new generation of writers – thus linking both purgatorial and poetic progress.

79-90. Taking up Dante's indirect reference (ll. 79-81) to Florence's decline into 'ruin' – one of the many references to his native city's troubles to be found in all three parts of the *Commedia* – Forese now prophesies the death of his kinsman Corso Donati. Corso was leader of the faction of 'Black' Guelfs (Papal supporters, opposed to Dante's party), was condemned as a traitor in 1308 and, according to contemporary chroniclers, was killed as he fled on horseback. Dante's version is imbued with additional symbolism: being dragged at the tail of a horse was a punishment for traitors; and the scene is transformed 'into a prophetic image', showing 'the mighty and ruthless wrecker of the city being dragged from the earth directly into the infernal abyss by a diabolical beast' (*CL* 2: 716). The 'wheels' of the sky (88) are the spheres of Paradise, signifying divine judgement upon Corso – hence making Forese's prophecy of vengeance similar to that of Hugh Capet in *Purg.* 20. 94-6.

99. The two 'marshals' are Virgil and Statius in their role as leaders and guides to Dante and others.

103-17. The 'verdant tree' (l. 104) is an offshoot of the Tree of Knowledge of Good and Evil (Genesis 2) which Dante imagines still growing 'further on high', that is in the Earthly Paradise at the summit of Mount Purgatory (*Purg.* 32. 37-42).

121-6. Warnings against gluttony, drawn again from classical and biblical sources, refer here to the drunken Centaurs punished by Theseus (Ovid, *Met.* 12. 210-535); and to the Israelite soldiers who failed Gideon's test of temperance and caution (Judges 7: 4-7).

150. The scent of 'ambrosia' (food of the gods) signals the presence of the divine (here the angel guarding the ascent to the next terrace) – as it did in the appearance of Venus to Aeneas in *Aen.* 1. 403-4.

151-4. The canto and the encounter end with a summary of the fourth Beatitude (Matthew 5: 6), celebrating those who 'hunger and thirst after righteousness'.

CANTO 25
Andrew Fitzsimons

Now there was nothing to halt our climb:
the sun had left the meridian circle
to Taurus, and to Scorpio the night-time;

thus, like the man who'll neither dither nor stall
but stick to his own path no matter what,   5
if propelled by the goad of a grail,

so we too through the narrow gap made
our way, one behind the other ascending,
the strait so narrow we had to divide.

And like the young stork who raises its wing   10
with desire to fly but then will not dare
abandon the nest, its wing lowering,

thus was I, the desire to ask and seek answer
lit then quenched, arriving as far as the mark
of an orator about to take the floor.   15

Not to leave me so, though our pace was brisk,
my sweet father says, 'Release the arrow
of your thought, since you have drawn to the nock.'

Emboldened, I could open my lips now,
and began: 'How can this be so, that they thin   20
here where the need for nourishment does not grow?'

'If you call to mind Meleager, the one
consumed as the fiery brand was consumed,
then this should not be a troubling question,

and if you think of how, at your own whims   25
your image swims within a mirror
what now seems hard will be no problem.

But so as to becalm your desire
Statius is here; and I call and beseech
him to be to your wound the healer.'   30

'If I reveal to him eternal justice,'
Statius responded, 'here in front of you,
let my obedience be my excuse.'

He then began: 'If the words I say,
son, can enter your mind and your regard,   35
they will illuminate your wondering why.

The part most perfected of the blood
which isn't drunk in by the thirsty veins
remains, as on a table leftover food,

and within the heart, and for each human   40
limb, acquires the power of informing life
to which that same blood flows as in a chain.

Digested again, it descends to whereof
better to be silent than speak, and then travels
to that other's blood, its natural wife.   45

Together in that vessel they mingle,
one disposed to endure, the other do,
due to the perfect place from which both hail;

and being conjoined begin to go
to work, first to thicken then to vivify   50
that which their own material has made so.

The informing life become a soul thereby
(as in a plant but with a difference:
the plant's complete, this just begun its journey)

works within so that it moves and senses,   55
like a marine sponge, and into form blends
then for the faculties it seeds, organs.

Now it expands, my son, now distends,
this virtue flowing from the begetter's heart
to all the human members, as nature intends.   60

But how animal becomes child that's the part
you cannot yet comprehend, where one more wise
than you was in error from the start,

for in his doctrine he distinguishes
possible intellect from soul, since   65
he could find no organ for that purpose.

Open your breast to the truth I will evince:
know that, as swiftly as in the embryo,
the articulation of the brain happens,

then the Prime Mover turns to it, in joy   70
at such art in nature, and he breathes
new spirit therein, with power imbued

and of what it finds active there assimilates
the substance, to become a singular soul
that lives and feels and self-contemplates.   75

And so you'll be less stunned by the things I tell,
look to the heat of the sun which produces wine
when joined to the juice that through the vine travels.

When Lachesis reaches the end of her line
the soul departs the flesh entire,   80
carrying both the human and the divine:

all other faculties void of power,
memory, intelligence, and the will
are now more active, more keen than before.

Without cease, of its own weight, it falls,   85
marvellously, to one or other parting place
discovering there the next stage of its call.

Once there, within this surrounding space,
the informing life radiates all around,
just as in their previously living states.   90

And just as the air, when filled with rain,
within itself the ray of another reflects
and with diverse colours becomes adorned,

just so the enveloping air affects
itself into that form itself imprinted   95
by the soul's power as it comes to rest;

and resembling the flame that slants
and shifts following its fire wheresoever,
the soul and its new form are entwined.

From then on possessing an exterior   100
form it is called a shade, and every
sense, even sight, possesses once more.

We can speak and we can laugh and we cry
and perhaps the tears we shed, and our sighs,
you've heard as you climbed Mount Purgatory.   105

The shade assumes the form of its desire,
and feels the force of other emotions,
and this it was that occasioned your surprise.'

We had arrived by now at the last turn
and veering as usual to the right   110
came upon a new preoccupation.

Here from the embankment flames shoot forth
while from the ledge blasted air shoots up
to bend the flames back and forge a path,

and on this edge we were forced to step,   115
one after the other, in fear of fire
the one side, on the other, of falling off.

He who led me said: 'In this place here
you'll need to keep your eyes in your head
for one small slip might be your final error.'   120

'*Summae Deus clementiae*' I heard,
from the heart of the great flame, voices singing,
and more wanted to turn from what lay ahead.

And I beheld souls through the flame walking,
for I looked to them as I watched my own   125
steps, now one, now the other, my gaze dividing.

After they had come to the end of their hymn
'*Virum non cognosco*', they screamed out loud,
and then, with low sound, began the song again.

That over, they screamed once more: 'To the wood   130
tended Diana, who chased out Helice,
the one who had Venus' poison in her blood.'

Then went back to the hymn, then of ladies
they screamed and of husbands who were chaste,
as decreed by virtue and by marriage laws.   135

And this ritual, I believe, lasts
for as long as the fire around them glows,
it is their cure and the food they must taste

that their open wound at last should close.

NOTES TO CANTO 25
Nick Havely

2-3. The position of the sun and of 'night' (envisaged as a diametrically opposite point on the other side of the globe) suggests to some commentators that the time is now 2 pm, but *DM* (2: 428) argue that because of the date of the equinox in 1300, it is 'shortly after noon'. On the registering of time in Purgatory through periphrases like this, see above, *Purg.* 2. 1-6 and note.

10-12. The hesitant Dante-persona is likened to a fledgling stork as he pauses before raising the complex question that forms the main subject of this canto. The comparison of mental or spiritual development to flight is especially recurrent in these later cantos of the *Purgatorio* (see note on *Purg.* 19.61-6).

22-3. Virgil compares the emaciated state of the starving gluttons to the fate of Meleager in *Met.* 8. 515-25. Melager's mother on hearing that he had killed her brothers, avenged them by kindling a magic brand which would take as long to burn as he had to live.

28-30. To answer Dante's question about the souls' capacity to suffer apparently physical torment (ll. 20-1) requires an explanation of human procreation and the relationship between body and soul that draws upon 'illumination by revelation and faith' (*DM* 2: 429). For this purpose Virgil calls upon the Christian Statius whose explanation has two interlinked sections: on the development of the foetus (ll. 37-78) and the state of the soul after death (79-108).

37-51. Following Aristotle and his 13th-century scientific disciples, Statius describes the formation of human semen as a process of 'digestion' in several stages – leading from the stomach to the heart, then the testicles – and how at conception it was thought to 'mingle' with an equivalent kind of female blood in the uterus (Boyde 271-3).

61-78. In Statius's account of the soul and its reasoning powers, Dante addresses several interpretations of Aristotle's views. The one said to be 'in error' is the 12th-century Islamic commentator Ibn-Rushd ('Averroes') whom Dante here as elsewhere speaks of with respect (*Inf.* 4. 144; *Mon.* 1. 3. 7-9; and *DE* 79). Ibn-Rushd held that humans share thought with a single universal and eternal 'possible intellect' (l. 65) and that individual humans are not immortal. Against this, Dante has Statius develop a lyrically Christian narrative of the infusion of the rational soul into the foetus at a key stage of its development, in a sentence (ll. 67-75) that – with its allusions to the Creation, the Incarnation and the mystery of the Trinity – 'contains perhaps the single most important doctrinal statement in the *Comedy*' (Boyde 279).

79. The three Fates who spin the thread of human life (Clotho), measure it (Lachesis) and cut it (Atropos) feature in Greek and Roman mythology and initially in Plato's *Republic* (10. 617b-621a). As Dante may have recalled, Ovid describes them as present at the birth of Meleager (see ll. 22-3, above) giving him an equal span of life to the wooden brand which, when burnt, causes his death (*Met.* 8. 451-7). Here, as often in the poem, at the beginning of Statius's account of the soul's afterlife, the pagan / Ovidian allusion serves a Christian purpose.

86. Points of embarkation for Hell has been imagined in the *Commedia* as the 'sad shore' of the Acheron from the classical underworld (*Inf.* 3. 78); whilst for Purgatory and (eventually) Paradise souls leave from the mouth of the Tiber (*Purg.* 2. 100-1).

121. 'God of boundless mercy' is a hymn 'associated liturgically with Saturday night' (*DM* 2: 435). Its third stanza appeals for help to resist sexual temptation.

128. 'I have no knowledge of man' (Luke 1: 34) is the Virgin Mary's first response to the Angel Gabriel's annunciation of the birth of Christ.

130-2. Helice was an Arcadian nymph who was seduced by Jupiter, expelled by Diana from her company and finally transformed by Juno into a bear. Jupiter finally changed her and her son into constellations: the Great and Little Bear (*Met.* 2. 409-507).

CANTO 26
Alvin Pang

So along the edge, one after the other, we went
and as we walked the good master cautioned
often: 'Watch your step. Stay vigilant.'

The entire western sky had been turned
from blue to white by the sun's dazzlingly   5
bright rays. My right shoulder burned,

and where my shadow fell the flames seemed subtly
more intense. I saw that many a passing soul,
having taken note of this faint anomaly,

had begun to gather and gabble   10
about me; I overheard their chatter
on how my body 'didn't seem virtual',

then a few approached me, or as near
as they dared without ever
stepping over the fiery frontier.   15

'You there, trailing behind the rest; you show vigour
but perhaps defer to those ahead. Answer
me this, who burns with thirst and fire –

and there are many others here also eager
for explanation, thirsting for it more than   20
parched India or Ethiopia craves cold water –

tell us, how is it your body can block the sun
as if you have not yet been caught
in the web of death?' So asked one

of the curious mob. Indeed, had not   25
the strangest sight distracted me just then,
I would have given them what they sought:

there, coming from the opposite direction
down the middle of that fiery road, new
figures had appeared. I stared in fascination   30

as the spirits in each group (as if on cue)
exchanged brief kisses, then with no time to lose
for a lengthier welcome, immediately withdrew;

they looked like ants, who in their teeming queues
would touch faces briefly upon meeting   35
as if to ask for directions or the latest news.

Once the spirits were done with their friendly greeting,
each shouted out a phrase as loud and as best
they could before moving on, their cries competing:

'Sodom and Gomorrah!' roared the newcomers. The rest   40
bellowed in response: 'Pasiphae enters the cow to
lure the bull into charging her lust!'

Like a flight of cranes parting ways – some veering to
the Riphaean heights, others to the desert,
avoiding either the sun's heat or the highland cold – so   45

both groups of spirits broke off and moved apart,
each of them returning to their appropriate
songs, respective lamentations. On my part,

the spirits that had begun to interrogate
me earlier drew near again, eager to resume   50
their audience. I did not let them wait,

having twice noted their enthusiasm.
So I began: 'You souls, most assured
of final peace, whenever it may come,

my limbs are neither new-sprouted nor withered   55
but are here alive with me, intact. Yes,
with all their joints and all my blood.

I climb now to cure my blindness.
There is a lady above this tier; my fleshly, bodied
self was brought into your world by her grace.　　　60

So that your greatest wish may be soon fulfilled,
and you ascend into heaven's true
reaches, which are so full of love and so wide,

tell me, that I may record it in my pages: Who
are you all, and who are those now fading　　　65
almost out of view behind you?'

An uncouth hermit hillbilly wandering
into city streets could hardly have been more
dumbfounded than these gathered spirits, gaping

with amazement at my words. Before　　　70
long, however, they recovered from their shock,
being the stout noble hearts that they were.

'Blessed are you, who, to die a better death, look
to take on board what you might from our experience,'
the one who first questioned me soon spoke.　　　75

'Those walking away from us? Their offence
was the same as Caesar's; at the height of his fame
there were those who called him "Queen". Hence

they cry "Sodom", as you heard when they came,
reproaching themselves for that particular sin　　　80
and feeding the fires with their burning shame.

Our own crimes were heterosexual in origin
but we put human limits to the test,
indulging our most animal appetites. Now in

our disgrace when we split off from the rest　　　85
we must exclaim the name of her who
debased herself inside that wood-framed beast.

So that's what we've done; that's our guilt. Should you
wish to know all our names, there are too many,
and not time enough to tell them, even if I knew.   90

As for myself, I'll satisfy your curiosity:
I am Guido Guinizelli, and because I was contrite
before death, I am well on my way to recovery.'

Like the sons who found their mother alive despite
the rage of Lycurgus, so I became, barely   95
restraining myself when his name came to light

since I recognised him immediately
as father to me and many a better name
that ply love's sweet and supple prosody.

I gazed upon him for the longest time,   100
lost in thought; struck deaf and silent
yet not approaching him because of the flame,

admiring him for an age until, at last content,
I offered my service to him, and mustered
my sincerest vows to convince him of my intent.   105

He said: 'You've impressed me with every word;
Not even the Lethe could abrogate
the clarity and conviction of what I've heard.

But if all you've spoken is the truth, state
why it is you regard me with such love as   110
your speech and manner demonstrate.'

And I replied: 'It is because of your exquisite verses
which, by the standards that we still hold dear,
make even the ink they're written in seem precious.'

'My Brother,' he said, 'this one I'd point you sooner   115
to', and he indicated a spirit ahead of us,
'as a better crafter of the vernacular.

His verses of love and tales of romance
were finer than anyone's. Let fools prattle on
about how great a bard was that chap from Limoges: 120

it's popular gossip that informs their opinion,
not the truth; they're passing judgment
that has no basis in artistic merit or reason.

The same happened with Guittone, in ancient
days: praise after praise was heaped on him, until   125
in time people came to a more sober assessment.

Now, should your privilege prove so ample
as to let you into that cloister where
Christ himself is abbot of the collegial

halls, say there for me a *Paternoster*   130
or whatever might best serve us in this place,
where sin is no longer within our power.'

Then as if someone else needed the space,
he disappeared quickly through the fire,
the way a fish darting through water might race   135

to the bottom. Edging forward, I stated my desire
to the one he'd pointed out, declaring myself ready
to make a welcome for his name. His answer

came freely: *'Your suit is fair and full of courtesy,*
so shroud myself from you I neither would nor may.   140
If it so please to know my name: Arnault I be,

who weeps and sings while making his way;
who sighs at sins past, each wrong-wrought thing,
and thrills in true hope of joy to come. I pray,

by the blessed power that shall soon bring   145
you to the summit of this winding spire,
you'll save some time to salute my suffering.'

And with that he faded into the purifying fire.

NOTES TO CANTO 26
Nick Havely

12-24. Dante's shadow is once again drawn attention to, as for instance in *Purg.* 5. 4-9, and the reminder of his bodily presence seems particularly appropriate in this part of Purgatory. The speaker in ll. 16-24 will name himself in l. 92 (see also below, ll. 73-5 and note).

40-2. The two examples of unbridled homosexual and heterosexual lust are Sodom (Genesis 18: 16-27 and 19: 1-29); and Pasiphae, wife of Minos, king of Crete, who was fated to lust after a bull and thus to give birth to the Minotaur (Ovid, *Met.* 8. 131-3 and 9. 735-40). The artificial wooden 'cow' into which Pasiphae entered to enable the bull to mount her (also mentioned in ll. 86-7 below) was designed by the mythical inventor Daedalus, and the allusion to the device may reflect upon the artistry of the love-poets here: their ingenuity glorifying a base urge.

43-5. Cranes are here imagined migrating in two directions: to escape the cold of the Riphean Mountains (believed to mark the northern boundary of Europe); and to flee the heat of the Egyptian desert. Lustful souls are also compared to a flight of cranes in *Inf.* 5. 46-8, but there the comparison focuses on the desperate sound of the souls' outcries; whereas here, as often in these later cantos of the *Purgatorio* (see the note on *Purg.* 19. 61-6, above), it conveys purposeful movement and direction.

73-5. The speaker here – as in ll. 16-24, above – is the Bolognese poet, Guido Guinizelli (d. 1296). His role as father-figure to Dante and others writing in the 'new style' of love poetry is obliquely reinforced in the original by rhymes which echo those of a sonnet Guinizelli wrote to his own poetic 'father', Guittone d'Arezzo (translated in the Postscript, no. 7a). Dante, as is evident here (esp. in ll. 97-9 below) greatly admired Guinizelli, especially for the latter's *canzone* 'Love finds its way into the noble heart' (also translated in the Postscript, no. 8). But he also recognizes certain limitations to the earlier poet's understanding and expression of love – as has been suggested by Virgil's comments on inadequate guides (*Purg.* 18. 18, above).

77-8. Julius Caesar was rumoured to have had a homosexual relationship with an Asian king and was thus mockingly hailed as *regina* (Suetonius, *De Vita Caesarum* 1. 49).

94-5. Hypsipyle's sons rescued her from execution which had been ordered by Lycurgus, King of Nemea (Statius, *Theb.* 5. 718ff.).

115-17. The 'better crafter' mentioned here by Guinizelli will name himself in l. 141 as Arnaut Daniel (c.1180-c.1210), another Occitan troubadour, who had been noted as a love-poet by Dante in *DVE* 2. 2. 9.

120. The 'chap from Limoges' is the Occitan troubadour, Giraut de Bornelh (c.1138-1215), who is referred to more respectfully by Dante as a moral poet in *DVE* 2.2.9.

124-6. Guittone d'Arezzo's limitations have already been emphasized in *Purg.* 24. 55-7, but his importance is also acknowledged by Dante, for instance through the oblique reminder of Guinizelli's respect for him (ll. 73-5, above; see the exchange of sonnets in the Postscript here, nos 7a-b).

139-47. The original has Dante's Arnaut speaking in his native Occitan and echoing the style of his love-poetry whilst transcending it. 'Dante endows no other soul in the *Purgatorio* with such beauty and fluency of expression in verse nor such concentrated and meaningful brevity' (*CL* 2: 789).

CANTO 27
Alvin Pang

As when the first rays of light scatter
over where the Maker's blood was
shed, and under high Libra falls the Ebro river

while the ninth hour parches the Ganges,
so stood the sun; here, day was departing,   5
when a glad angel of God appeared to us

Perched beyond the flames, he was singing
'Beati mundo corde!' with an air
more alive than the living.

Then: 'No way ahead nor around, fair   10
souls, but through the maw of flame: so brave
the blaze, and heed what's chanted there,'

he said when we were not far off;
when I heard him, I fell in such a state
I became as one given to the grave.   15

Holding out my hands against the heat,
I stared into the fire; my thoughts riven
with bodies I'd seen burning; charred meat.

My thoughtful escorts turned to me then;
and Virgil said: 'Son, here   20
there may be torment, but not death. Even

on Geryon's back – remember? Remember –
I led you safely on. What more
now, when God is near?

You can rest assured that even were   25
you to spend a thousand years within
this flame's bowels, you wouldn't miss a hair.

And if you think I am perhaps mistaken,
prove it to yourself. Hold up to the blaze
a corner of your clothing; see what will happen.   30

Put aside, put aside your dread. Face
the fire, and stride in, confident!' But still,
I was mulish, disregarding conscience.

He eyed me, all seized up and stubborn, until,
a little vexed, he said: 'Look, son: 35
between you and Beatrice stands this wall.'

As, hearing the name of Thisbe, nigh-gone
Pyramus opened his eyes, the day
the mulberry turned vermilion,

so too did my resistance fall away   40
as I turned to my mentor, at mention
of the name that in my thoughts ever holds sway.

At which he shook his head: 'Go on,
are you just going to stand there?'
he smiled, as at a child won over by an apple. Then   45

he stepped right into the fire,
asking Statius, who had been walking
between us, to bring up the rear.

As soon as I entered, I felt like throwing
myself into molten glass for solace,   50
so immeasurably intense was that blistering

heat. My kind father kept speaking of Beatrice
along the way, to comfort and cheer
me, saying: 'I can almost make out her eyes.'

A voice in song guided us from the other   55
side. Following attentively, we
emerged where the path led higher.

'*Venite, benedicti Patris mei*'
the voice sang, from within a light
so intense that it blinded me.   60

'The sun is setting and here comes night,'
went the song. 'Do not dally, pick
up your pace, lest the west fade from sight.'

The path climbed straight through the rock
at such an angle I saw my shadow before   65
me, with the low sun at my back.

We had barely gone a few steps further
when the sun set behind us: as I and the wise
ones realised, once my shadow was no more.

Before all of that immense   70
sky had become a single shade,
and night could rule the whole expanse,

each of us made a stretch of stair our bed;
for the nature of the mountain took from us
the will and power to move ahead.   75

Grazing goats are impetuous
and swift as they skip and sally
over the hilly peaks, but as soon as

they are sated, will lie placidly
in shade as their herdsman, leaning   80
on his staff, keeps watch quietly;

and as a shepherd, closely guarding
his flock, stays by them all night, lest
some beast sends them scattering,

so all three of us were there at rest: 85
I the goat, and they the herdsmen, watchful,
while on either side of us rose a rocky crest

obscuring my view; from what little
I did see of the stars, they seemed to me
brighter, clearer and larger than usual.   90

So, gazing upon and thinking about the
firmament, I fell asleep; the sleep that often
brings true tidings of what has yet to be.

It was the hour, I believe, when over the eastern
peaks first appears the light of Cythera, who   95
with the fires of love is always ardent,

that a lovely young woman appeared to
me in a dream; walking through a meadow,
she was gathering flowers and singing so:

'Whoever asks for my name, know   100
that I am Leah, and with my fine
hands a garland I now sew.

To look good in the looking glass, I adorn
myself, but my sister Rachel does not rise
from the mirror; she sits all night and morn   105

gazing upon her own beautiful eyes,
even as I beautify myself with my hands.
She is busy with reflection; I with enterprise.'

And now a predawn glow ascends,
the splendour that makes pilgrims happy   110
as, returning, they near their homelands,

and with the darkness fleeing on every
side, my sleep fell from me; I woke to see
the great masters already risen and ready.

'That sweetest of fruit, sought on so many   115
a branch to cure mortality's hunger, shall
today satisfy your craving fully,'

were the words bestowed on me by Virgil
and there was no gift I might have received
that could have been their pleasing equal.   120

More and more I meant to climb, moved
with each step by such an urge to rise
I felt my feet had grown wing-hooved.

Soon the entire stairway was below us
and we stood on the final step. That was   125
when Virgil turned to fix me with his eyes

and said: 'The temporal and the eternal blaze
you have seen, my son; now you have arrived at
the place past which my power cannot gaze.

I've led you here with intellect and art;   130
now let pleasure be your guide,
for you are past the steep and narrow rut.

See how the sun shines on your forehead;
look at the grasses, flowers and shrubs, that from
this soil have spontaneously sprouted.   135

While waiting for those fair eyes to come
whose tears dispatched me to your side,
you may sit or stroll among them.

Wait no longer for my word or nod;
your will is free, righteous and true,   140
so to do as you will is fitting and good:

Over yourself I crown and mitre you.'

NOTES TO CANTO 27
Nick Havely

1-4. Sunset in Purgatory is thus indicated cosmographically by the references to time at three other points (north, west and east) on the globe: Jerusalem, Spain (the Ebro) and India (the Ganges).

8. 'Blessed are the pure in heart' is the sixth of the Beatitudes in Matthew 5: 8. It is the last to be heard in the *Purgatorio*, and the rest of the verse ('for they shall see God') points forward to the completion of the souls' journey and to Dante's own visions in the Earthly Paradise and the *Paradiso*.

22 'Geryon's back' recalls the monster which carried Dante and Virgil down the abyss between the seventh and eighth circles of Hell. There, as here, the terrified Dante-persona was called upon to trust Virgil's judgment (*Inf.* 17. 79-99).

37-9. The story of the doomed lovers Pyramus and Thisbe and the tragic misunderstanding that leads to their suicides is told by Ovid in *Met.* 4. 55-166. The moments paralleled here are: when Pyramus, who has stabbed himself, thinking that Thisbe has been killed, momentarily revives when she returns and calls his name (*Met.* 4. 145-6); and when the mulberry tree which was their place of rendezvous has its berries turned from white to dark (*Met.* 4.165).

54. Virgil's reminder of Beatrice's 'eyes' both here and at the end of the canto (l. 136) draws its force from the image in medieval love-poetry, including Dante's.

58. 'Come, you blessed of my Father' is part of Christ's address to the redeemed souls in his prophecy of the Last Judgment (Matthew 25: 34).

91-6. Dante here imagines the planet of Venus (Cythera, l. 95) as appearing in the early morning, which was the time when dreams were believed to foretell the truth (compare *Purg.* 19. 1-6).

97-108. The dream about Leah and Rachel is the third and last of the pilgrim's morning-visions in the *Purgatorio*; the others are at the openings of cantos 9 and 19. This vision – with its contrasting images of action and contemplation – points forward in several ways to the Earthly Paradise in the following cantos and to the figures of Matelda and Beatrice whom Dante will encounter there.

110. Pilgrimage is a recurrent metaphor for the journey through Dante's Purgatory (for instance in *Purg.* 2. 63 and 8. 4-6), and it reinforces the sense of community as well as of renewal.

125-42. Virgil's speech is, as he announces in line 139, his final 'word' in the *Commedia*, although he will accompany the pilgrim into the Earthly Paradise, leaving only at the advent of Beatrice in *Purg.* 30. The lines embrace the span of the journey in the first two parts of the poem: the 'eternal' torments of hell and the 'temporal' ones of Purgatory (as at the start of this canto) in l. 127; the 'steep and narrow' paths of the mountain (132); and finally (136-7) it looks towards the reunion with Beatrice, who in *Inf.* 2 was said to have 'dispatched' Virgil to guide Dante up to this point.

CANTO 28
Percy Bysshe Shelley

Earnest to explore within and all around
The divine wood, whose thick green living woof
Tempered the young day to the sight, I wound

Up the [green] slope, beneath the [forest's] roof
With slow soft steps, leaving the abrupt steep   5
And the   aloof.

A gentle air which had within itself
No motion struck upon my forehead bare,
The soft stroke of a continuous wind

In which the passive leaves tremblingly were   10
All bent towards that [part], where earliest
That sacred hill obscures the morning air;

Yet were they not so shaken from their rest
But that the birds perched on the utmost spray,
[Incessantly] renewing their blithe quest   15

With perfect joy received the early day,
Singing within the glancing leaves, whose sound
Kept one low burden to their roundelay,

Such as from bough to bough gathers around
The pine forest on bleak Chiassi's shore,
When Aeolus Scirocco has unbound.   20

My slow steps had already borne me o'er
Such space within the antique wood, that I
Perceived not where I entered any more;

When lo, a stream whose little waves went by,   25
Bending towards the left the grass that grew
Upon its bank, impeded suddenly

My going on – waters of purest hue
On earth, would appear turbid and impure
Compared with this, whose unconcealing dew   30

Dark, dark yet clear moved under the obscure
Eternal shades, whose   [glooms]
The rays of moon or sunlight ne'er endure.

I moved not with my feet, but amid the glooms
I pierced with my charmed sight, contemplating   35
The mighty multitude of fresh Mayblooms;

And then appeared to me, even like a thing
Which suddenly for blank astonishment
Dissolves all other thought,

A solitary woman, and she went   40
Singing and gathering flower after flower
With which her way was painted and besprent.

'Bright lady, who if looks had ever power
To bear <firm> witness of the heart within,
Dost bask under the beams of love, come lower   45

[Towards] this bank, I prithee let me win
Thus much of thee, that thou shouldst come anear
So I may hear thy song; like Proserpine

Thou seemest to my fancy, singing here
And gathering flowers, at that time when   50
She lost the spring and Ceres her ... more dear.'

Michael O'Neill

    In the way, dancing, a woman
pivots, feet on the ground, close by each other,
    neither foot moving before the other one,

she turned to me upon the red flowers   55
    and on the yellow too, with the air
of a graceful maiden whose eyes are lowered;

and brought appeasement to my prayer,
    approaching me so closely her soft voice
was audible, its meanings clear.   60

    Soon as she'd reached the place where grass
starts to be washed by the shining river's tide,
    she granted me the gift of her raised eyes.

I don't believe so brilliant a light
    gleamed below the eyelids of Venus   65
when, by mistake, her son's barb hit.

    She smiled, upright, from the opposite side
as she gathered flowers with her hands,
    flowers the high earth grows without seed.

The river put between us three steps' distance;   70
    but Hellespont, where Xerxes once passed over,
a tale that still curbs human arrogance,

    did not endure more hatred from Leander,
because of the spate between Sestos and Abydos
    than I felt at that separating river.   75

'You're new,' she ventured, 'and perhaps because
    I'm smiling in this place chosen to be
the nest of all the human race,

    some doubt besets you wonderingly;
but what will give you light and banish clouds   80
    is the psalm entitled *Delectasti*.

And you who, asking me, have stepped forwards,
    tell me if you wish to hear more;
I came to satisfy you with my words.'

And I: 'The water and the forest choir   85
battle against a new faith in a thing
   of which I've heard the contrary before.'

Then she: 'I will give the reason explaining
   that which makes you wonder;
I'll purge the fog that lunges at your seeing.   90

   The Highest Good, whose being's its own pleasure,
made humans good, and for good, and He gave
   this place to man, eternal peace's forerunner.

But man defaulted soon and had to leave.
   But he defaulted, and chose tears and sweat   95
in place of joy and virtuous laughter.

   In order that the storms, created out
of breathings from the water and the ground
   that, to the degree they can, follow heat,

should cause no harm to human kind,   100
   the mountain rose this high towards heaven;
above the storms is where it is positioned.

   Now since all the air must turn
in a circle driven by the primal motion,
   unless the circuit is at all broken,   105

the motion, striking this mountain
   as it dwells freely in the living air,
then touches into music vegetation.

   And the struck forest has such power
it diffuses through the air its quality,   110
   essences the spinning air will scatter,

until the earth below, to the degree
   its soil is suitable and its climate,
conceives and rears tree-rich diversity.

If this were understood, then it   115
wouldn't seem strange down there how, without seed
   apparently, a plant will have its root.

You must have understood that the sacred
   fields where you stand are full of every seed,
and yield fruits which, down there, are not picked.   120

   The water which you see has not appeared
from a source nourished by rain's condensation
   like a river whose force has grown or faded,

but flows, strongly and steadily, from a fountain
   which regains as much by the will of God   125
as it spends on both parts of the terrain.

   On one side it pours down a powerful good,
that of erasing memory of sin;
   on the other, it restores any fine deed.

   On this side Lethe, Eunoë on   130
the other are the names, and neither functions,
   unless tasted on both sides in turn.

The taste outdoes gustatory sensations,
   and though your own thirst may now have passed,
and though I'll offer no more revelations,   135

   I'll give you a follow-up (you are graced);
and I don't think my words will be less dear
   to you if they exceed what I had promised.

Poets of old times, with their idea
   of the golden age and its happy state,   140
perhaps dreamt in Parnassus of this place here.

   Here human innocence took root;
here spring is lasting and each kind of fruit;
   this is the nectar of which poets write.'

Then I made a right-round, total   145
     turn to my poets, and saw that with a grin
they'd heard this last proposal;

then turned my face back to that courteous woman.

NOTES TO CANTO 28
Timothy Webb & Nick Havely

INTRODUCTORY NOTE TO LINES 1-51:

Percy Bysshe Shelley did not translate the whole of this canto (or any other), only the passage now widely known as 'Matilda Gathering Flowers'. Shelley's interest in Dante received a noticeable impetus when he moved to Italy at the end of March 1818 and within a few days started reading the *Divine Comedy*, which he soon finished. In spite of his critical attitude to Christian orthodoxy, its 'distorted notions of invisible things' and the traditional structures of its theology, Shelley was increasingly susceptible to a reading of Dante which recognized the pioneering importance of his writings and particularly the imaginative force of his poetry. Yet, for all his evident and sustained enthusiasm, this remarkable translation is Shelley's only known extended rendering from the *Divine Comedy*. Whether Shelley chose this passage simply because it was one of the acknowledged 'beauties' of Dante; or whether he discussed with Mary, when reading Dante together, the darker possibilities of the Proserpina story (the subject of one of her plays and the admitted centre of *Matilda*, her autobiographical fiction), must remain frustratingly uncertain. Alternatively, Percy Shelley's translation may once have been intended to illustrate a never-written essay on certain aspects of Dante (like his projected essay on versions of the devil which occasioned translations from Goethe and Calderón); or it may have been a self-delighting enterprise; or perhaps a poetic exercise, or an experiment in translation.

     The text in ll. 1-51 of the canto here follows Timothy Webb's edition of the manuscript (Oxford, Bodleian Library, MS Shelley adds. e. 6, fols 39-42) in *The Violet in the Crucible: Shelley and Translation* (Oxford: Clarendon Press, 1976), pp. 313-14, where minimal punctuation has been provided. Square brackets indicate a cancellation; angled brackets indicate an editorial conjecture. Further comments on the translation are on pp. 317-25 of Webb's study. The notebook in which the manuscript appears seems to point towards 1819 or 1820, although

Thomas Medwin attributed it to 1822. Crucially, though, Medwin didn't allow for the possibility that the poem dated from an earlier period and that Shelley had forgotten or discarded it, or did not think it sufficiently important for publication. No fair-copy seems to be extant, which strongly suggests that (just like one of Shelley's translations from Virgil, also in *terza rima*), this poem was not primarily intended, or still not ready, to appear in print.

Shelley's version is obviously unpolished, although for many years this was not apparent to readers since, when Medwin published a partial version in 1834, he filled in the gaps and rephrased the lines according to poetic convention. Shelley's version supplies several adjectives, which was also his usual practice with Greek texts and standard procedure for contemporary translators, who often allowed themselves considerable liberties. Sometimes he is troubled by the need to find a balance between a strict rhyme-scheme and the apparent import of the original. Although it may seem obvious now, Shelley's selection of *terza rima* (still highly uncommon in English poetry of that time) gives to his version formal resemblance to the Italian original together with freshness and fluency; this is often lacking in the versions of predecessors and contemporaries, such as Henry Francis Cary (much admired by Coleridge and Keats) whose blank verse is damagingly Miltonic in flavour, rhythm and phrasing and, for all its clarity and apparent simplicities, strikingly different from Dante.

EXPLANATORY NOTES:

6. Shelley did not complete this line, which in the near-contemporary version of *Purg.* by Cary (completed c.1807, publ. 1814) is translated as: 'the ground, that on all sides / Delicious odour breathed.' Shelley's *aloof* at the end of the line (like the cancelled readings in ll. 2 and 4) does not correspond to any words in Dante's original text; it signifies here that this kind of rhyme would eventually be needed.

11-12. The paradisal breeze blows from the east, associated with dawn and creation.

18-20. Chiassi is Classe, the port of Ravenna on the Adriatic coast, where the pine forest is said to rustle in response to the south-east wind ('Scirocco') which has been let loose by the god of the winds ('Aeolus').

32. Another line left incomplete in Shelley's translation. Cary's version has the stream flowing 'beneath perpetual gloom, which ne'er / Admits or sun or moon-light'.

39. The line is left unfinished, but is nonetheless highly successful in suggesting the effect of 'blank astonishment'. The translation is actually concise and complete, although it lacks the rhyme with *contemplating* (l. 35) and *thing* (l. 37).

40-2. The 'solitary woman' is not named (as Matelda) until the last canto of *Purg.* (33. 119); on her role and possible symbolism, see *DE* 599-602. Her appearance in the springtime scene here recalls 'the [lyric] *pastourelle* tradition, in which the narrator meets a beautiful shepherdess in a *locus amoenus* [idyllic place] and usually gains her favours; the most famous Italian example is [Guido] Cavalcanti's "In un boschetto", to which Dante here makes several allusions' (*DM* 2: 485). Cavalcanti's lyric is translated (as ' In a grove I saw a shepherdess') in the Postscript to this volume (no. 11).

48. Proserpina, daughter of Ceres (l. 51), goddess of crops, was abducted by Pluto, god of the underworld, and released for only part of the year: spring and summer (*Met.* 5. 385-571).

64-6. Venus's passion for Adonis was caused by an accidental grazing by one of Cupid's arrows (*Met.* 10. 519-32).

71-5. The Persian king Xerxes bridged the Hellespont strait separating Greece and Asia during his campaign against the Greeks (Lucan *DBC* 2. 672-3), but he was subsequently defeated at the battle of Salamis in 480 BCE. Leander of Abydos (ll. 73-4) was the lover of Hero, priestess of Aphrodite in Sestos, on the other side of the strait (Ovid, *Heroides* 18 and 19).

80-1. 'You have brought me joy (*delectasti*), Yahweh, by your deeds, at the work of your hands I cry out' is the fourth verse of Psalm 92 (*JB* version; Ps. 91 in the Vulgate), in which humanity praises divine creation. Matelda's allusion thus points Dante to the significance of what he is witnessing: the soul's recovery of Paradise as originally created before the Fall.

97-101. As Statius has explained earlier, normal effects of earthly weather extend only as far as the gate of Purgatory (*Purg.* 21. 46-51). According to medieval meteorology (deriving from Aristotle), phenomena such as storms were 'exhalations' of vapours from beneath the earth and sea.

130-2. The two rivers of the Earthly Paradise thus flow from a divine source (ll. 21-6), and, as the pilgrim will experience in cantos 31 and 33, immersion in them erases the memory of sin (Lethe) and restores that of good deeds (Eunoë).

139-47. 'Poets of old times' who imagined the Golden Age would, in Dante's book, have included Virgil (*Eclogues* 4) and Ovid (*Met.* 1. 89-112).

CANTO 29
A. E. Stallings

And thus she spoke, her words hovered,
and then she sang as one in love,
'Blessed are those whose sins are covered.'

And as nymphs in a dappled grove
would wander singly, one in gleam,   5
and one in gloom, so did she move,

along the riverbank upstream,
I kept pace on the other shore,
small steps in tandem like a team,

fifty steps, or scarcely more,   10
when both banks of the river bent,
so that I faced East as before.

It was not very far we went,
she turned and faced me in full sight.
'Look, brother, listen,' as she sent   15

my gaze to something sudden, bright,
that radiated through the wood,
much as a bolt of lightning might,

except a bolt of lightning should
cease soon as coming, this endured   20
and glowed the stronger – Oh what could

this be? I thought, and then I heard
a sweet tune through the bright air weave,
whence a good envy in me stirred,

to rue the recklessness of Eve,   25
in days when earth and heaven obeyed,
a woman, lone, new-formed, naïve,

could not stand any veil, a shade
that under which, had she been true,
I'd have lifelong a bower made   30

and tasted sweets untold and new.
And as among first fruits galore
delights eternal, I passed through,

wholly enchanted, wanting more,
beneath green boughs, air seemed to burn,   35
song was the sound we'd heard before.

If, Holy Virgins, you discern
I ever fasted, thirsted, lay
sleepless for your sake, in turn

I ask for my reward. Now may   40
Helicon's waters spring with ease,
and Urania's chorus help me say

things hard to think. Now seven trees
of gold appeared, so I believed,
since distance tricked the eye, but these,   45

on closer look no more deceived,
the first impression had been wrong,
and now my reason's power perceived

their common form – for all along
they were branched candlesticks… And soon   50
I heard '*Hosanna!*' in the song.

Above now, blazing light was strewn
brighter than cloudless skies are bright
at mid-month at the midnight moon.

And all amazement at the sight   55
I turned to Virgil; my good guide,
was no less stunned to see this light.

I turned my face to watch them glide,
the things on high: they moved so slow,
more slowly than a new-wed bride.   60

My lady then reproved me so:
'Why gaze at living lights in vain
and not what follows as they go?'

I saw the people in their train,
arrayed in white of such perfection   65
no earthly whiteness could attain.

And on the left, on my inspection,
the river held, as in a mirror,
my left side in its bright reflection.

I edged, till I could get no nearer   70
to the stream's bank, and closer to
the scene, my sight of it was clearer:

I watched the flames come into view,
the way they seemed to paint the air
like paint brushes of every hue,   75

the air above them kept the flare
of seven colours, like Heaven's bow,
or ribbons Delia would wear,

these seven banners stretched back so
I lost sight – but only ten, no more,   80
paces from outer glow to glow.

Beneath this fair sky, twenty four
elders were walking two by two,
and crowns of lily flowers wore.

They all were singing, 'Blessed are you   85
among the daughters of Adam – may
your beauty be blessed ever, too!'

The chosen people did not stay
and left the river bank still bright
with flowers and grass, and went their way.   90

As in the sky, light follows light,
so after them, four living things
came, in green leafy crowns bedight,

and each one had six feathered wings,
each feather full of many eyes   95
like Argus with his peacock rings.

More rhymes I cannot authorize
dear reader, on this theme alone.
I'm running low on rich supplies.

Go read Ezekiel, who has shown   100
them as he saw: with wind and cloud
and fire, dropped from the frozen zone,

as on his page these are avowed,
just so they were, with plumes to spare,
which John, along with me, allowed.   105

These creatures four marked off a square
in which a two-wheeled chariot flew,
drawn by a griffin through the air.

The griffin lifted up his two
wings in the mid-most band of light,   110
and cut no other light bands through,

so high, the wings were lost to sight.
His avian parts were gold, the rest,
mixed with vermilion, was white.

With no such chariot Rome impressed   115
Augustus or Scipio, none so grand;
the Sun's would seem but second best,

the Sun's car, which careened toward land,
and at the holy Earth's appeal,
was burnt by Jove's arcane command.   120

Three ladies by the right-hand wheel
came dancing, one so red was seen
that fire itself would near conceal;

another's flesh and bones were green
as though of emerald, and the last   125
shone white as snow's new-fallen sheen.

Sometimes the white or red one passed
to lead the dance; with song, the red
controlled their movements, slow or fast.

At the left wheel, with dancing tread,   130
four ladies whirled, in purple hue,
while one, with three eyes in her head,

kept time. Two men came into view,
old men, most differently arrayed,
though like in bearing, sombre, true.   135

The first was of the healer's trade
as great Hippocrates would seem,
by Nature formed for creatures' aid.

The second had a different theme,
he held a sword so sharp and bright,   140
I feared it, though across the stream.

Four humble men came into sight,
then after them an old man came
and seemed to walk asleep, despite

his keen look. This group dressed the same   145
as that first group of seven before,
except their crowns were red as flame,

and roses red, not lilies, wore;
above their eyebrows all would seem
ablaze, seen from the other shore.   150

The chariot stopped across the stream;
the thunder boomed: the noble crowd
came to a halt, so you would deem

passing those first banners not allowed.

NOTES TO CANTO 29
Nick Havely

3. *Beati quorum tecta sunt peccata* is the first verse of Psalm 32 (31 in the Vulgate). Matelda's song corresponds with the sequence of Beatitudes as pronounced by the angels on the terraces of the mountain.

25-30. The 'veil' that Eve is said to have spurned (l. 27) is probably a metaphor for the prohibition against eating the fruit from the tree of the knowledge of good and evil (Genesis 2:17). Dante's reversion here to the traditional anti-feminist trope of blaming Eve for the loss of Paradise (27-30) contrasts with the embodiment of Eden in this episode through prominent female figures such as Matelda (canto 28 and here), the Virgin Mary (85-7), the seven Virtues (121-32), and ultimately Beatrice (canto 30).

37-43. In Christianizing the nine classical Muses as 'Holy Virgins', Dante portrays the poet's vocation as comparable with religious devotion. 'Helicon's waters' (l. 41) were those of a mountain spring held sacred to the Muses and said to have flowed when the hooves of Pegasus, the winged horse and symbol of poetry, touched the ground. Urania (42) was the Muse of astronomy, and the appeal for her aid in expressing 'things hard to think' foreshadows the coming journey through the spheres of Paradise and the difficulty of describing it. As far as is known, Dante is the earliest writer in Italian to invoke the Muses (for example, in *Inf.* 2. 7 and *Purg.* 1. 7-9).

51. *Hosanna*, the Hebrew exclamation (originally meaning 'Save') greeted Christ at his entry into Jerusalem (Matthew 21: 9) and here celebrates the arrival of the symbolic pageant which will bring Beatrice. The beginning of the same biblical verse ('Blessed is he that comes in

the name of the Lord') will announce Beatrice's arrival in the next canto (*Purg.* 30.19).

54. The light of the seven 'candlesticks' blazing in the forest is thus compared with that of the moon when at its fullest.

78. 'Delia' is another name for Diana / Artemis, born on the island of Delos (*Purg.* 20. 132 and note) and associated with the moon. The 'ribbons' are therefore the rainbow colours visible in a lunar halo.

82-4. The language and imagery recall Revelation 4: 4, where the twenty-four elders represent the Books of the Old Testament. Their white crowns are the colour traditionally attributed to faith (as in l. 121, below).

85-7. The song combines the praise of an Old Testament heroine (Judith 13:23 and 15: 11) with the angel's greeting of the Virgin Mary as 'blessed among women' (Luke 1: 28). It also prefigures the appearance of Beatrice in the next canto (*Purg.* 30. 19).

91-3. The four 'living things' are emblems of the four Evangelists: the man (Matthew), the lion (Mark), the ox (Luke), and the eagle (John). Their appearance is compared to the way in which constellations appear to wheel around the sky 'light after light', and the green of their crowns suggests the hope for humanity conveyed by the gospels.

95-6. Argus was the shepherd with a hundred eyes who was assigned by Jupiter to guard the nymph Io (*Met.* 1. 68-746). Here the eyes on the wings of the Evangelists reflect how 'the Scriptural vision probes deeply into all things' (*CL* 2: 866).

100-5. In his portrayal of the four Evangelists Dante consciously draws upon prophetic visionaries of the Old and New Testaments (Ezekiel 1:4 and Revelation 4: 6-8), audaciously aligning his vision with those of the Scriptural authorities.

106-20. At the centre of the symbolic pageant, the 'chariot' displays affinities with the Hebrew Ark of the Covenant (see above, *Purg.* 10. 55-66), as also with the Ark of Noah and the Ship of St Peter, both of which came to symbolize the Christian community. Its two wheels (l. 107) signify how Christianity draws upon both the Old and the New Testaments. The 'griffin' drawing it is a mythical beast which was believed to combine features of two 'primate' creatures – the eagle and the lion – and it may here symbolize the two natures of Christ (divine and human), corresponding to the gold and red / white colours of its body (112-14), but for alternative interpretations see *DE* 454-6. The chariot itself surpasses two celebrated classical vehicles (115-20): that which featured in Roman victors' triumphs; and that of the Sun, which Phaethon attempted to drive with disastrous results (Ovid, *Met.* 2. 150-

328; Dante, *Inf.* 17. 106-8).

121-9. The three women dancing beside the chariot's right wheel symbolize, through their colouring, the three 'theological' virtues: Charity (red); Hope (green); Faith (white). A leading role is shared by the first and third of these (ll. 127-8), but the primacy of Charity, controlling the dance with her song, is acknowledged here (128-9), as it is by St Paul (1 Corinthians 13: 7 and 13).

130-2. Similarly, the four 'cardinal' or moral virtues (Prudence, Temperance, Fortitude and Justice) follow the chariot's left wheel. Prudence, like Charity (above), conducts the dance, following the traditional prominence given to this among the moral virtues (as in *Conv.* 4. 27. 5). Her three eyes (l. 13 2) represent awareness of past, present and future. On the relationship between the cardinal and theological virtues, see *Purg.* 8. 85-95, above.

133-41. The two 'old men, most differently arrayed' – one healer, the other a sword bearer – are identified with St Luke (described as 'the beloved physician' in Colossians 4: 14) and St Paul (often depicted with a sword, following Ephesians 6: 17 and the instrument of his beheading). They represent the sequence of New Testament books after the Gospels (Acts, composed by St Luke, then the Pauline Epistles), but the pairing also 'perhaps signifies that in God the inclinations to mercy and justice are always combined, cf. *Par.* 7. 105' (*CL* 2: 871).

142-50. The 'four humble men' following Luke and Paul represent the Epistles which (in the Vulgate) follow the Pauline texts – viz.: James, Peter (1-2), John (1-3) and Jude. The final solitary somnambulist with the 'keen look' (ll. 142-5) is the Apostle John, believed to have been the author of the visionary Book of Revelation, the last of the Scriptural texts. The crowning of all seven elders (including Luke and Paul) with roses 'red as flame' signifies their embodiment of Christian charity.

CANTO 30
Jane Draycott

And so the seven lights of Heaven came
　　to rest, those stars which never rise or set
or fade unless behind a mist of sin and shame,

those guiding lights that keep each spirit's sights
　　on track, just as our seven earthly stars　　　　5
mark out our safe route home and back to port.

The elders of the Truth now turned to face
　　the chariot from their place between the Griffin
and the stars, as if to face their peace.

And a voice among their number sang, like an envoy　10
　　sent from heaven, *'Veni, sponsa di Libano'* –
three times he sang, three times the others joined him.

Just as all blessed souls on Judgement Day
　　will rise from their darkened sepulchres and caves
and with re-embodied voices sing in praise,　　　　15

so now a hundred angels, ministers
　　and messengers of eternal life, rose
from the chariot to give that ancient call their answer:

in a single voice 'Blessed art thou that comest,'
　　they sang and scattered flowers to fill the air　　20
and ground, *'Manibus o date lilia plenis.'*

I have seen at the beginning of the day
　　the eastern sky a haze of rosy red
while all the rest serene and cloudless lies

and how the sun's face rising through the air　　　25
　　is shadowy and veiled, and how the mist
allows the eye to rest and linger there.

So in the same way, behind that cloud of flowers
　　which blossomed from the angels' hands and fell
below them in the chariot and around　　　　　　30

the figure of a woman appeared to me,
　　her dress like a live flame beneath her cloak
of green, her white veil wreathed in olive leaves.

And at that moment, although so much time
　　had passed since when I last stood trembling　　35
in her presence, dazed and overcome

even without looking at her now
　　my spirit felt the fire of that first love
once more, touched to the core by her hidden power.

In the instant that vision struck my heart again　　40
　　with all the force that first transfixed me then
when I was still a boy and hardly grown

in that very instant I looked to my left for Virgil
　　– just as a trusting child might run to find
his mother to tell her he's afraid or ill –　　　　45

to say to him 'Not a drop of blood remains
　　within my veins that isn't trembling now.
I know too well the signs of the old flame!'

But Virgil had left us there, diminished, small,
　　bereft – Virgil who'd been my dearest father,　　50
to whom I gave up both my self and soul.

Not all the Eden that Eve lost could now
　　prevent the tears from darkening these cheeks
which not so long before he'd washed in dew.

'Dante, now is not the proper time　　　　　　　55
　　to weep: though Virgil's gone, hold back your tears
for weeping at the cut that's still to come.'

At the sound of my own name (which I note
    here only because I must) I turned again
and there to the left side of the chariot,   60

like a great sea-captain pacing fore and aft
    on deck to oversee and stir the hearts
of men on other ships within his fleet,

I saw the lady, the *donna* I'd first seen
    veiled behind the angels' hail of flowers,   65
now gazing directly at me across the stream.

Even though her veil, crowned with a circlet
    of Minerva's leaves, fell down around
her face and kept her almost hidden from sight

still she held herself like a young queen,   70
    her voice severe and strict as if holding back
the even fiercer words she'd like to speak:

'Look closely. See who I am – I am your Beatrice.
    How do you dare to venture on this mountain?
Do you not know that here we live in bliss?'   75

I lowered my eyes to the clear stream between us
    but seeing my own face there, weighed down with shame
I moved my gaze towards its bank of grass.

Just then she seemed to me as a harsh mother
    seems toward her son; the taste of her disquiet,   80
sharp and deep, was the taste of all that's bitter.

At her silence, the angels sang: 'I put my trust
    in Thee' – '*In te Domine speravi*' –
but sang no further than 'Thou hast set my feet...'

Imagine how the snow on Italy's vaulted spine   85
    is frozen on the branches of its living beams,
blown and turned to ice by Russian winds

234 / After Dante: Poets in Purgatory

and how it melts then, trickling within itself
    when the breath of shadeless Africa returns,
as beneath a flame a candle burns and melts.   90

So I myself was frozen without tears
    or sighs until I heard that singing – note
for note the sound of the eternal spheres.

Something in the sweetness of their tone
    which seemed to speak of pity for me, as if   95
they sang: 'Lady, why do you shame him so?'

melted the ice which gripped me deep inside
    until it flowed from me as breath and water
from my mouth and eyes, and from my agonised heart.

The lady stood motionless, remained exactly   100
    in her place beside the chariot, then turned
her words on the angels who had shown me pity:

'In eternal daylight you all remain awake
    so neither sleep nor darkness can obscure
any step on the road the world below might take.   105

And so in answering I shall take great care
    to help this weeping man here understand
how guilt is bound in equal measure to tears.

Blessed by the workings of the wheeling planets
    that direct each seed toward its destined end   110
in conjunction with the course the stars have set

and also by the gifts of Heaven's graces
    whose showers fall like rain from clouds in regions
far too high for human eyes to trace

this man whose future looked so very bright   115
    should surely through good living and right action
by now have reaped the most miraculous harvest.

In truth however the richer the quality
    of soil, the wilder and more rank the growth
when an untended garden goes to seed.   120

For a time, I sustained him simply by my face:
    I turned my young eyes on him then and led him
in company with me along the paths of grace.

But once I crossed the threshold, travelling further
    onwards to my second life, he turned   125
his back on me and gave himself to others.

From flesh I rose to the spirit you see here,
    far greater now in virtuous power and beauty
though to him I seemed less lovely and less dear.

He turned his steps to wild and fruitless wandering,   130
    chasing illusive images of good
which promised much but always came to nothing.

I prayed I might inspire him through dreams
    and visions calling him back to me – but my prayers
were useless, so little did I matter to him then.   135

He had fallen so far I had only one last resort,
    one final strategy by which to save him:
to show him the fate of the souls already lost.

So I visited the gateway of the Dead,
    and to the spirit who has guided him up here   140
my prayers were carried with the tears I wept.

But the laws of God will not have been fulfilled
    if this man's allowed to cross the Lethe here
or drink the life-giving water from its pools

without first paying in tears his penitential dues.'   145

NOTES TO CANTO 30
Nick Havely

1-6. The 'seven lights' are those which have been seen leading the procession in canto 29 (ll. 43-54 and 73-8).

11. The first of several Latin quotations in this canto is from the Lover's address in the third poem of the Song of Songs: 'Come from Lebanon, my promised bride' (*JB* translation, 4: 8). The 'bride' was commonly allegorized as the Church, but here and in *Conv.* 2. 14. 20, Dante suggests that she represents divine wisdom (*CL* 2: 903), as the 'circlet / of Minerva's leaves' worn by Beatrice (l. 68) may confirm.

19-21. *Benedictus qui venis [in nomine Domini]* (quoted by Dante here again in Latin) are the words said to have greeted Christ on his entry into Jerusalem (John 12: 13). The biblical quotation is quickly followed by a classical one. 'Bring me handfuls of lilies' (l. 21) was part of a lament for the early death of Augustus's son Marcellus in *Aen.* 6. 867-86, and came near the end of the underworld encounter between Aeneas and his father Anchises. Here it acts as tribute (to Beatrice by way of Virgil) whilst foreshadowing another necessary departure: that of Dante's 'father', Virgil.

31-3. The colours of Beatrice's white veil, green cloak and red dress, are those of the three 'theological virtues' of faith, hope and charity (see above, *Purg.* 8. 85-93 and note).

34-42. Facing the shock of recognizing Beatrice after 'so much time', the Dante-persona recalls his early prose and verse work, the *Vita Nova*, which described his 'trembling' responses to her 'hidden power' in childhood and youth (*VN* 2. 4 and 14. 4). The drama of *VN*, which hinges upon the death and immediate afterlife of Beatrice, will also be recalled by her when reproaching him for his infidelity at the end of this canto (ll. 115-35).

46-8. Dante's proposed appeal to the now absent Virgil combines a further recollection of a scenario in *VN* ('trembling', l. 47) with a further tribute to the Roman poet (see l. 21, above) and his treatment of love and memory. Virgil's widowed queen Dido of Carthage acknowledges the force of her nascent passion for her Trojan guest Aeneas as the rekindling of a former flame: *adgnosco veteris vestigia flammae* (*Aen.* 4. 23).

53-4. The recollection here on the summit of the mountain of how his guide had cleansed the grime of Hell from Dante's cheeks at its foot (*Purg.* 1. 124-9) also acts as a recognition of the extent of the Virgil-character's role in the journey.

55. *Dante* is Beatrice's first word to be addressed to her lover in the *Commedia* and begins a ritual of penitence and reconciliation that continues into the next canto. Speaking of oneself without due cause was disapproved of by medieval rhetoricians (as Dante had noted in *Conv.* 1.2. 1-3), but naming as part of the penitential process is seen as necessary here (ll. 58-9), and this is the one time that Dante's name appears in the poem, perhaps as a kind of re-baptism.

68. Associated with the Greco-Roman goddess Minerva (Athene), the circlet of olive leaves (as in l. 33 above) signifies Beatrice's wisdom which will be drawn upon in the rest of the *Purgatorio* and almost all of the *Paradiso*.

82-4. The first eight verses of Psalm 31 (30 in the Vulgate), as sung by the angels during Beatrice's silence, are an expression of trust in divine guidance.

85-9. The 'spine' of Italy is the chain of the Apennine mountains, whose northern passes Dante would have crossed a number of times during his years of exile. The thawing of frozen snow on the trees ('living beams') in spring reflects the process of contrition (also seen as melting ice in ll. 96-9).

93. The angels' singing is said to mirror the pattern of the divinely determined cosmic order ('the eternal spheres') that will be experienced in the *Paradiso*.

115-35. Beatrice now revisits the scene of *VN* as Dante had done earlier (above, ll. 34-42 and 46-8), and she even uses the title of the work (*vita nova*) in l. 115 to refer to his 'bright' early promise; but her main concern is with Dante's straying from the path that could have been taken. His pursuit of 'illusive images of good' could in part refer to his devotion to Lady Philosophy, as celebrated in the third part of the *Convivio* – see *Purg.* 2. 112 and the poem prefacing *Conv.* 3, translated in the Postscript to this volume (no. 2). Beatrice's early guidance of her lover (ll. 121-3), her transformation from 'flesh to spirit' (ll. 124-8), and her appearance to him then in dreams and visions (ll. 134-5) are all features of *VN* (e.g., in chapters 11, 33, 39 and 51), and her words here can be seen as 'throwing a bridge over the years between that "little book" and this poem' (*CL* 2: 899).

139-41. Beatrice's descent through the 'gateway of the Dead' to Limbo and her tearful appeal to Virgil for help are reported by him at length near the beginning of the poem (*Inf.* 2. 52-117). That passage, like Beatrice's own version here, reinforces a sense of the journey's ultimate purpose.

CANTO 31
Jane Draycott

Without a trace of hesitation on her lips
    Beatrice continued, turning the sword-edge
of her speech full force towards its tip:

'Let's hear your thoughts from there across
    the river: tell the truth, and to gain pardon   5
facing such a charge, you must confess.'

I stood confused, all force drained out.
    I strained to speak – my words
were spent before they left my throat.

She waited just a moment – then asked, 'So?   10
    Is it not the case, the water hasn't yet erased
your darkest memories from you?'

Fear and panic together drove my faint reply,
    a 'Yes' so quiet on my lips
as to be audible only with the eyes.   15

You'll know how a crossbow drawn too hard
    will shatter string and bow and even arrow
making only the feeblest impact on its mark –

well, that was me as I broke beneath the stress
of her attack in floods of tears, my voice   20
a frail thing on my breath.

'And where,' she asked, 'in all your love
    for me – which taught you the greatest Good
we can hope for here or above –

where were the chains or fords across your path   25
    which proved so impassable as to make you
lose all hope of progressing farther?

What stronger fascination in the eyes of others
    lured you so strongly that you couldn't help
offering yourself up as a potential lover?'   30

I drew a long sigh, bitter, inward.
    My lips formed my reply
although I barely had the voice to answer:

'Instant pleasures, shallow things, misled
    me then' (I was weeping now). 'Once   35
I had lost sight of you, they turned my head.'

'Even if you'd not confessed,' came her reply,
    'your guilt would be no secret from Him
who sees everything you may try to hide

though if the sinner with his own lips self-accuses freely   40
    then the sword of justice, its blade reversed
against the whetstone, will cut less sharply.

Even so, to feel true shame and be the stronger
    for it, prepared against the next time
you might be tempted by those sirens' song,   45

you must stop sowing these tears and hear the ways
    you could have taken guided by my spirit
once my body lay in its grave:

nothing in art or nature pleased your mind
    more than the lovely framework of my limbs,   50
so soon to be scattered in the ground

so how, after what you treasured came to dust
    so plainly, could you trust in any earthly thing
to replace the happiness that you'd lost?

Once the vanity of earthly things had hurt   55
    you with its arrow you should have risen
above it – as I did when I left this mortal world –

instead of settling your feathers in the path
    of further hurt from some young girl or other,
pleasures of such short-term worth.   60

Only a fledgling who knows no better
    gets caught a second time, but the adult bird
has too keen an eye and ear to be shot again or netted.'

Like a young child silenced by their shame,
    eyes cast downward to the ground   65
and crying, knowing they are to blame

I stood there as she spoke: 'If what I now say
    makes you grieve, then raise your bearded chin
and see a sight to really make you cry.'

The sturdiest oak tree braced against   70
    gales from both our North and Africa
could not show more resistance than I did then

when on her orders I finally raised my eyes,
    so deeply wounded by her mocking reference
to my beard, my growing adult years.   75

I lifted my face, my gaze: I saw how
    the angels – beautiful, first-created beings –
were no longer scattering their flowers

and through my blurred, uncertain vision
    realised that Beatrice stood turned toward   80
the creature of two-natures-in-one-person.

Behind her veil across that stream she eclipsed
    the beauty even of the girl she'd been, more still
than she had outshone others when she lived.

Now the nettle-stings of regret hurt deeply in me   85
    and all I had been most inclined and drawn
to love became my hateful enemy.

Consumed with guilt, my heart now failed
    and felled me. What happened next is best
known to the woman who caused it all.   90

As I came to I saw above me the woman
    I'd earlier encountered on her own, saying
to me, 'Just hold on to me – hold on!'

as she pulled me across the river's drift
    behind her, up to my neck in water   95
as she skimmed the surface like the lightest skiff.

A sound of singing came from the sacred shore
    ahead: 'Purify me: a*sperges me.*' No words
to say how sweet that was to hear.

At this the lady stretched her arms out wider,   100
    gripped my head and dipped me deep
into the stream to make me drink its waters.

Then pulling me to shore she led me to the dance
    of the four lovely women, who made an arch
above me with their four raised arms.   105

'Here we are nymphs,' they sang, 'and in heaven
    we are stars. Before Beatrice descended to the world
we were her appointed hand-maidens.

We'll take you to meet her eyes: what's hidden
    in their radiant light's to be revealed by three   110
with deeper sight who will refine your vision.'

So they sang on and took me to where Beatrice
    was standing close near the Griffin's breast –
Beatrice, who now turned her face toward us.

'Don't be afraid to look at her,' they said, 'now   115
    that we've brought you here, in sight of those emerald
jewels from where love once aimed his arrows.'

A thousand longings burning worse than fire
    transfixed my eyes on her eyes as they gazed
without the slightest stirring at the Griffin there.   120

Like the sun in a mirror, that two-being'd creature
    shone reflected in her eyes, first in one form
then in the other aspect of its double nature.

Imagine, reader, the wonder of this being
    which in its deepest self remained the same   125
while in its image changed and changed again.

While my soul, astonished and delighted,
    fed on that nourishment which renews
appetite just as fast as it is sated

the other three moved forward, higher among   130
    the rest in rank and bearing as they danced
to the accompaniment of their own angelic song:

'Turn your eyes,' they sang, 'blessed Beatrice,
    toward your faithful follower, this man
who's travelled so very far to see your face.   135

And in your graciousness reveal
    your mouth and lips so he may see their beauty
also, kept hidden till now behind your veil.'

Ah! Brightest, timeless light! Any writer
    working in Parnassus' shadow, growing pale   140
there, drinking deeply from its waters

would visibly feel imagination's burden
    trying to find the right words for the way
you looked just then, the image of harmony in heaven

as in the clear air you unveiled your face.   145

NOTES TO CANTO 31
Nick Havely

11-12. The 'water' that washes away the 'darkest memories' (i.e., those of misdeeds) is that of the river Lethe, which as Dante imagines it here, flows between him and Beatrice (see below, ll. 94-102).

41-2. The image of the blunted blade signifies the tempering of justice with mercy (contrast Deuteronomy 32: 41, Isaiah 34: 5-6). Blunted blades are also wielded by the guardian angels in *Purg.* 8. 27 (and compare *Par.* 22. 16).

45. Dante's beguilement by the 'sirens' song' is a further allusion to the voyage of Ulysses, whose wanderings are evoked as a contrast to Dante's journey – as in *Purg.* 1. 130-3 and 19. 19-24.

59-60. Speaking of this 'young girl', Beatrice is probably referring to the female figures who had displaced her in Dante's poetry following the *Vita nova*. The 'other pleasures' would include those of earthly fame and knowledge – the latter celebrated through his praise of Lady Philosophy in the *canzone* prefacing *Conv.* 3 ('Love, speaking of her now within my mind', translated in the Postscript to this volume, no. 2).

80-1. The 'creature of two-natures-in-one-person' is the Christ-like Griffin, first described in canto 29 (108-14), and Beatrice's turning towards it probably reflects her role as intermediary between Christ and Dante.

91-2. The woman whom Dante has 'earlier encountered on her own' (see *Purg.* 28. 40-2) is Matelda.

96. The lightness of Matelda skimming the surface of Lethe may recall the angelic 'vessel so light and speedy' that brings souls to Purgatory in canto 2. 16-45.

98. *Asperges me* is part of the *Miserere* (Psalm 51: 7; 50: 7 in the Vulgate) and is a verse that has to do with rites of purification.

100-2. Matelda continues to act as a kind of priestess on behalf of Beatrice.

103-11. The 'four lovely women' are the four 'cardinal' or moral virtues, who were earlier portrayed dancing beside the left wheel of the pageant's chariot (*Purg.* 29. 130-2 and note). Their presence as 'stars' in the sky of Purgatory is mentioned earlier (*Purg.* 1. 22-7). The 'three with deeper sight' (ll. 110-11 here) are the 'theological' virtues (see *Purg.* 29. 121-9 and note).

124-6. Here as elsewhere in the *Commedia* (see above, *Purg.* 8. 19-30), a direct address to the reader highlights a moment of wonder.

136-8. The two main features of Beatrice's face that are evoked by the dancing Virtues – her eyes (l. 133) and mouth (here) – are those thought to reveal most clearly the workings of the soul, as Dante notes in *Conv.* 3. 8. 8.

139-45. The last tercets and the final line of the canto show Dante transcending the praise of the exalted, quasi-divine woman in earlier lyric poetry, such as Guinizelli's *canzone* and his own earlier poems; see the examples in the Postscript, nos 2 (ll. 23-56); 5 (ll. 15-50); and 8 (ll. 41-50). The 'timeless light' (l. 139) is that of divinity transmitted through Beatrice, and the expression of it strains the resources of the poet, even one who is granted inspiration from Parnassus (140), the mountain sacred to the Muses. The notion here of transcending the Muses in order to express what is ineffable in the vision points forward to language of the *Paradiso* – e.g., *Par.* 23. 55-66.

CANTO 32
John Kinsella

My eyes stick as tongue to pump nozzle,
that decade of thirst demanding relief
when overload leads to a collapse of the sensual,

when from every direction the weave
of holy face-off, of walls closing in without   5
an actual care for the world, the belief

forced on me via having my sight
twisted left to right, right to left, by a trio
of goddesses bullying me with 'You fixate!'

What can you expect when the ratio   10
of light to dark is tilted by a sunblast
that deprives me of my sight, here & now;

but the semantics of visuals recast
to suit the holier than thou, the diminution
compared to the intensity I had passed?   15

The rightwing always put on a vision-
splendid to leave sun-lookers awe-struck,
faces sevenfold-rampant with their flame-shine,

much like those tricks of battle that fuck
with our sense of good order, of accomplishment – 20
the lies of about-face and shields interlocked – luck

having nothing to do with celestial armaments,
the cannon fodder having advanced before the heavy
armour turns on a pinhead and augments.

And though these women are reduced to a 'bevy',   25
of interstices with the twist of the machine's wheels,
not a feather on the Griffin was ruffled by its levy.

And she who impelled me across the forgetful
waters now gathered us – Statius and myself –
within the circuit of the wheel within a wheel.   30

And with Eve-blame stimulated by the forest, himself
over herself like shelf fungus, the angel-music
suppressing serpents and denying her the rights of self.

And as time plays distance so it plays the politics
of measurement – the arrow in triplicate   35
is the spatiality of Beatrice's aeronautics.

And caught in the gender binary with the constellate
Adamic, they oscillate about the tree
whose limbs have been shaved of leaves and florets.

And this is what becomes of the tall trees   40
that spread a marvellous canopy as they grow –
the people whose land they share are robbed of liberty.

'But we untangle our thanks, O Griffin, as you sow
good by not consuming the lush and juicy foliage –
the greed that strips them is not Eve, but the middlebrow.'   45

And letting reality lapse we fall into the image
and allow the tree to remain upstanding and healthy:
'And so a record of past life is life for future's wreckage.'

And so to unravel the irony of the stealthy
loggers and miners and developers, he hauled   50
the shaft below the bough in ironic empathy.

As if the bulldozed are merely pollarded,
as if they'll burst again with growth and light,
(the allusion to Lasca falls as industry rewarded)

so our trees glisten in their fallen state,   55
so they grow briefly tense(s) before the sap fades
and dries and skins let the sun go back to its grate:

and the array of colours that are made
through decay – rose-violet enhancements –
are a surprise to those who believe what's filtered.   60

And though a music of achievement
is extracted from the screeds of *nature writing*,
it's hard to catch the sweetened tune and not lament.

And it's so easy to be lured into a feinting
sleep, a painted sleep, a setting of a model   65
that's all permissions and not the exploiting

eyes that wander across the rise & fall
of the heaving body, this hoodwinking, this
sleep while tuned to a better telling of Syrinx's tale.

But it's all in the waking and not the mist   70
of sleep, this confrontation with harsh light
outside the sheets, the guilt of 'Why *not* rise?'

It's the apple tree that holds the rights
to marriages made in heaven – a counter
story of who gets fed from what's   75

available as Peter, John and James appear
and though shocked pull themselves together
and reassess the cost of their siesta,

waking to a diminished number –
the absence of Elias and Moses;   80
and the refashioning of their Master;

so I quickly came to my senses
and saw she who had guided me with tolerance
along the river standing over me – 'Where is Beatrice?'

I asked while troubled by my conscience;   85
and she replied, 'There, follow the ascending
flock down to the seat beneath the now verdant branches,

fresh roots have sent new growth flowing
as her companions alongside the Griffin
sing earthsongs that reach out ring by ring.'   90

What she said was more complex than
my rendering as bathos, and it's only because
another woman comes into focus that I turn

to study *her* seated in the dust
as companion to the armoured car   95
which the hybrid creature had cause

to abandon there. But she was far
from alone – protected by a chorus
of those seven girls whose hands glower

safe from the biting easterlies and southerlies   100
'And so the forest becomes the sacristy
in which Christ joins Rome and you serve us.

And so to benefit a world that lives dishonestly,
consider the nature of that car and how it presents.
When back with *people* tell them of violence's ubiquity.' 105

And so, Beatrice. And so, I, who cannot prevent
the word of peace being rewritten as a permission
to ignore what she's suggesting could be heaven-sent.

And in the reversals characteristic of military nations,
the eagle is said to fall fast to rend the tree's regrowth 110
when in fact it is only a bird in image, a camouflaged drone

called Jove that fires and burns like the truth
that's acid rain, stripping away *real nature*
to its utilit, to its semantics of 'claw' vs. 'tooth'.

And he (the field marshal of space) made sure   115
the armoured car was left a smoking mess
amongst the storm of gases dust and manure.

And then, seriously, into that wreck's
burning frame I saw a Fox take cover,
a Fox that had been fed on depleted uranium bullets.   120

But as writer of the history with one over
him, my lady forced him out,
and pushed him as hard as he could suffer.

And then the drone dropped into the casket
of the car and spread an eagle's plumes –   125
a distraction while it gathered data to retort.

And the emblem of the heart that makes room
for compassion as all codes of war dictate said:
'What was heaven sent has been turned into a tomb.'

But where the seeds of conflict are laid for dead   130
between the wheels I see rise the Dragon,
a hypersonic 'rumour' that fills the West with dread,

and that the West will configure an equally malign
wasp with an individualised sting, a marvel, a joy
of measure, countermeasure, of retaliation   135

in the murk of annihilation, in the ploy
of better off dead, in the power holding on to power
globalism of capital shifting as feather and grass and toys,

as gentle as an arms conference, a war museum tour,
the shaft the drive the tracks pistons and bearings   140
that dress and redress the final gasp through lips of the other.

And you call this holy or is it just me that sings
its changes overwhelmed by heads appearing
on the edges and three from its driveshaft couplings?

All the hallucinogens they dish out in the making   145
of monsters – honestly, horned as oxen
and four like obscene unicorns (time / setting)!

And then slut-shaming, they *(they)* dish up a vixen,
a *whore* to wobble the nuclear family,
eyes everywhere, staring down from her mountain,   150

and then, laid on as conservatives reply
to accusations of branch-stacking, a giant is conjured –
and *they* were said to indulge in sex for *pleasure's sake* and to ply

each other with kisses, and then I see her lust-fired
eye on *me*, and though later it will be reported   160
that 'a giant' beat her, it was the righteous mob that attacked.

And in the turnings of truth, the fury unleashed
at the pacifists, the giant was monstered
and said to release a monster that burnt the forests to the ground.

And thus the NRA made capital from the dead.   165

NOTES TO CANTO 32
Nick Havely

The title of John Kinsella's version is: 'Terror of Capital and Dante's *Purgatorio* Canto 32'.

2. Dante's 'decade of thirst' ran from the death of Beatrice (1290; recorded in *VN*) to the imagined date of his otherworld journey (1300).

8. The 'trio of goddesses' are once again the 'theological' virtues of Faith, Hope and Charity, seen as classical deities. Their accusation of 'fixating' perhaps applies to Dante's harking back to his past and to the Beatrice of *VN*.

16-30. Like an army on the march, the chariot drawn by the Griffin (see *Purg.* 29. 106-30) now moves to the right, and Matelda, who has led Dante over the 'forgetful waters' of Lethe, guides him and Statius on its right-hand side.

31-42. On the 'blaming' of Eve along with the exaltation of Beatrice (l. 36) compare canto 29. 25-40. The return to Eden and the re-enactment of of the Fall are signalled by the encounter with the now denuded Tree of Knowledge (38).

43-60. Praise of the Griffin by the followers of the chariot focuses on Christ's obedience, avoidance of 'greed' (l. 45) and concern for justice (48), as indicated in Matthew 3: 15. The tethering of the chariot to the tree and the latter's subsquent renewal reflect the energies of the early Christian community. 'Lasca' (54), which in Tuscan dialect means 'fish' refers to the zodiacal sign of Pisces (Feb 19-March 20), preceding Aries and signalling Spring, renewal, 'growth and light'.

64-9. As the narrator falls into 'sleep', the strangeness of the vision that follows is signalled by the allusion to myth. How Mercury lulled to sleep Argus (guardian of Io, as in *Purg.* 29. 95-6) by telling the tale of Pan's love for Syrinx (l. 69) is described by Ovid in *Met.* 1. 671-721.

76. Peter, John and James were the apostles who witnessed Christ's transfiguration on the mountain (Matthew 17: 1-8, Mark 9: 2-8, Luke 9: 28-36) and are here emblematic of the early Christian church.

83-90. As in ll. 28-30, the unnamed guide is Matelda, waking the dreamer within the dream and pointing to Beatrice, who is placed humbly 'in the dust' (94) and is associated with Christ-like qualities (the Griffin) and with the moral and theological virtues, the 'seven girls' (99, as in *Purg.* 30. 129-32 and 31. 110-11 and 130).

103-5. Beatrice's words endow the dreamer with an authority comparable to that of Old Testament prophets such as Isaiah, and apostles such as St Paul and St John of Revelation.

109-65. Dante's vision imagines four main crises for Christianity, each portrayed by assaults on the chariot. The descent of the Eagle represents the ambiguous role of the Roman Empire as both persecutor and propagator of the faith (ll. 109-12). The subversion by the fox suggests division and heresy (118-23); whilst the other assaults recall visions of evil in Revelation: the Dragon in ll. 131-5 recalls Rev. 12: 3-9; the seven heads (143-7) are like the seven-headed beast in Rev. 17: 3-17; whilst the 'whore' who with the giant dominates the end of the canto evokes the *meretrix magna* of Revelation 17: 1-6 and 15-18.

CANTO 33
Patrick Worsnip

'*Deus, venerunt gentes*' – so began
    the women's sweet psalm; groups of three and four
    chanted alternately as their tears ran;
Beatrice, compassionate to her core,
    was downcast listening to them sing, and sighed – 5
    Mary at the cross was scarcely altered more.
The seven virgins paused now, to provide
    the chance for her to say what she would say;
    standing erect, her face fired, she replied:
'*Modicum, et non videbitis me*   10
    et iterum, beloved sisters of mine,
    modicum, et vos videbitis me.'
She placed all seven before her in a line,
    then moved the woman, the savant who'd stayed
    and me behind her with a single sign.   15
And on she went; I don't believe she'd made
    more than ten paces on the ground than she'd
    met my eyes with her own eyes and surveyed
me calmly, saying: 'Walk with greater speed,
    so that, if I should want to speak with you,   20
    you will be readier to pay me heed.'
When I had joined her, as I had to do,
    she said to me: 'Brother, do you not dare
    to ask me questions, now you're able to?'
Like those who have too reverent an air   25
    before superiors, and when they speak
    their voice comes to their mouth but lingers there –
that's how I felt: my tone halting and weak,
    I stammered out: 'My lady, you can see
    how to address my need, and what I seek.'   30
She said to me: 'I want you now to free
    yourself once and for all from fear and shame,
    and not keep talking in some reverie.
This I will say to those who bear the blame
    that the vessel the serpent broke is gone: 35
    the vengeance of the Lord comes just the same.

The eagle that had left its feathers on
    the chariot, which became a monster, then
    a prey, won't lack an heir a whole aeon;
stars are approaching that will grant to men –   40
    I see it clearly and can therefore state –
    free from all check and hindrance a time when
Five Hundred, Ten and Five, the delegate
    of God, will kill the thieving whore and hence
    the giant with whom she loves to copulate.   45
Perhaps you find my prophecies as dense
    as Themis' and the Sphinx's were; they block
    belief because, like theirs, they cloud the sense;
facts will soon be the Naiads that unlock
    the enigma I have posed, however hard,   50
    and without injury to grain or flock.
Note down the words I spoke in this regard;
    report them as they stand to those who race
    to live a life that ends in the graveyard.
Remember, when you write this, to leave space   55
    to include the tree – and how you witnessed it –
    which twice now has been plundered in this place.
To rob or damage it means to commit
    a sacrilege that treats God with disdain:
    He made it holy for His benefit.   60
For tasting it, Adam, in grief and pain,
    yearned five millennia for Him who redeemed
    that taste in His own person, being slain.
There is a special reason that tree seemed
    so lofty, with its roots upon its head: 65
    if you could not guess that, you must have dreamed.
Had not your idle notions overspread
    your brain, like Elsa's water, and their delight
    matched Pyramus tingeing the mulberry red,
you'd grasp, merely from that tree's form and height,   70
    how, placing it off-limits to mankind,
    the justice of the Lord was morally right.
But since I see stone set within your mind,
    and that you are both calcified and stained,
    so the light of my utterance made you blind,   75

I want these words sketched out, if not ingrained
   in you to take back, as a pilgrim's pole
   is wreathed round with a palm frond he obtained.'
I said: 'As sealing wax reflects the whole
   of the shape that's impressed on it, with no   80
   distortion, what you've said has stamped my soul.
But why do your words, which I wanted so,
   soar way above my sight? The more I force
   my eyes to follow them, the higher they go.'
'That's so you understand,' she said, 'the source   85
   of learning you pursue, and to make clear
   how far it lags, compared with my discourse;
and how remote the pathway that you steer
   is from the road of God – as long a haul
   as from earth to the highest heavenly sphere.'   90
To which I answered her: 'I don't recall
   estranging myself from you on even one
   occasion; conscience does not prick at all.'
'If you cannot remember what you've done,'
   she answered with a smile, 'then recollect: 95
   today you drank Lethe's oblivion;
if fire is proved by smoke – cause by effect –
   from so forgetting, guilt for your desire,
   that turned elsewhere, is what one would expect.
From now on, my pronouncements will aspire   100
   to be stripped bare, to disclose what I mean
   as clearly as your crude vision could require.'
With slower steps and with a brighter sheen
   the sun was hugging the meridian ring,
   which varies by the point from which it's seen, 105
when, as an escort who's accompanying
   a group, walking before them, often will
   stop if he finds a trace of some strange thing,
just so the seven women here stopped still
   near thin shade like mountains cast, under trees' 110
   green leaves and black boughs, on an icy rill.
In front I thought I saw the Euphrates
   and Tigris issue from one origin,
   then flow off, like friends parting ill at ease.

'You light and glory of all people in   115
   the world, what are these waterways that well
   up here, then split from where they both begin?'
The answer to my question was: 'To tell
   you that, request Matelda to reply.'
   As though she had some censure to dispel,   120
the lovely woman said: 'He has had my
   account of this and much else; I've no doubt
   that Lethe's water did not veil his eye.'
Beatrice said: 'Perhaps thinking about
   more pressing things, which are well known for slowing 125
   the memory, blocked his mental vision out.
But see Eunoë – over there it's flowing:
   lead him to it, and then, as is your use,
   contrive to get his failing powers going.'
Like noble souls, which offer no excuse,   130
   but take their plan from what another planned
   as soon as outward signs have set it loose,
the moment she had taken me in hand,
   the lovely woman moved and said to Statius
   'Come with him', in a womanly command.   135
Reader, if my manuscript were more capacious
   to write on, I'd describe – if not in full –
   that nectarous draught that left me still voracious.
But, as it is, this second canticle
   has run through all the pages designated: 140
   art's bridle, then, makes that impossible.
I made my way back feeling renovated
   from that most holy stream, as new plants rise,
   green with new shoots and reinvigorated,
pure and prepared to scale the star-filled skies.   145

NOTES TO CANTO 33
Nick Havely

1-3. In response to the desolation wrought at the end of the previous canto, the seven Virtues sing the psalm which laments the desecration of the Temple and the sacking of Jerusalem: 'O God, the nations have come into your inheritance' (Ps. 79; 78 in the Vulgate). The psalm later appeals for divine intervention and deliverance, as Beatrice will do in this canto (ll. 34-57), and with its mixture of despair and hope, it is the last of the biblical and liturgical songs to be heard in the *Purgatorio*.

10-12. Beatrice's response to the psalm is to quote Christ's words before the Crucifixion: 'In a short time you will no longer see me, and then a short time later you will see me again' (John 16:16) – once more (as in ll. 1-3) combining the experiences of loss and hope.

13-15. Beatrice choreographs the scene, with the seven Virtues in front of her and Matelda, Statius ('the savant who'd stayed') and Dante behind.

23. Addressing Dante as 'brother' recalls the use of the term by other souls (see *Purg.* 11. 82 and note). Here it admits Dante to a quasi-religious role as acolyte of Beatrice.

34-51. Beatrice's prophecy summarizes the damage done to the Christian community at the end of the previous canto, whilst also foretelling its deliverance. The agent of that deliverance is portrayed in deliberately cryptic terms as 'Five Hundred, Ten and Five' (DXV in Roman numerals, so perhaps an anagram of 'DUX' [leader]). Prophecies of divine intervention and vengeance recur throughout the *Commedia*, but here – as with the mysterious 'Greyhound' in *Inf.* 1 – the scale of the futurity envisaged renders the terms of the prophecy obscure, and Beatrice compares her words with the riddles of classical antiquity: those of Themis (*Met.* 1. 347-415) and the Sphinx at the gate of Thebes (*Met.* 7. 759-61). The obscurity she acknowledges is not helped by her identification of 'Naiads', the river nymphs (l. 49) as solvers of the riddle of the Sphinx (the mistake derives from a corrupt medieval version of *Met.*, where 'Laiades' [the patronymic name of Oedipus] was mis-spelled). The solving of the riddle and the subsequent death of the Sphinx was avenged by Themis through the devastation of the Thebans' 'grain' and 'flocks' (51).

52-78. The symbolism of the 'tree' of knowledge of good and evil (l. 56), which in the previous canto has been 'plundered' by both the Eagle and the Giant, here becomes a key element in Beatrice's interpretation of the vision. On one level it is associated with divine 'justice' (72), whose workings Dante will continue to wrestle with in the *Paradiso*. The 'idle notions' (67) which prevent Dante from understanding the significance of the 'lofty' inverted tree (64-5) will be linked more broadly to the limitations of his philosophy (85-90, below). Here in ll. 68-9 they are compared to the calcifying effect of the river Elsa (tributary of the Arno) and the staining of the mulberry at the death of Pyramus (see *Purg.* 27. 37-9 and note). The allusion to the Pyramus story (*Met.* 4. 55-166) draws together the ideas of misunderstanding and self-destructiveness.

Beatrice's emphasis here on Dante as the 'pilgrim' making sure to report her words (56) and get them right (76-8) takes up the *Purgatorio*'s recurrent image of pilgrimage (e.g., in *Purg.* 2. 63, 8. 4, 13. 96, 23. 16, and 27. 110), whilst also reflecting this final canto's consciousness of acts of interpretation and of writing, as in ll. 136-41, below.

85-90. The 'source of learning' that Beatrice rejects was probably a form of Aristotelianism associated with Ibn-Rushd ('Averroes'), to which Dante had earlier been attracted and according to which 'human reason was in itself adequate for the understanding of universal truths' (*CL* 2: 974).

104. The apparent slowness of the sun's movement around its zenith at mid-day is the first signal of the passing of time since Dante's entry into the Earthly Paradise.

112-13. The two rivers of Mesopotamia were thought to have their common source in the Earthly Paradise (Genesis 2: 10-14).

115-16. Praise of Beatrice as 'light and glory' of humanity recalls Virgil's tribute to her at the start of Dante's journey (*Inf.* 2. 76-8).

118-27. The Dante-persona has, appropriately, forgotten Matelda's explanation about the sources and features of the rivers in the Earthly Paradise (*Purg.* 28. 121-33). Eunoë – the river that restores the memory of goodness, as Matelda had explained there – is an invention of Dante, whereas Lethe ('erasing memory of sin') derives from classical myth.

136-45. The final address to the reader draws further attention to the act of writing through its emphasis on poetic direction through 'art's bridle' (l. 141). It combines with the subsequent images of renewal, growth and ascent (143-5) to end the *Purgatorio* with a sense of dual purpose through the linkage of the poem's two I's: the pilgrim and the poet.

Postscript: Around *Purgatorio*

*Poems by Dante, his predecessors
and contemporaries*

translated by
Peter Hainsworth and Nick Havely

1. Dante to Guido Cavalcanti

Sonnet 'Guido i' vorrei'
translated by Nick Havely

Guido, wouldn't it be wonderful if we
were all swept up by Merlin's magic spell,
launched in a bonny boat, skimming the swell,
sailing just where we pleased – you, Lapo, me –   4

where stormy skies, or turmoil out at sea
would not disturb our voyage nor dispel
our growing wish that we might always dwell
like that, close friends in perfect harmony?   8

To complement our friendly sorcerer's crew,
Vanna and Lagia could both come – and she
whom once I listed thirtieth in that song;   11

and love would be our subject all day long –
which would ensure that each of them would be
happy, just as, I think, we should be too.   14

2. Dante

Canzone 'Amor che ne la mente mi ragiona'
translated by Nick Havely

Love, speaking with great yearning in my mind,
breeds such strong memories of her in me
with images of her, so frequently
that following them my thoughts run all astray.
Such is the sweetness of his speech, I find,   5
that, though I listen so attentively,

my soul laments its inability
to follow what his words about her say.
And so I fail utterly to portray
in writing what those things Love told me were; 10
for human understanding cannot reach,
nor can my powers of speech
voice even partly what I heard of her.
Hence, if my verses cannot here find ways
to speak of her, let my weak wits incur 15
the blame for failing to express her praise –
and our language that lacks the resource
to render what Love said in all its force.

Nor as the sun spins round us in its sphere
does it see anything on earth as fine 20
as at that hour when it lets radiance shine
on the woman of whom Love has me tell.
The minds of angels turn to her; and here
on earth her image is firm-fixed sign
for her true followers when their hearts incline 25
to love, and when Love casts his peaceful spell.
Her soul's Creator finds himself so well-
pleased that on her bounteously
he pours more power than humans could expect.
So, having no defect, 30
her soul draws on God's grace continually,
revealing it through actions every day:
beauties abound in her so potently
that, when they shine on us, they make their way
straight to the heart, images from the eyes 35
that breed desire that then draws breath as sighs.

Upon her such celestial powers flow
as with the angels gazing on God's light;
and those who do not recognize such might
should follow her and see it openly. 40
And when she speaks, bending to us below,
love's messenger appears now to our sight
affirming that her virtue has attained a height
surpassing this world's worth immeasurably.

Her gentle gestures when in company   45
vie with each other, calling on Love's grace
with eloquence demanding to be heard.
So you may trust my word:
womanliness here finds its noblest place;
beauty is only what resembles her.   50
And we affirm that looking on her face
makes us believe that miracles occur
through which our faith is now sustained;
for thus it was eternally ordained.

Wonders shine forth in her appearance   55
and figure forth the bliss of Paradise;
for in her eyes and smile I recognise
that Love makes manifest his presence there.
They overcome our weak intelligence
like sunlight dazzling enfeebled eyes;   60
hence, as my sight itself does not suffice
to render them, my words must seem threadbare.
Her beauty rains sparks of fire, and there
nobility burns as in a constant flame,
breeding the aspirations that win praise.   65
Those lightning shafts erase
the innate faults that give us such deep shame.
So, madam, should you be criticised
– your lack of modesty open to blame –
see in her modesty eternalised.   70
She makes humble those who're wilfully blind:
she was the thought in the First Mover's mind.

My song, you seem to take a different view
from that of your own sister; she would say:
'This modest woman that you here portray   75
I should instead call arrogant and loud.'
But as the heavens remain clear and blue,
unmarked by flaws they might seem to display
to our eyes, which for many reasons may
find the stars darkened as by cloud –   80
so, when that other poem calls her proud,
it does not see her in the proper light,

but only as she might then have appeared.
Indeed my soul once feared,
and yet again fears what once had given fright,   85
for in her sight those feelings still may stir.
So make your case, if it seems to you right,
then say, as you present yourself to her:
'I worship you, and, if you wish it so,
shall speak of you wherever I may go.'   90

3. Sordello

Planh, 'Planher vuelh en Blacatz'
translated by Peter Hainsworth

I want to weep in simple song for Sir Blacatz,
with a bleak, baffled heart, and in that I'll be right,
since with him I have lost a lord and a fine friend,
and every sign of value with his death is lost.
So deadly is the damage that I am afraid   5
only in one way can it ever be made good;
cut out his heart, I say, for the great lords to eat,
who've lost what heart they had, then they'll get some heart back.

Let first eat of the heart, since he has serious need,
the Emperor of Rome, if he will force defeat   10
upon the Milanese, who hold him beaten down,
deprived of his inheritance despite his Germans.
And close behind let the French king come to eat.
Then he'll recoup Castille which folly's let him lose,
though if his mother frets, he will not take a bite,   15
since it's well known he dares do nothing to upset her.

I want the English king, since he is feeble-hearted,
to tuck into it hard. Then he'll be strong and fit,
and get the country back, and not be so ill thought of,

being robbed by the French king, who knows how null he is. 20
And the Castilian king should really eat for two,
because he has two kingdoms and can't manage one.
But if he wants to eat, he ought to eat in secret,
for if his mother heard, she get a stick and beat him.

I'd like the king of Aragon to eat some too,   25
for it would lift the weight of shame from off his back
for Marseilles and Millais round here, since otherwise
nothing he says or does can now restore his honour.
And then I'd like some heart for the king of Navarre,
who was a better count than he is king, I hear.   30
It's criminal when God lifts someone to great grandeur,
for their own feeble-heartedness to pull them down.

The count of Toulouse must eat up a largish portion,
if he compares his present and his past possessions.
For if another's heart doesn't make good his losses,   35
I think he'll hardly manage it with just his own.
And the count of Provence should eat some too, recalling
that losing your inheritance makes your life worthless.
Although he struggles valiantly and keeps on going,
he needs to be fed some heart given all his burdens.   40

Great lords will wish me ill for what I say so well;
I tell them they're as low for me as I for them.

Fair Recompense, so long as you will show me mercy,
I'll write off anyone who's not a friend of mine.

4a. Bonagiunta da Lucca to Guido Guinizelli

Sonnet, 'Voi ch'avete mutata'
translated by Peter Hainsworth

You are the one who's made a change
in the love poetry that we once enjoyed,
giving its being a quite different form,
in order to surpass all other poets.   4

What you have done is what the light can do
that gives brightness to places that are dark,
and yet not here where the high sphere is shining
with a surpassing, supreme clarity.   8

You are supreme in complicatedness,
and no one can be found to make it plain,
so dark is the discourse that you deliver.   11

It's widely held wrong-headed aberration,
even with learning that comes from Bologna,
to draw out poems from texts that one has read.   14

4b. Guinizelli's reply

Sonnet 'Omo ch'è saggio'
translated by Peter Hainsworth

A man who's wise doesn't start running lightly,
but marks his steps as measure tells him to.
And after thinking, he holds back his thought
until there's confirmation that it's true.   4

He's mad who feels only he sees the truth
and doesn't think it interests others too.
A man must not esteem himself too highly,
but bear in mind his status and his nature.   8

Birds fly the air in their peculiar ways
and have quite varied modes of operation;
not all have the same flight or the same mettle.   11

God set the world and nature on a scale,
and made wit and intelligence unequal.
Therefore a man must not say what he's thinking.   14

5. Dante

Canzone 'Donne ch'avete intelletto d'amore'
translated by Peter Hainsworth

Ladies who have some insight into love,
I want to say a poem to you about my lady,
not that I think I can do her full justice,
but speech can maybe give the mind relief.
I tell you when I think how superlative she is,   5
I feel Love send such a sweet surge through me
that if I then did not lose confidence,
people would fall in love to hear me speak.
I shan't aim though at such exalted discourse
that nervousness would rob me of resolve.   10
My treatment of her nobleness will be
a light one, considering what she is,
and addressed to you, ladies and girls in love,
since it's not something for the world to hear.

An angel calls out in the mind of God,   15
saying, 'Sir, we can see down in the world
a marvel being realised and it's from
a soul whose radiance reaches even here.'
Heaven, where no defect can be found except
she is not there, requests her from its Lord,   20
and every saint shouts for him to show mercy.
On our side we have only Pity, in the words
that God (who fully knows my lady) says:
'My loved ones, now accept it peacefully
if your hope stays as long as pleases me   25
there where there's someone who expects to lose her,
and who will say in Hell, "You ill-born souls,
I saw her whom the blessèd hope to see."'

My lady is desired in highest heaven.
I want to tell you now about her virtues.   30
I mean, that a lady wanting to impress as noble
should go with her, for as she walks down the street
Love injects a chill into ignoble hearts,
that makes all their ideas ice up and perish.
Any of them who could bear to look at her   35
would either become noble or else die.
And when she does find someone who deserves
to see her, they feel her virtue take effect:
something happens to make them better people,
humbling them so they forget any slight.   40
What's more God has given her a greater grace:
a few words with her rules out ending badly.

Love asks of her, 'How come a mortal thing
can be both so lovely and so pure?'
Then he looks again and swears to himself   45
God's purpose was to make her something special.
She has almost a pearliness, the kind
a lady should have, not excessive.
She is all the best that Nature can create,
the standard by which beauty should be measured.   50
With every single movement of her eyes,
spirits of love come from them all ablaze
that wound the eyes of those who see her then,

and pass through, every one finding the heart.
You ladies see Love's image in her face,   55
there where no one can bear to look for long.

I know, my poem, that you will go and speak
with numerous ladies, once I set you free.
My admonition now, since I have raised you
as one of Love's young, unassuming daughters,   60
is that you ask, whatever place you reach:
'Teach me which way to go, for I've been sent
to find her with whose praises I'm adorned.'
And if you don't want to go on in vain,
don't stop off where ignoble people are.   65
Do what you can to let yourself be seen
only by ladies or a gentleman,
who'll take you to her by some rapid route.
You will discover Love is there beside her.
Remember me to him as is your duty.   70

6. Giacomo da Lentini

Sonnet 'Io m'aggio posto in core'
translated by Nick Havely

I'm set on serving God so very well
that I'll go straight to heaven, come the day:
to paradise where, as I have heard tell,
blest souls remain eternally at play.   4

Yet that would surely be no place to dwell,
if her bright face, blonde hair were far away.
Bliss there, unpartnered, would be more like hell;
parted from her, I don't think I could stay.   8

But saying that, of course I wouldn't mean
to commit sin of any sort up there.
I only want her beauty to be seen: 11

her sweet face and her quiet, thoughtful stare.
Then all my thoughts would stay calm and serene,
Seeing her rise to brightness in the air.   14

7a. Guido Guinizelli to Fra Guittone

Sonnet 'O caro padre'
translated by Peter Hainsworth

O my dear father, starting praising you
is not a thing for any to embark on,
for your mind's not a place that vice dare enter,
before the arrows of your wisdom see it off.   4

It slams the door on every sort of evil
although there's more about than cash in Venice.
Your soul has joy among the Friars Joyous
whose joys I think are superjubilant.   8

Accept this poem that I submit to be
chiselled and polished by your know-how,
for you are the one master that I turn to.   11

It's certainly not bound together firmly,
so check each bracket holding it together
to smoothe the flaws with your adjustments.   14

7b. Fra Guittone's reply

Sonnet 'Figlio mio'
translated by Peter Hainsworth

Delightful son of mine, the praise you fire
at me is not, I think, shot with discretion.
It is unwisdom to enjoy hearing praises,
even if the praiser really hits the mark.   4

And so my heart won't praise me praising you,
although you merit praise and do praise well.
Praising makes a fine man seem less praiseworthy,
and it's the wise who say that, not the asses.   8

But if I take you for a worthy son,
I don't wish to diminish you at all,
and hurry happily to sing your praises.   11

That generous grace of calling me your father
(which signals a contented son) I welcome,
so long as there's some truth in your perception.   14

8. Guido Guinizelli

Canzone, 'Al cor gentil'
translated by Nick Havely

Love finds its way into the noble heart,
as birds in leafy forests find their nests;
Nature did not create love before
the noble heart, nor did that precede love;
for when the sun first shone,   5
brilliance of light was born at the same time,
where no light was before;

and love forms part of true nobility
just as, inherently,
heat glows within the brightness of a flame.   10

The flame of love kindles the noble heart
like magic power in a precious stone;
for that power is transmitted by a star
only when the sun's rays have ennobled it;
when they have fully drawn   15
out of the stone all its unworthiness,
the star then gives it worth:
so, for the heart that Nature has created
distinct, pure, and fine,
the loved woman acts just like that star.   20

And love thus lights upon the noble heart
as a flame does upon a torch's tip,
dancing and flickering there, gleaming and clear,
by nature destined to burn only there.
But when unworthy souls   25
meet love, it's water cast on fire,
or heat clashing with cold.
Whilst love finds refuge in the noble heart,
that is its kindred form,
as iron-ore in the mine bears diamonds.   30

The sun may shine all day upon the dirt;
dirt it remains, nor does the sun's heat fail.
The vain man says: 'I'm noble from far back',
but he's just dirt; true worth is like the sun.
And one thing is for sure: 35
that true nobility dwells in the heart,
nor can it be passed on
to those who are not noble in themselves,
for pure water reflects
the radiance that heaven's stars retain.   40

Brighter than sunlight dazzling our eyes below,
God the creator shines upon heaven's powers.
Heeding their maker, mover of heaven's spheres,

the stars and planets wheel at his command;
And as, immediately,   45
our God's just will is perfectly fulfilled,
so it is right that she
whose beauty dazzles her noble lover's eyes
kindles in him desire
never to disobey what she commands.   50

Love, as I meet my maker at the last,
he may well ask my soul: 'What did you mean?
You scaled the heavens all the way up here
to use me as a profane simile.
Such praise should be for me   55
and for this noble kingdom's worthy Queen
who puts falsehood to flight.'
I'd answer him: 'An angel from above
is how she seemed to me;
I was not then so wrong to fall in love'.   60

9. Guido Guinizelli

Sonnet, 'Chi vedesse a Lucia'
translated by Nick Havely

Looking at Lucy with that fur-trimmed hood
framing her face, perfect in every way,
you'd say: from Naples to this neighbourhood,
no bloke would not be smitten straightaway.   4

In that cute trim she surely looks as good
as any French or German posh girl may.
And a snake's head severed never could
throb like she makes my heart do every day.   8

Taking her then, even against her will,
kissing her mouth and that cute face of hers,
and then that pair of fiery, sparkling eyes   11

But stop – don't do it, don't fulfil
that urge: it might make things much worse;
That way, my friend, far greater trouble lies.   14

10. Arnaut Daniel

Sestina 'Lo ferm voler q'el cor m'intra'
translated by Peter Hainsworth

My heart's let a fixed fancy enter
that beak cannot tear out of me, nor nail
of meddler with vile tongue arming his soul.
Since I can't risk hitting with branch or stick,
at least by stealth, there where I have no uncle,   5
shall I enjoy love's joy in bower or chamber.

When I call back to mind the chamber
where to my cost I know no man can enter,
(all treat me worse than brother could, or uncle),
I've no limb not a-shake, no, not a nail,   10
more than a child who has to face the stick,
so scared am I she too much owns my soul.

Her body take me, not her soul!
And cunningly conceal me in her chamber!
It hurts my heart more than blows from a stick   15
that where she is her servant cannot enter.
I'll always be to her as flesh to nail,
indifferent to reproof of friend or uncle.

Even the sister of my uncle
I did not love so much, by this my soul.   20
As close to her as finger to its nail,
if she agreed, I'd be within her chamber.
Love twists me since my heart has let it enter
more than a strong man playing with a thin stick.

Since flower bloomed first on a dry stick   25
and from Sir Adam nephew came or uncle,
a love as fine as that my heart feels enter
was not I think in body nor in soul.
Whether she goes about or stays in chamber,
my heart stays closer to her than a nail.   30

My heart thus fits and clamps its nail
to her more tightly than bark to a stick.
She is joy's tower, its palace and its chamber.
I love her more than cousin of mine or uncle,
and Paradise will doubly joy my soul,   35
if there by fine love ever man may enter.

Arnaut despatches song of nail and uncle
to please her with the stick that arms his soul,
his Desirée, by merit entering chamber.

11. Guido Cavalcanti

Ballata, 'In un boschetto trova' pasturella'
translated by Nick Havely

In a grove I saw a shepherdess,
a star, I guess; no less she seemed to be

I saw below her fair and curly hair
her eyes alive with love, cheeks rose and white;

a crook to keep the young lambs in her care;   5
her feet unshod, bathed in the dew of night.
She sang as though her heart were set alight,
her beauty bright with such variety.

Greeting her then, just in a friendly way,
I asked if she was wandering on her own,   10
and sweetly she answered: yes, that day
she was there in the forest all alone,
and said: 'But when the chirping bird has flown
it shall be known, a love will come for me.'

Once she had told me what was in her heart,   15
and when I heard birds in the forest sing,
I told myself: 'It's time to make a start
and taste the joy this shepherdess may bring.'
So I implored her for a single thing:
a kiss in Spring – if she would willingly.   20

Most willingly she took me by the hand,
declaring: 'Now I give my heart to you',
and led me through that leafy springtime land,
through grass where flowers of all the colours grew
and where I felt joy and delight and knew   25
the God of Love still flew, as I could see.

12. Cino da Pistoia

Canzone 'Su per la costa, Amor, de l'alto monte'
translated by Nick Havely

Up there, Love, on the crags of that high peak,
using the skill and style of poets' speech,
who can still climb,
now that the wings of genius lie broken?

I know well that the waters have run dry   5
within the spring where all who gazed might see
their flaws exposed,
if they looked carefully upon that glass.
    O, just, true God who pardons graciously
all those who reach repentance at the end,   10
take this keen soul,
who throughout his whole life tended the plant
of love, to Beatrice's arms at last.

NOTES ON POEMS 1-12
Nick Havely

1. Dante to Guido Cavalcanti, sonnet, 'Guido i' vorrei'.
Addressed to Guido Cavalcanti, the sonnet is a 'wish-poem' celebrating friendship between poets. The imagined voyage will be developed somewhat differently by the metaphorical 'little skiff 'of *Purgatorio* 1. 2, but the idea of the magic boat continues to fascinate Dante in the *Commedia* (for example in *Purg.* 2. 22-45 and *Par.* 2. 1-18). Guido himself is mentioned a number of times in Dante's work (see the note on no. 11, below). In chapter 6 of the *Vita Nova* Dante mentions having written a poem listing 'the names of the sixty most beautiful women in the city [of Florence]'. Beatrice is there said to have been be placed ninth, so the woman 'listed at thirtieth' must be someone else, possibly the *gentil donna* whom Dante says he made a 'screen' for his love of Beatrice (*Vita Nova* ch. 5-6).

2. Dante, *canzone*, 'Amor che ne la mente mi ragiona'.
The lyric that Dante's Casella begins to perform in *Purgatorio* 2. 112-14 is this *canzone*, placed at the beginning of the third treatise of Dante's earlier work: the incomplete *Convivio* (c.1304-7) and celebrating a figure whom Dante later identifies as 'that lady of the intellect who is called Philosophy'(*Conv.* 3.11.1). Without actually naming Lady Philosophy, the *canzone* begins to assert what the third treatise of the *Convivio* will go on to demonstrate: her supreme role in reflecting and communicating divine power in the created universe (ll. 37-72). Expression of that supremacy and ineffability becomes in Dante's poem a tense and challenging exercise – and in order to convey some of that tension the translation has here attempted to replicate the complex rhyme-scheme of the original.

3. Sordello, *planh*, 'Planher vuelh en Blacatz'.
In *Purg.* 6 (ll. 58 onwards) Dante imagines an encounter with Sordello – the 13th century Lombard poet who wrote entirely in Provençal. In this 'complaint' on the death of Blacatz, the concerns with inadequate rulers reflect those expressed in the 'Valley of the Princes' (*Purg.* 6-8) and must have prompted Dante to portray Sordello as his guide in those three cantos.

4a. Bonagiunta da Lucca to Guido Guinizelli, sonnet, 'Voi ch'avete mutata'.
In *Purg.* 24. 50 and 57, Dante's Bonagiunta praises the 'new rhymes' and the 'style so sweet' of the love-poetry produced by Dante and his circle – in direct contrast to what the historical Bonagiunta says here about such verses (by Guinizelli and others) being obscure, over-complicated and an 'aberration'.

4b. Guinizelli's reply, sonnet, 'Omo ch'è saggio'.
Guinizelli's somewhat evasive answer – perhaps suggesting that the 'man who's wise' could say more but won't – is perhaps comparable to the Dante-persona's somewhat offhand treatment of the Bonagiunta of *Purg.* 24.

5. Dante, *canzone*, 'Donne ch'avete intelletto d'amore':
In *Purg.* 24. 51, Dante's Bonagiunta quotes the opening line of this *canzone*, which is the first lyric in this form to feature in *VN* (ch. 19). In *VN* it occupies a key position in the work's development of verse praising Beatrice and associating her with divine love, power and creativity (ll. 15-56). It is probably Dante's earliest serious venture in a form which he was to describe in *DVE* 2.3.3 as 'far and away the most excellent'; and it helped to establish his reputation as a love-poet, circulating separately, for instance in a late 13th-century Florentine manuscript (now Vatican MS 3793).

6. Giacomo da Lentini, sonnet, 'Io m'aggio posto in core'.
In *Purg.* 24. 55-7, Dante's Bonagiunta speaks of 'the knot / that held back the Notary, Guittone and me / from getting to that style so new so sweet'. The 'Notary' was Giacomo da Lentini who was mentioned as the Emperor Frederick II's 'faithful scribe' at the Imperial court in Sicily between 1233 and 1240. Giacomo's poems include 38 sonnets (a form which he probably invented) and this example plays with the idea of transforming erotic passion in a way that anticipates the more serious explorations of the 'new style' poets, such as Guinizelli and Dante.

7a. Guido Guinizelli to Fra Guittone, sonnet, 'O caro padre'.
In *Purg.* 26. 73-5, Dante's Guinizelli, amid the flames in the circle of those expiating lust, greets the pilgrim with images and rhyme words that echo the historical Gunizelli's tribute to Guittone d'Arezzo in the first of these sonnets. The father-son relationship between poets is also adopted by Dante when speaking of Guinizelli in *Purg.* 26. 97-8,

although the latter (like Bonagiunta in *Purg.* 24. 55) will address his fellow-poet as 'Brother' (115).

7b. Fra Guittone's reply, sonnet 'Figlio mio'.
Guittone is under-rated by Dante in *Purg.* 24. 55-7 and by Dante's Guinizelli in *Purg.* 26. 124-6. His sonnets, political poems and letters represent a significant achievement, which Dante seems to have needed to downplay, in order to stake a claim for the new generation of poets. He adopts a somewhat tortuously modest stance, particularly in the second quatrain of this sonnet, perhaps reflecting the 'knotty' style criticized in *Purg.* 24. 55-6.

8. Guido Guinizelli, *canzone*, 'Al cor gentil'.
In *Purg.* 26. 112-14, the Dante-persona acknowledges the influence of Guinizelli's 'verses which ... make even the ink they're written in seem precious.' This *canzone* was well-known to Dante and he quotes from it a number of times: in the tenth sonnet of *VN* (ch. 20) and on several occasions in *DVE*. It encompasses a transition from the old to the new style: moving from the imagery and concerns of earlier Tuscan poetry to the transformation of the lady and of love in the last two stanzas (ll. 41-60). The first *canzone* of Dante's *VN* (above, no. 5) builds upon Guinizelli's scenario here.

9. Guido Guinizelli, sonnet, 'Chi vedesse a Lucia'.
In *Purg.* 26 the Dante-persona has to leave Guinizelli behind on the terrace of souls expiating lust, as he moves through the wall of flame separating him from Beatrice, and it was obviously important for Dante the poet to transcend his predecessor. There is no specific evidence about what the historical Guinizelli might have needed to be 'contrite' about (*Purg.* 26. 91-3), but several commentators have suggested that the contemplation of sexual assault in the sestet of this sonnet may to Dante have indicated an instinct needing to be refined.

10. Arnaut Daniel, *sestina*, 'Lo ferm voler q'el cor m'intra'.
Near the end of *Purg.* 26, Dante's Guinizelli introduces the Provençal poet Arnaut Daniel (b. 1145/50) as 'a better crafter of the vernacular' whose 'verses of love [...] were finer than anyone's' (ll. 117-19), and the latter then uses his own (Occitan) language to seek the pilgrim's prayers before disappearing again 'into the purifying fire' (139-48). Dante was himself influenced by Arnaut in the use of the difficult *sestina* form (using six rhyme-words in intricate permutations) which the latter probably invented, and he lists the Provençal poet among the practitioners of 'illustrious *canzoni*' in *DVE* 2.6.6 and 2.13.2. The *sestina* above displays Arnaut's technical skill and in its sixth stanza raises the question of how 'fine love' might relate to the quest for 'Paradise' (ll. 35-6).

11. Guido Cavalcanti, *ballata*, 'In un boschetto trova' pasturella'.
In *Purg.* 28 (especially ll. 37-75) the encounter between the Dante-persona and Matelda, precursor of Beatrice, amid the idyllic landscape

of the Earthly Paradise can be seen as Dante's deliberate transformation of the erotic scene in this contemporary *ballata*. Guido Cavalcanti here adopts the *pastourelle* form (where a footloose male narrator meets a lone woman in a spring setting and wins – or seeks to win – her love); and he uses an intricate verse form, including *rimalmezzo* (rhyme in the middle of lines). Cavalcanti is named as one of Dante's poetic colleagues and rivals in *Purg.* 11. 97-8 (as also earlier in *Inf.* 10. 60-3). Like Dante, he was of a Florentine mercantile family with some claims to nobility, and he is also referred to as a friend in the commentaries to Dante's love poems in the *Vita Nova* (chapters 3, 25 and 30). His work (also referred to in Dante's treatise on language and poetry, *De vulgari eloquentia*) was usually in a more serious vein and came to be seen as key to the development of learned love-poetry in what Dante's Bonagiunta calls the 'sweet new style' (*Purg.* 24. 57).

12. Cino da Pistoia, *canzone*, 'Su per la costa, Amor, de l'alto monte'.
Cino (1270-1336/7) was a contemporary of Dante: a friend who is mentioned a number of times in *DVE*, a fellow-exile and a poet in the 'new style'. This *canzone* on the death of Dante (1321), of which the first of three stanzas is translated here, develops its tribute through a series of allusions to the *Commedia* – beginning by merging the mythical mountain of Apollo and the Muses with the 'high peak' of Purgatory, on which the Dante-persona encounters – among others – the souls of contemporary poets in the course of his ascent to Beatrice. Cino was master of a cogent, plain and harmonious style, which is evident in his poems on the departure of Beatrice, on exile, and in commemoration of the emperor Henry VII. As this *canzone* also shows, he was particularly good at goodbyes.

MARY JO BANG (cantos 1, 4-5 and notes) is the author of eight books of poems, including *A Doll for Throwing*, *Louise in Love*, *The Last Two Seconds*, and *Elegy*, which received the National Book Critics Circle Award. Her translation of Dante's *Inferno*, illustrated by Henrik Drescher, was published by Graywolf Press in 2012. Her translation of *Purgatorio* is forthcoming from Graywolf in 2021. She has co-translated, with Yuki Tanaka, *The Poetic Experiments of Shuzo Takiguchi 1927-1937*. She has received a Hodder Fellowship from Princeton University, a Guggenheim Fellowship, and a Berlin Prize Fellowship. She teaches creative writing at Washington University in St. Louis.

COLIN DONATI (cantos 19-20) is a Scottish poet of third-generation Italian descent who lives somewhat precariously in Edinburgh. He is a regular performer of his work and has issued collections with Kettillonia and Red Squirrel Press. As musician, he performs his songs and song settings in the duo 'Various Moons' with cellist Robin Mason. He is also a translator of Dostoevsky into Scots, editor of the collected dramatic works of Robert McLellan, *Robert McLellan, Playing Scotland's Story* (Luath, 2014), and currently serves as trustee on the board of Scottish PEN.

JANE DRAYCOTT (cantos 30-1) is a UK-based poet with a particular interest in audio and collaborative work. Her most recent collections from Carcanet include *Over*, short-listed for the T. S. Eliot Prize, *Pearl*, her award-winning translation of the medieval dream-elegy and *The Occupant*, written following her time as Writer in Residence in Amsterdam. A Next Generation poet, her work has been nominated three times for the Forward Prizes for poetry. Her 2017 translations, *Storms Under the Skin: Selected Poems of Henri Michaux (1927-1954)* is published by Two Rivers Press.

STEVE ELLIS (cantos 13-14, 16-17 and notes) is Emeritus Professor of English Literature at the University of Birmingham. Among his many volumes of poetry and books of criticism is *Dante and English Poetry: Shelley to T. S. Eliot* (1983, reprinted 2010). His verse translation of the *Inferno* was published in 1994 and has been reprinted several times, and was extensively revised for inclusion in his translation of the complete *Divine Comedy* (Vintage Classics, 2019).

ANDREW FITZSIMONS (cantos 23-5) was born in Ireland and lives in Tokyo. His books include *What the Sky Arranges* (2013), *A Fire in the Head* (2014) and *The Sunken Keep* (2017), a translation of Giuseppe Ungaretti's *Il Porto Sepolto*, all from Isobar Press. His translation of *The Complete Haiku of Bashō* will be published by the University of California Press in Spring 2022.

JONATHAN GALASSI (canto 18) has translated the poetry of Eugenio Montale, Giacomo Leopardi, Primo Levi and others, including most recently a selection of Montale's poems for Everyman's Library's Pocket Poets (2020). He has also published several volumes of poetry and a novel, MUSE (2015), and serves as president of the American publishing house Farrar, Straus & Giroux in New York.

LORNA GOODISON (canto 12) is the Poet Laureate of Jamaica 2017-2020. She is the recipient of the 2019 Queen's Gold Medal for Poetry and the 2018 Windham Campbell Prize for Poetry from Yale University. The author of twelve collections of poetry including *Collected Poems* published by Carcanet Press in 2017, three collections of short stories, an award winning memoir, *From Harvey River*, and a collection of essays, *Redemption Ground*, she is Professor Emerita in the Department of English and the Centre for African and Afroamerican Studies at the University of Michigan.

PETER HAINSWORTH (Postscript nos 3-4, 7 and 10) is an Emeritus Fellow of Lady Margaret Hall, Oxford. After lectureships at Hull and Kent Universities, he taught at Oxford until retiring in 2003. As well as *Petrarch the Poet* (Routledge, 1986), he has written widely on other Italian authors, medieval and modern. He co-edited, with David Robey, *The Oxford Companion to Italian Literature* (OUP, 2002) and co-authored with him a *Very Short Introduction to Italian Literature* (OUP, 2012) and a *Very Short Introduction to Dante* (OUP 2012). He has also published two volumes of translations: *The Essential Petrarch* (Hackett 2012) and *Tales from the Decameron* (Penguin 2015).

NICK HAVELY (editor; Introduction, Notes and Postscript nos 1-2, 5-6 and 11) is Emeritus Professor of English and Related Literature at the University of York. His recent publications include *Dante* (Blackwell Guides to Literature, 2007) and *Dante's British Public: Readers and Texts, from the Fourteenth Century to the Present* (OUP, 2014). He has received Leverhulme and Bogliasco Fellowships and was recently elected an Honorary Member of the Dante Society of America. Current projects are a collection of essays, *Dante Beyond Borders: Contexts and Reception* (to be published by Legenda in 2021) and a book on travellers in the Apennines.

JAN KEMP (Prelude, poem 1) was born in New Zealand and granted an MNZM in the Queen's Birthday Honours 2005. She lives in Germany where she is preparing a Dante Video 2021 with musicians and readers based on poems from *Dante Down Under* (2017). Recent publications are her collected short fiction *Spirals of Breath* (2019) and her ninth collection of poems *Black Ice & the Love Planet* (2020); see www.tranzlit de. *Raiment – a Quarter Century as a Kiwi: a memoir 1949-1974* is forthcoming in April 2022 (Massey University Press). Kemp is writing new poems for *the dancing heart.* See also https://poetryarchive.org/poet/jan-kemp/.

JOHN KINSELLA's (canto 32) most recent poetry volumes include *Drowning in Wheat: Selected Poems* (Picador, 2016), *The Wound* (Arc, 2018), *Insomnia* (Picador, 2019) and *Brimstone: A Book of Villanelles* (Arc, 2020). He has also written fiction, criticism, and plays, and often works in collaboration with other writers, artists and musicians. He is a Fellow of Churchill College, Cambridge, and Professor of Literature and Environment, Curtin University, Western Australia. His many encounters with Dante include the book-length works *Divine Comedy: Journeys Through a Regional Geography* (W. W. Norton, 2008) and *On the Outskirts* (University of Queensland Press, 2017), an engagement with William Blake's illustrations to the *Divine Comedy.*

ANGELA LEIGHTON (Prelude, poem 3; cantos 9-11) is a critic and poet at Trinity College, Cambridge. She has published many critical works, among them *On Form: Poetry, Aestheticism, and the Legacy of a Word* (OUP, 2007) and *Hearing Things: The Work of Sound in Poetry* (Harvard, 2018), as well as five volumes of poetry. Her fourth volume, *Spills* (Carcanet, 2016), includes poems, memoirs and short stories, as well as translations, both strict and free, of the poetry of the Sicilian author, Sciascia. Her most recent (fifth) volume, *One, Two* (Carcanet, 2021) contains translations of the poetry of Pirandello.

ROB A. MACKENZIE (canto 15) is from Glasgow and lives in Leith. He is reviews editor for Magma poetry magazine and runs literary publisher, Blue Diode Press. His poems and translations have appeared in many publications and anthologies, including a translation of Salvatore Quasimodo in *The FSG Book of Twentieth Century Italian Poetry* ed. Geoffrey Brock (Farrar, Straus & Giroux, 2012). His most recent poetry collections are *The Good News* (2013) and *The Book of Revelation* (2020), both published by Salt.

JAMIE MCKENDRICK (Prelude, poem 2; canto 8) was born in Liverpool in 1955, has published seven books of poetry, most recently *Anomaly*, and two *Selected Poems*. He edited *The Faber Book of Twentieth-Century Italian Poems* and has translated poetry from Valerio Magrelli (*The Embrace*) and Antonella Anedda (*Archipelago*) as well as the six books of Giorgio Bassani's *The Novel of Ferrara*. His book of essays about art, poetry, and translation, *The Foreign Connection*, was published by Legenda in 2020.

BERNARD O'DONOGHUE (co-editor; cantos 2 and 6-7) is Emeritus Fellow of Wadham College Oxford. He has published ten collections of poetry, including *Gunpowder* which won the Whitbread Poetry Award in 1995 and *Selected Poems* (Faber 2008) and he has translated the great Middle English romance, *Gawain and the Green Knight* for Penguin. He is currently translating another major medieval poem, Langland's *Piers Plowman*, whilst also working on a comprehensive new edition of Seamus Heaney (both for Faber). He is a Fellow of the Royal Society of Literature and Honorary President of the Irish Literary Society of London.

MICHAEL O'NEILL (Prelude, poem 4; cantos 21-2 and 28, ll. 52-148) was Professor of English at Durham University. His critical studies include *Romanticism and the Self-Conscious Poem* (OUP, 1997), *The All-Sustaining Air: Romantic Legacies and Renewals* (OUP, 2007) and *Shelley's Reimaginings and Influence* (OUP, 2019). He was the co-editor of *The Oxford Handbook of Percy Bysshe Shelley* (2013), and an editor on the multi-volume Johns Hopkins edition of Shelley's poetry. His poetry includes *The Stripped Bed* (Collins-Harvill, 1990); and *Wheel* (2008), *Gangs of Shadow* (2014), *Return of the Gift* (2018) and *Crash & Burn* (2019), all published by Arc.

ALVIN PANG (cantos 26-7) is a Singaporean poet and editor, and an Adjunct Professor of RMIT University. Featured in the *Oxford Companion to Modern Poetry in English*, and the *Penguin Book of the Prose Poem*, his writing has been published in more than twenty languages, including Swedish, Macedonian, Croatian and Slovene. He is a Fellow of the Iowa International Writing Program, and a board member of the International Poetry Studies Institute. His collection *When the Barbarians Arrive* was published by Arc in 2012, and his latest books include *What Happened: Poems 1997-2017* (Math Paper Press: Singapore, 2017) and *Uninterrupted Time* (Recent Work Press: Australia, 2019).

A. E. STALLINGS (cantos 3 and 29) is an American poet and translator who lives in Greece. Her most recent poetry collection, *Like* (Farrar, Straus and Giroux), was a finalist for the Pulitzer prize. Her recent verse translations include *Hesiod's Works and Days* (Penguin Classics) and an illustrated version of the pseudo-Homeric *Battle Between the Frogs and the Mice* (Paul Dry Books). She has received fellowships from the Guggenheim, United States Artists, and MacArthur foundations.

TIMOTHY WEBB (Note on an edition of canto 28, ll. 1-51) is a Senior Research Fellow and Professor Emeritus at the University of Bristol. He has written and lectured widely on Romantic topics (especially Mary and Percy Shelley, Byron and Leigh Hunt), and on Irish topics (especially Joyce and Yeats, whom he has edited for Penguin). He has particular interests in classical and in particular Greek influences on English writers, in Italian dimensions to Romanticism, and in translation. His two-volume annotated edition of Leigh Hunt's *Autobiography* is soon to be published by Oxford University Press. Work in progress includes an investigation of English Romantic writers and Ireland.

PATRICK WORSNIP (canto 33) read Classics and Modern Languages at Merton College, Oxford and now lives in Cambridge. He worked for more than forty years as a foreign correspondent for Reuters, reporting from over eighty countries and covering stories ranging from the collapse of the Soviet Union to the conflicts in the Gulf. Since retiring in 2012, he has devoted himself to translation, mainly of poetry. His version of the complete poems of Propertius, published by Carcanet Press in 2018, was a Poetry Book Society recommendation. Apart from Dante, he is currently working on the poetry of Umberto Saba.

To begin with, Bernard O'Donoghue must be acknowledged as a begetter and nurturer of the present venture. From the start, his inspiration, advice and encouragement – as well as his practical assistance in enlisting contributors – have been invaluable. As the title-page acknowledges, without his companionship and collaboration the idea of this book would never have taken shape nor continued to publication.

This version of the *Purgatorio* has developed over more than a decade. Among the earliest contributors was Michael O'Neill who sadly did not live to see it published, although his verse still travels Dante's hillside here. Michael's 'poem about Purgatory' was written while he was re-reading Dante in 2008, and it now features in the 'Prelude' to the translations. He then contributed versions of cantos 21, 22 and (following Shelley) the second half of canto 28; and the whole book is dedicated to his memory.

Early impetus and support was also given to the project by two experienced poet-translators of Dante: Mary Jo Bang and Steve Ellis, both of whom have subsequently gone on to translate the whole of the *Purgatorio*. We should like to thank them and their publishers for permission to reprint cantos 1, 4 and 5 from Mary Jo's *Purgatorio* (Graywolf Press, 2021) and cantos 13-14 and 16-17 from Steve's Dante: *The Divine Comedy* (Vintage Classics, 2019).

Part of Bernard O'Donoghue's version of canto 2 appeared as 'Casella' in his collection *Farmers Cross* (2011), and we are grateful to Faber & Faber for permission to include it here. For permission to publish the four poems about the *Purgatorio* that feature in the 'Prelude' here, we are grateful to their publishers: Puriri Press (for Jan Kemp's 'Crux Australis'); Faber & Faber (for Jamie McKendrick's 'il tremoto'); Carcanet (for Angela Leighton's 'Dante on Reflection'); and Arc Publications (for Michael O'Neill's 'Detained').

Contributors to this volume have used a variety of editions, commentaries and translations, but in our conversations about 'Dante's original' (and in the references to that in the Notes to cantos) much is owed especially to two recent works: Anna Maria Chiavacci Leonardi's edition with commentary and the parallel text and commentary, edited by the late Robert Durling and Ronald Martinez (both cited in the 'Abbreviations' at the beginning of the book).

At Arc, the book has been fortunate to find the ideal general editor (for the 'Arc Classics: New Translations of Great Poets of the Past' series) in Jean Boase-Beier. Since taking on the project in 2018, Jean has been unstinting – as well as astonishingly swift – with support, advice and guidance. It has been a privilege to draw upon her experience as a distinguished translator and writer about translation. Also at Arc, Angela Jarman's perceptive and meticulous work during the production process has been very much appreciated.

Finally, conversations about Dante and translation with the entire group of poets involved have made the work of editing this *Purgatorio* enlivening and enlightening. As this collaborative version goes into production during the coronavirus 'lockdown' and looks to publication in the 700th year after Dante's death, the medieval poem of exile seems increasingly pertinent to a world struggling to muster resources, sustain contacts and renew purposes. As one of the contributors put it recently, we can only hope that it will in some way help 'to keep the cultural fires burning'.

Nick Havely

CPSIA information can be obtained
at www.ICGtesting.com
Printed in the USA
LVHW111142060721
691970LV00005B/457